the ROAD TO BAU

the AUTOBIOGRAPHY OF JOELI BULU

Titles in The Missiology of Alan R. Tippett Series

The Jesus Documents (2012)

The Ways of the People: A Reader in Missionary Anthropology (2013)

the ROAD TO BAU

THE MISSIOLOGY OF ALAN R. TIPPETT SERIES
DOUG PRIEST, SERIES EDITOR

WILLIAM CAREY
LIBRARY

Published by William Carey Library
1605 E. Elizabeth Street
Pasadena, CA 91104 | www.missionbooks.org

Kelley Wolfe, editor
Brad Koenig, copyeditor
Pourio Lee, cover concept
Josie Leung, designer
Wisnu Sasongko, cover art, courtesy of Overseas Ministries Study Center

William Carey Library is a ministry of the
U.S. Center for World Mission
Pasadena, CA | www.uscwm.org

Printed in the United States of America
17 16 15 14 13   5 4 3 2 1 BP250

Library of Congress Cataloging-in-Publication Data

Tippett, Alan R. (Alan Richard), 1911-1988.
  Road to Bau : the life and work of John Hunt of Viwa, Fiji / by Alan R. Tippett, Delanikoro, Bau, Fiji, 1955.
      pages cm
  Also contains "The Autobiography of Joeli Bulu" by Alan R. Tippett.
  Includes bibliographical references.
  ISBN 978-0-87808-476-0
1. Hunt, John, 1812-1848. 2. Bulu, Joel, 1810?-1877. 3. Missionaries--Fiji--Biography. 4. Methodist Church--Missions--Fiji--History--19th century. I. Tippett, Alan R. (Alan Richard), 1911-1988. Autobiography of Joeli Bulu. II. Title.
  BV3680.F5T57 2013
  266'.7536092--dc23
  [B]

2013011903

CONTENTS

130077

SERIES FOREWORD

Always the creative thinker, Alan Tippett, transplanted to the United States from Australia (never really integrated), is the originator of the concept of cultural fatigue which continues after culture shock has passed. One afternoon he walked the entire midtown business district of Pasadena seeking "a reel of cotton." Returning in despair, what was he asking for? Well, of course, a spool of thread. However, in the field of anthropology, he didn't miss a thing and had a compendious knowledge, especially of the Southern Pacific sphere.

His alert mind took him in many directions, some complete surprises, and from volume to volume in this series you will find very little overlap and much that is rich for contemplation. Thanks to Doug Priest as well as Darrell Whiteman, Charles Kraft, and Greg Parsons for making sure these gems of thought are still available.

Ralph D. Winter
Pasadena, California
May 2009

FOREWORD

The printing of these works by Alan R. Tippett and, in the case of the Joeli Bulu autobiography, also by Tomasi Kanailagi, has great value in its own right, but it also brings certain issues in missiology, anthropology, and theology full circle.

The Fiji Mission began in 1835 as a project of the Tongan Mission, which itself was begun in 1826 by the newly created (1822) Australasian Methodist Missionary Society, which itself was a project of the Wesleyan Methodist Missionary Society of the Methodist Church in Great Britain. This "genealogy of mission" reveals one of the strengths of nineteenth century Wesleyanism, and that is its willingness to replicate the district structure wherever it went and to empower the district itself to move out in mission.

Joeli Bulu (ca. 1810–77) became a missionary to Fiji just a few years after his conversion in the Tongan Great Awakening. In his lifetime he saw the conversion of the Fijian people, including the great chief Cakobau, as well as the sending of the first Fijian missionaries on to German New Guinea. A few years after Bulu went to Fiji, the mission there was augmented by the arrival of newly commissioned missionary John Hunt (1812–48) and his teammates. Through great sacrifice by both British Methodist and Fijian Methodist missionaries, the church took strong root among the Fijian people at a time when cannibalism, local political intrigue and wars, and a strong system of traditional priests created barriers that would have made most missionaries turn back.

Alan Tippett arrived in Fiji over one hundred years later, serving as a missionary there for twenty years (1941–61). Tippett found that the church was still run by missionaries, somewhat counter to the empowering strategy of the first missionaries. Ahead of his time, he insisted that the missionaries shed their colonial paternalism and embrace the emerging indigenous church. Other mission groups did not begin to do this until they moved into the decade of decolonization (the 1960s), and even then, many were shamed into following the lead taken by the politicians. Tippett took a postcolonial posture long before the term became current in the missiology literature. His partnership with Tomasi Kanailagi to edit the autobiography of a Tongan missionary shows that he recognised the contribution of "native" missionaries as well as his willingness to share editorial control over mission materials with indigenous historians.

Tippett was also in on the ground floor of the emerging discipline of missiology. He was one of a handful of missionaries who earned doctorates in anthropology at secular universities. His work with Homer Barnett created in him an energetic fusion that brought anthropological methods and theories to bear on the study of mission and local expressions of Christianity. He was at the center of a generation (in the 1960s and 1970s) that exuded a kind of "hybrid vigor," producing a flurry of anthropological insights for mission work. Missiology is in need now of a new generation trained not in yesterday's missiology, but in today's anthropology and theology in order to once again reap the benefits of academic hybrid vigor.

Tippett bridged the world of the academy and the world of the seminary. He had a continuing link with anthropology, particularly through Barnett and his theories of culture change, and, with his other hand, held on to missiology and theology at Fuller with Charles Kraft and Donald McGavran and his theories of church growth (1965–77). His research and publications were respected within anthropology as well as used in missiology. To an outsider it may have looked like he lived in two different worlds, but his network was seamless because he knew that anthropology was critical to the proclamation of the gospel.

Tippett found and used the methodological and theoretical tools that were appropriate for the work that he was called to do. He worked both in anthropology and ethnohistory, and both genres are evident in this volume. Ethnohistory spans the boundary between anthropology and history; in short, it is writing history using ethnographic categories. Thus, the ethnohistorian uses both documentary sources and oral traditions, still tries to understand culture in terms of the culture itself, and foregrounds not a monolithic voice, which was usually a colonial voice in the past, but rather reveals many voices, especially indigenous voices. Beyond the events and categories, today's ethnohistorian tries to discover and deploy indigenous notions of what events are, which events are important, and how they might be brought together in an appropriately indigenous way. This approach is foreshadowed in Tippett's first few chapters here. History is constructed, always, and so the ethnohistorian not only gives voice to, but also reflects, the structure of the indigenous narrative. Tippett's work was widely respected, and his publications show up in anthropological as well as missiological bibliographies.

One might well ask: why is it that missiology's best work, the work that has advanced the discipline, has come from people, like Alan Tippett, who have long-term missionary experience that is then refined by serious academic work in anthropology and history? Tippett was such a person whose life came to bear rich missiological fruit in the 1960s and 1970s. Tippett mastered the discipline of anthropology and kept up with advances in the discipline by engaging and contributing to the literature. With him, the insights never grew old. What young person is now being trained in anthropology so that they will be able to continue the hybrid vigor that has, at the right time, brought new life to missiology?

> Therefore every scribe who has been trained for the kingdom of heaven is like the master of a household who brings out of his treasure what is new and what is old. (Matt 13:52 NRSV)

Michael A. Rynkiewich
Professor of Anthropology
E. Stanley Jones School of World Mission and Evangelism
Asbury Theological Seminary
Wilmore, Kentucky

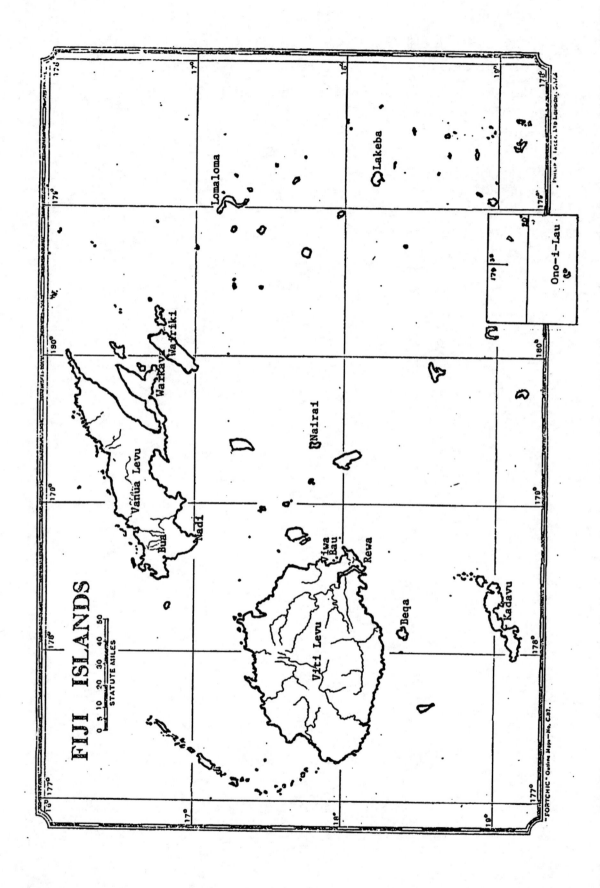

INTRODUCTION

If my critic asks if the world needs another biography of John Hunt, I shall defend myself by pointing out how much yet remains to be said about him that is not only in danger of being lost, but is still vitally relevant today. This in itself both justifies the book and indeed makes it imperative that someone should make the attempt.

Another obvious criticism will be that I have allowed my own self to be projected into the pages here and there. Were this biography purely a work of library research, such subjectivity by the author might be quite unjustifiable, but there are biographies in which it is inevitable—for example, a biography by a wife or a son.

The same applies when a man follows the footsteps of another, as I have followed Hunt's. The work he began, I try to carry on; I work among the grandsons and granddaughters of folk to whom he gave assignments; I know his handwriting well and have been carefully over the records he left behind for those of us who would follow; many things he handled, I too have handled; and I live today in the place he strove to conquer, and gaze out each morning at the island of Viwa where his greatest work was done.

Yet even beyond this, Hunt—as a man, as a Bible student, and as a missionary—has been a continual source of inspiration to me; my life has been better on his account, and my Bible study more diligent, and my evangelism among the Fijian people more effective. He has been to me as Paul was to Timothy.

I have one advantage over John Hunt. I am able to look back on his work and see it in perspective, as it were, observing also its results, as he was not permitted to see. I venture to believe that there is much worth saying still on this point.

Three lives of Hunt have been written in English, yet none of them have really said what I feel in my heart to say. Very soon after his death, *The Life of John Hunt, Missionary to the Cannibals* (1860) was written by George Stringer Rowe, a well-known missionary biographer of the period. This book was written to be an inspiration to the young men of the following generation. It was a study in saintly living, and was somewhat introspective in character, but for all this was well documented and compiled from Hunt's own journals. The book served a good purpose in its day. A version in French also appeared at the time.

Half a century later Joseph Nettleton's *John Hunt: Missionary Pioneer and Saint* (1906) appeared in the Library of Missionary Biography. It was a much smaller work, but breathed far more naturally the air of Fiji itself than did Rowe's work, which was obviously written from a distance. Nettleton was a missionary and knew both Viwa and the fruit of Hunt's work. He had also witnessed revivals. I would that Nettleton had tackled a really big work on Hunt.

And now, in our own time, comes a third, Birtwhistle's *In His Armour* (1954), a most useful catalogue of the life and work of John Hunt; an accurate and chronological record. It seems to me to be written for the students of missions in England. Its introduction shows it has an axe to grind and an application to modern missionary thinking. It is indeed a thesis on missionary policy, with the evidence coming from the life and ministry of John Hunt.

Each of these works had its place for the days in which it was written, and I heartily approve them all. What then, the reader will ask, remains to be said?

In the first place, there has been no really constructive attempt to paint the background against which the picture of Hunt must stand, nor has there been any real evaluation of the permanence of his work. As the years go by and young Fiji itself comes to study its past and its foundations, it will indeed be a sad state of affairs if there is no record of this. Nor do I think that sufficient light has been thrown on the place taken by Hunt's Fijian lieutenants in this great drama—one of the greatest of the South Seas.

Furthermore, it seems to me that some understanding of the Fijian background, against which Hunt and his colleagues laboured, is important to modern missionaries, especially those who labour in partly Westernised fields without bothering to enquire thoroughly into the nature of the place whence their flocks have come.

Again, I do not think it has been fully appreciated that a missionary's real service does not begin when he arrives on the field. He is still being prepared, even though he may be in the front lines. We are living in days when ten-day tourists write travel books, when universities give students a few courses on method and send them out among primitive people to expect a reliable thesis in a couple of years. If they bother learning the language at all, many get it the wrong way round and, no doubt, they go back to civilisation to become authorities. The missionary life of men like John Hunt serves as a corrective to this unfortunate state of affairs. Hunt's real missionary work did not begin until God called him to Viwa; prior to that, everything was preparatory.

It is the thesis of this book that Viwa represented the task for which God brought Hunt into this world, and his remarkable accomplishments were due to the absoluteness of his surrender to God, his willingness to be led anywhere, and his ready responsiveness to that divine guidance. Prior to that all, was training. The evidence to follow shows many factors by means of which he was prepared for the great task ahead, even factors within Fiji itself, and how they were all brought to bear on his Viwa ministry. He went to Viwa a man in the prime of life; he died, worn out, after six years. Yet in that six years he set the directions and lay down the criteria for what was really an indigenous church in Fiji from the beginning.

Alan R. Tippett
Delanikoro, Bau, Fiji, 1955

1

"THE END OF THE AGE! ALAS!"

I

I cannot tell you the year of this tale, though one who knows the stars might help to find the answer. I only know that it was the year in which the comet with three tails appeared in the heavens, when people awaited its meaning with fear—did it spell tragedy or some amazing achievement? They were not kept in suspense for long, for it was also the year the first white man's ship appeared in those parts. It might have been the *Pandora* (1791), the *Providence* (1792), or the *Arthur* (1794); or it may have been some other vessel. I do not know. I only know that three events are told together in the songs of the minstrels—the comet with three tails, the first white man's ship, and the wasting sickness.

A strange disease indeed was this legacy of the white sailor whom they took ashore from the white man's ship.

"Our fathers," so say the storytellers of the tribe, "felt their legs go from under them, and as they walked they swayed and fell, and where they fell they lay. Not many of them died of the disease—but their friends had need to strangle them because of their weakness. They became such a burden to everyone. Prior to that, few but widows were strangled, and that to accompany their dead husbands into the next world. But from this time there began our custom of strangling the sick. Both customs we retained until Christianity came."

Another song tells of havoc caused in Naitasiri, until a plant from which a potent medicine was made, was found, and gave relief and eventually cure. Its name, *Vueti Naitasiri*, is remembered to this day.

Two old women, captured in the wars half a century later, brought with them from their village an ancient lament, and as they performed their rhythmic body movements they chanted these words:

> Great is the sickness lying at the masthead,
> Swollen like food-baskets their heads,
> And hoarse indeed their voices;
> They fall, and helpless and pitiable they lie.

Degei[1] is put to shame.

A noble thing indeed is the strangling rope.

So ran the story of Vunivasa. At Vunivia it was the same:

What is this sickness that smites them?
I remember!
The wasting sickness, that spreads far and wide.
I remember!

And again at Kura the doleful melody is heard:

The old men are listless,
I remember!
Terrifying indeed the sickness,
I remember!
We do not die. We do not live.
I remember!
Our stomachs ache. Our heads ache.
I remember!
The strangling cords creak.
I remember!
Spirits flow away like running water.
I remember!

Everywhere throughout the country the same miserable tale is told and sung of the wasting sickness which came with the first white man's ship and the comet with the three tails.

Have we fallen upon a new age? Alas!
We lie down. We grow torpid. Alas!
Many die. A few live on. Alas!
Many die indeed only by the rope. Alas!
Their girdles rot around their waists. Alas!
The women despair. Alas!
Their grass skirts unloosed. Alas!
And we wonder at it all.
What can it mean?
Is it a sign of death to the chiefs?
Is it the end of the age? Alas!

II

Maybe ten years later. Again I cannot tell the date with certainty. One thing only I know—that the tale is told together with that of an eclipse of the sun and a tidal wave. It is said

---

1   Degei is the name of their god.

that Chief Naulivou was installed into office as chief warlord of Bau on the day of the eclipse (some say it was 7 September 1802), and he had followed Chief Banuve, who had died a victim of another white man's disease. The eclipse, the tidal wave, a second white man's ship—and death.

Slowly once more the graceful brown bodies begin to sway, and arms move to the rhythmic beat of another dirge.

> Loudly roar the waves of the trade winds,
> Breakers chase each other in quick succession,
> To burst over the end of the canoe shed
> Shaking a shower of berries from the *vetau*
> Into the open doorway.
> Mother of No'wester collects them
> Bringing them within the house to me
> To be my playthings.
>
> Quickly run out the neap tides
> New is the tale we hear
> As a ship comes up from the ocean.
> They launch the *Word of the Chief*
> And sail out of the Kabara Sea.
> Where they lower the sail at the stern.
> O, you, who travel the ocean.
> There is Rotuma and Galagala.
> On Distant Reef the surf boils
> This is the place where canoes anchor.
>
> The foreigners have returned
> And anchor at Blowing Sand.
>
> *   *   *   *   *
>
> The sickness has come among us
> Empty is every district.
> Our warriors by it are bound
> Their heads droop and wither
> As the *diaga* plant droops at sunset,
> And are buried in the place of the dead.
>
> The foreigners have sailed away.
> Our men are swept away.
> Our women are swept away.
> They are as withering plantains.

There is a story told in Nakelo that the epidemic of dysentery was eventually cleared away only by a great flood, a higher flood than ever before or since, when whole villages were swept out to sea and the mangroves were buried in silt. Much of the lower Rewa delta is said to have been built up at the time. The Bauans have a similar tale.

III

On 10 September 1808: Valevatu, a petty chief, entertains a party of visitors led by the paramount chief of the district. There has been a conference of the old men. They have promised to set their defences in order and to aid their overlord in war. They have feasted together on yams and breadfruit, and the remainder of the night is spent in dancing in the moonlight.

The ancient faith of their fathers has ordained that they dance while the moon shines, the men and the women in separate groups, to the tune of the bamboo nose-flute. The visitors are armed with the ancient weapons of war, manufactured according to the traditional arts handed down from their ancestors. Indeed, is it not from their great ancestor, whose famous exploits are sung in the tribal ballads, and whom they have since deified, to whom they now give worship very similar to that given to the ancestor spirit himself?

Yet there is one among them who seems a little less at ease than the rest, and his weapons are new and strange—a musket on his back, and a pair of pistols at hand. Beneath the black paint that covers his body lies a white skin.

He is now asked to demonstrate the magic of his instruments of war, and having previously taken care to place more than one ball in each, he proceeds to sink some into nearby trees and cause damage which truly astonishes his hosts. Though the paramount chief knows the secret, no other person can be induced to even touch a pistol.

For the time being the support of this tribe is assured, though later they found it favourable to aid the enemy, for which double dealings they paid dearly by a punishment inflicted by the white man's weapons.

IV

The date is about a month later. A fleet of canoes prepares to attack an island, and the island canoes come out to meet their invaders. There is a preliminary skirmish with bows and arrows and stone-slinging, and as they draw closer, with spears and clubs. The spears are pointed with guardfish bills and many, finding their marks, are surgically extracted by the victims themselves by means of sharp pieces of shell or bamboo. A prisoner is taken. It is said his wounds will be dressed in the morning (but actually he will be clubbed and eaten). One hundred and fifty war canoes surround the island. The attack lasts three days and leaves the island devastated. Hogs, plantains, yams, mats, baskets, and fishing nets are plundered, and every house is burnt, and the food trees are cut down. The hideout of the old men and women and children is discovered, and these are lashed to poles like pigs and carried away among the plunder. Some die of the treatment. Others are clubbed. No one is shown any respect, save a grotesque, deformed boy, who is respected only because his malformed body indicated him to be spirit-possessed.

In the intense excitement the cries of the dying are hardly distinguishable from the bloodthirsty yelling of the victors. A warcry rings out with every new victim, the war songs begin, and the war dances follow—filthy and lewd.

On one canoe stands a white man; beside him, forty-two bodies. All night the wild rejoicing continues. Then another day—a day spent in cutting up and cooking bodies. There is dexterity in it.

White men, clad and painted as the natives, find their participation in native war takes them further than they want to go. There are no food supplies from the uartermaster in native war. For four days there has been no prepared meal, which possibly explains the disgusting gluttony which follows plunder and massacre.

One of the white men has the initiative to say that the eating of human flesh is forbidden by his God, and this alone saves him, but his only food is yam cooked in the same pots as human bodies.

V

It is another month later.

A white man bargains with a native chief. He offers many costly presents—presents much better than he usually gives away. But the chief drives a hard bargain. He may not fully understand what lies behind the China sandalwood trade, but he does know the white man will do almost anything to get this timber.

So the white man accepts the terms and agrees to fight a native war, and accordingly a native army of some 1,800 is joined by a white man's launch, with sixteen white men armed with muskets and cutlasses, and another launch with a 12 lb. carronade and a swivel and fourteen men.

It is an attack on an island fortress, and ammunition supplies are sent from the white man's ship. The fortress falls before the firearms, but it has been desperately defended, and the capture reveals some two hundred corpses within—among them the body of the chief.

Though the chief for whom the white men fight promised to save the women and children, he can do nothing about it. War, as they know it, is savage war. There is no mercy.

The next day sees a Christian burial—the body of a white man killed in action. Afterwards white men stand and watch the preparations for cannibal feasting.

Within a few days they have their sandalwood—one hundred tons of it—which reached Port Jackson on 14 February 1809.

VI

On 20 June 1808, 11 p.m., S. Lat. 17.40, E. Long. 179: the *Eliza* is fast on the reef near Nairai, Fiji.

White men escaping to the shore are met by natives with bows and arrows, spears, and war clubs. Is it not their tradition that saltwater bodies are theirs by gift from their gods? The white men are relieved of their clothing and goods and left naked, but no life has yet been taken—the shipwrecked are not often so fortunate.

One of these is taken by the chief of Batiki to his island, where in a miserable state of health he lies up for a long time, almost at death's door. Nor are the natives helpful to his depressed spirit. They come and look at the poor wretch, almost blind with ophthalmia, the use of one leg gone, and internal pains from who knows what. Then they feel his legs and say, "White man, you are good to eat."

Whereupon the now long-repentant sailor becomes a preacher—perhaps the first in Fiji, if the truth be known.

He tells them of his great God, who disapproves of people eating human flesh, and adds that if they would only desist from the practise and open their land to the white men their God would surely send cattle, which are far better to eat. They say they want no cattle. If they are as big as he says, they would be afraid of them anyway.

The women see him lying there and ask him when he will die, for certainly were they so sick they would die right away. He answers that he will die when his God sees fit to take him out of the world. And they ask him about his land. Are there any women there? They will not believe him, for are not the white men chiefs from the sun?

He tells them of God again. He convinces them of the greatness of God. They compare this God with theirs. He turns opportunity to his own ends and warns them to do nothing that will rouse the anger of his God—certainly nothing so rash as killing a white man.

The women are kind to him. He keeps a record of time by making knots in a spear of grass. He keeps Sunday and remembers Christmas. At times the white man feels he will die, and then he blames the devil for these feelings, and he prays:

> O Lord, spare my unprofitable life and enable me to get off this savage island,
> and protect me once more over the boisterous ocean to my native country, and
> I will try by Thy assistance to seek religion and become what Thou wouldst have
> me to be.

The prayer was eventually answered, and he lived to see America again.

Sometime later, back in Nairai again he sees a man clubbed and about to be eaten. Again he tells how wrong it is and how God must certainly be angry with them if they eat their fellows. They gratify him by taking the body away for burial, but they eat it just the same. They listen to his preaching but go their own way.

VII

A child of four years, the half-caste daughter of a white man who has made himself the power and fear of Fiji, lies on her bed watching him go through his sea chest. He too comes from the *Eliza*, but his record is very different. A desperate adventurer, by guile and good shooting he has established himself as a Fijian hero and enjoys the privileges which go with the title. Two great ladies are given him for wives. For miles around he has brought tribes under the heel of Bau. His main business is war. In the winter months he follows the sandalwood ships, for wherever these ships go there is action, danger, and opportunity for good shooting.

Maraia lies watching her father and is attracted by the glittering contents of the chest. She startles her father who has thought her asleep. He is going away for a long time he tells her, and must hide her property in a safe place. So he poles over to some spot on the mainland, and next morning she discovers the Bauan canoes have sailed for Bua.

Here this adventurer, whose good marksmanship has consigned so many to the ovens, ends his own bodily existence in the same form of internment. Years later Maraia is forced to marry the captain of a Manilla ship, and her father's treasure of South American dollars still lies buried within the vicinity of Bau.

VIII

Things have gone wrong somehow with the plans of the white sea captain. The death of a chief with whom he had made a business deal threatens to rob him of his sandalwood cargo, and he goes ashore. The principal wife of the dead chief is to be strangled. She does not want to die, and the captain determines to try to save the lady purely because he sees a way of obtaining his cargo of sandalwood thereby, even though by doing this the woman also becomes his.

So taking his largest whale's tooth he goes to plead for her life, but the priest, his enemy and the enemy of all white people, who has repeatedly pointed out how intercourse with whites always brings trouble, hastens on the ceremony—for the rite means profit to him. The sea captain is too late. The fatal cord is drawn.

Somewhat sanctimoniously the priest explains that it is necessary. It is the law. He alone, as priest, knows the reason. Sacrifices will follow.

The captain is fifteen minutes late, and greatly agitated turns on the priest and upbraids him, but the priest is calm, for has he not won the encounter? "It is the law," he says.

Even so the captain finds a trick by means of which he gets his sandalwood.

IX

One thing leads to another.

The year is 1838, and this tale concerns a certain French brig, *L'Aimable Josephine*, whose captain, like so many others of his kind, has been partaking in native politics and wars.

His craft is at Viwa. His business relationships with the native people seem good. The Viwa chief is persuaded to allow his nephew to attack the vessel. He does so most efficiently, massacres the crew, steals the vessel, and thereby earns for himself the name Varani, after the Frenchman.

This sort of thing inevitably brings reprisals. Shortly afterwards there appears in these waters one M. Dumont d'Urville to avenge the death of Captain Bureau and the crew of his brig. The town of Viwa is bombarded from the sea and completely destroyed.

* * * * *

This sequence of vignettes of pre-Christian Fiji is a kind of filmstrip and introduces us to the main basic problems created in Fiji in the few decades immediately prior to the coming of Christianity. In the episodes I have sketched, I have purposely refrained from the use of any missionary sources or documents. Much has been said to the effect that the missionaries overpainted the picture; to avoid such criticism I have confined myself to native traditions and the written records of the seamen who witnessed these events. (I shall not subject myself to the same limitations however in subsequent chapters.)

We may now sum up the problems introduced:

(1) White man's disease and its social and psychological effect

(2) Introduction of firearms, and political importance of marksmanship

(3) Interference of white men in native wars

(4) Massacres of white men and reprisals

(5) Taking of native wives by white sailors and disputes arising thereupon

All these are apparent on the surface, but there were other factors less apparent to the casual observer. There was a growing realisation that these "men from the sun" had behind them some great power; be it a kingdom or a God, they seemed to have an unlimited supply of munitions and landships.

Again the Fijian was mystified by a dim idea that this power, whatever it was, disapproved of many of his own traditional rites; in particular, widow-strangling and cannibalism. Even when men of war shrank from eating human flesh and interfered with their sacred burial rites—and this before any missionary appeared. The episode of the French reprisals introduces another element which was a bitter issue in midcentury—French Pacific policy. This had a violent effect on the Protestant missionaries, and a native chief must have often wondered at the quarrels among the white men themselves.

At the same time it must have been hard for a friendly trader who had established good trade relationships with a tribe to return and find them openly hostile. One captain's greed for sandalwood might spoil intercourse for all strangers to follow.

There was no such thing as unity in Fiji in those days. Fiji was the world, with Tonga on the edge of it, and the white men came from beyond, from another world. The chiefs of Fiji were fighting among themselves; the stronger swallowing the others one by one. The greatest of these were Bau, Rewa, and Somosomo, at the time the missionaries came, but there were five or six others that had not yet been completely accounted for, and of the interior very little was known, even by the coastal Fijians. These chiefs were fighting for paramouncy, and if the white man could be persuaded to fight their battles, that was good, but otherwise they were best left alone. Kill a white man and something always seemed to go wrong. Perhaps it was the white man's God. Perhaps a landship would come and blast their village from the coast. Or perhaps some strange disease for which no forest cure was known. Was it not in their laments and songs?

Of course the white man brought other things—axes, knives, fishhooks, and many useful articles. And above all they would sell muskets. A musket could be obtained for as small a price as a slave woman.

And then there came the strangest white men of all—no doubt the priests of the white man's God. Fearless men who put no trust in firearms, but made new things called books, and taught new arts like reading and writing and sewing, and administered medicine to the sick, and set new words to their old melodies—new strange words of a teaching they had not met before. They brought their wives and raised white families in their midst.

They were new days—strange and terrible. They chanted—

> What can it mean?
> Is it a sign of death to the chiefs?
> Is it the end of the age? Alas!

—as their graceful bodies swayed to and fro in unison to the rhythm.

2
THE PLOUGHBOY OF LINCOLNSHIRE

I

At the time when Walter Lawry, despite the Wesleyan London Committee, was chartering a vessel to thrust Wesleyanism out from Australia into missionary work in the islands, a small Lincolnshire lad of ten, having completed his scanty education under the parish pedagogue, was beginning his life as a farm boy. A more obvious misfit would have been hard to find, clumsy in handling his tools, lacking the robustness required for farming, and advised by his fellow farm boys to take up tailoring. Yet his very clumsiness irritated him so much that with grim determination he set out to overcome his failings, and won thereby as a nickname "Farmer Jack."

Thus at the early age of ten we have the first public evidence of what was later to become a major element in helping him to do almost impossible things at the antipodes.

Yet it was not the lad's real desire to become a farmer. His father had not always been a farmer, and by far the most exciting tales he had from his father were connected with his army experiences as a young man before he deserted and joined the navy, and his naval reminiscences of engagements like the Battle of the Nile. These evening tales, told in the first person, made some impression on the mind of young John Hunt, the hero-worshipping son who dreamed, not of farming, but simply of being a hero. He kept his dreams secret, and for five years tried to improve himself as a farm boy. Of the precise nature of the great adventures which lay before him he had no possible idea, yet when the time came for him to choose the greatest adventure of all, it was not the element of "adventure" which made him do so, but rather a religious attitude to God which had no origin in his boyhood home.

In religion his parents were a strange pair, both strictly moral, teaching the children to do good and avoid evil, but poles apart from the Wesleyans to whom John became attached later. The children were taught to pray, yet neither could read, and neither made any real profession of religion. So John's prayers followed a more or less experimental line, and he prayed for protection from storms, animals, and Gypsies. Having learned to read from the parish pedagogue, he read the Bible, but found most of it beyond him. He found some interest in the historical sections.

At one time his father became taken up with a sect known as the Ranters, but John took a great dislike to the whole business. It put him off religion and he thought less of it, devoting his mind to improving his work. A serious illness at sixteen turned his mind again to religion.

A young friend of his died about this time. John turned more and more to prayer and Bible reading, though without a guide he was thrown purely onto his own devices as to how he used them. It should be noted perhaps that he was using the two means of grace, which in years to come became his fundamental method.

After recovery, when he joined his farm friends again, some of the fervour departed. He must have been a lonely youth. Not even with his mother could he share his experience. Once, when she heard he had been attending cottage prayer meetings, he confessed, but she could not help him.

His need was instruction. He hungered for knowledge. The sermons at church did not satisfy him. Eventually in company with a young Methodist he went to their chapel.

At Swinderby he eventually became a member of a class, but confessed afterwards that his service was more from a sense of duty than from the heart. Others spoke of joy and assurance. He was far from either.

Then came a memorable occasion when he found what he sought in a prayer meeting at Thorpe, where a little memorial chapel stands today. I record his own description as it retains something of the atmosphere of the occasion.

> Mr. Smith was praying with a poor woman who could not believe in Christ; and feeling what was needed, he cried out, with all his soul and might, "Send us more power!" I knelt near him, and remember, with some feeling I said, "Amen!" Immediately a most overwhelming influence came upon me, so that I cried aloud for mercy for the sake of Christ; while I was, in a minute, as completely bathed with tears and perspiration as if I had been thrown into a river. I prayed as in an agony, for a few minutes.

The whole passage is a long one. Smith brought him to the point of answering whether or not he believed the death of Christ provided forgiveness of his own personal sins, and Hunt found life.

It is important that we should note that Hunt did pass through such an experience as that, because in years to come in Viwa he saw hundreds of Fijians come to precisely the same point. John Smith knew well these signs, and many he has led that way had been ploughboys. But he could have had no idea what was to grow from this particular plough-boy's conversion in the brief twenty years that remained for his life to run its course.

Nor for that matter, did the boy himself.

II

John Hunt's library comprised a Bible, a copy of Bunyan's *Pilgrim's Progress*, the *Methodist Magazine* for 1812, and a few tracts. It was not a great deal for a young man with such a thirst for knowledge. One can understand his joy in discovering that the Mr. Wilkinson of Swinderby with whom he was engaged for one year owned a good library and opened it for the use of his servants.

Here Hunt discovered Horne's *Introduction* and the works of Wesley, Paley, and Dwight. Life opened for the studious farmer boy. Mason's *Self-knowledge* gripped him, and then Wesley's *Notes on the New Testament*. Beneath the farmer's blue smock beat a heart full of new discovery, and as he turned over sweet-smelling furrows of brown earth, he ploughed too new fields of thought, and especially did his mind turn steadily towards scripture exposition. He formed the habit of fixing his mind daily on some scripture passage. Nor was it long before the members of the Society observed a remarkable piety about young Hunt.

Yet he shrank from the holy work of preaching, which he felt was for them only who had a specific call to it. Most of his early attempts at preaching were because of appointed preachers being unable to fill their engagements, and though his early congregations felt his power and appreciation of Scripture, Hunt himself was far from satisfied. We note that right from this early period Hunt considered there was one qualification for the preacher—viz., the specific call to do so.

Hunt's conception of a call is a fundamental element of his life story, and it applied to other tasks besides preaching. It touches also on his conception of the will of God, and it was with some degree of hesitation that he allowed his name to be put on the circuit plan as an exhorter.

Upon the receipt of the first plan on which his name appeared, he took it to his room and spread it out before God, and prayed earnestly for the revelation of his will. And behind the closed door of that little room there came to him that day a clear conviction that God wanted him to preach the gospel—and until the day of his death he never doubted again.

At the same time he saw that his own personal effort had to play a part in effecting the divine programme. He believed that he who called him would provide the gifts needed, but it was his part to develop those gifts. He saw the shortcomings of his educational background and set out to improve his English by attending a night school.

His improvement astonished the village congregations who remembered the brogue and clumsiness of his earlier efforts. He set out to make himself a master of the works of Wesley, Fletcher, and Watson—in itself a formidable task. God blessed his studies and the people approved him.

In 1833 the new superintendent of the circuit (the Rev. W. Smith) heard Hunt preach and recognised his potential power. He was staggered to learn that he was but an ordinary ploughboy. It was Smith who put the thought of the ministry into Hunt's mind. It startled him at first, and he returned to his secret place. Was this perhaps the meaning of those confused movements in his soul? Was it this that stirred within him as he grappled with Wesley and Watson? Was it this which kept saying that ploughing a straight furrow in the brown earth was not the real purpose for which God had brought him into the world? Yet he trembled at the thought.

There has been a time when Laidman Hodgson, a missionary from South Africa, who had also ministered from time to time in Lincolnshire, had made some natural appeal to the spirit of young Hunt. He might well then have gone with him as his personal servant, gardener, or farmer, hoping also for some "teaching children in the Sunday School and preaching to the English settlers."

Smith made good use of the young preacher and saw he got opportunity in the larger chapels and in the city itself. His preaching had natural quality despite the shortcomings of his general education. Its discourse is said to have been logical and at the same time earnest from the fire in his heart.

If, as Rowe says, his early work was ungrammatical, he certainly corrected the matter as time went on, for there is no evidence of it in the work of the Fiji period. He was never blind to his failings and was diligent in correcting them. He never ceased to wonder that God would choose and use him in the service of the kingdom. His spiritual shortcomings he strove to correct by prayer, and his academic defects by study. He built his house on the two main pillars of prayer and study, and what an amazing house it turned out to be. This was, indeed, just the kind of man God needed for the work in faraway Fiji.

Hunt candidated for the ministry in 1835—the same year, as it happened, that Cross and Cargill launched out into the deep and established the Fiji Mission. The tales of adventure he had in childhood from his father and the memories of Laidman Hodgson had influenced the form of his candidature. It was his sincere desire to go to the Cape.

The story is told of how the letter Smith sent to the London Committee amused them, so extravagant it seemed to them, but theirs was the surprise when they came to examine the Lincolnshire ploughboy personally. He so impressed them that they determined to give him the opportunity he seemed to merit—a course in the Theological Institution recently established at Hoxton.

Many of Hunt's supporters were alarmed at this. They felt that his qualifications for the ministry were his natural piety and fire, not education. Yet many who watched his course through the institution with some degree of fear were led, through his stability, to see how such an institution in the right hands can cultivate a man's natural gifts and make him even fitter for service.

3
THE STUDENT OF HOXTON

I

Hoxton provided Hunt with opportunity to develop his own potentiality. It did not change him; it developed him. Long before his candidature, the desire for deeper holiness had grown in his heart. He never lost this desire, and not to his dying day did he cease striving towards this end. He longed for holiness. He believed the effectiveness of his service would be determined by his holiness in the Lord. "Let us not be satisfied with being ordinary Christians," he wrote to a friend, "Let us pray and believe until praying and believing becomes habitual. I believe it is possible to live in the Spirit to such a degree, that it would be as natural to pray and believe as to breathe."

This Hunt of Hoxton, feeling there is yet so much to be achieved, is the same as the ploughboy who felt himself unworthy to preach and determined to wait until he *knew* God had called him to do so. Here is a young man determined to relate his own will to God's will. It is the same man who later on shares with James Calvert his secret thoughts on holiness, born from prayer and intensive Bible study, and published after his death as *Entire Sanctification* (1849). Here is a man developing, not changing. Here is divine discontent; a passion for holiness; a continual consciousness of his own shortcomings, of his human frailty, of his utter dependence on God. Here is a choice seedling God raised in the fields of Lincolnshire, took and nurtured in Hoxton, transplanted in the cannibal Pacific—where some said he wasted his fragrance. But those of us who follow him know otherwise. It has been recently pointed out that Hunt carried the biblical doctrine of holiness further than the theologians of England at the time, especially in connexion with its social application (Birtwhistle 1954, ch. 14). This shows that Hunt was not a mere copyist of his tutors. The Bible itself was his standard. He drew much from the Hoxton tutors, especially from Hannah, but he drew only that which related itself to Scripture as he experienced it. His studies were experiential, not merely academic. He was quite satisfied with Christ as his Saviour; he was not satisfied with his own personal holiness.

Together with this we must consider also his studious nature. There can be no doubt about the young man being a "chosen vessel" like the Apostle Paul, and that God needed a man who continually strove for the holier life. But God also needed a student. Yet the kind of student God needed was of the practical rather than the academic kind. We have all seen men of great academic distinction who have been complete failures in the ministry at home and on the mission field. There are two forms of scholarship, one academic and the other practical. The authorities saw the value of Hunt's first year in the institution and granted him a second, and finally after two and a half years he left with a good biblical and linguistic background for his preaching and teaching, and when he came to translate the New Testament into Fijian he was able to work from the Greek itself, and in the parts of the Old Testament he translated, from the Hebrew. Having come from a lowly origin, he never lost touch with lowly people, and thus his scholarship was essentially practical.

The government of Hoxton was in the hands of Joseph Entwistle, to whom Hunt was much devoted, but it was from John Hannah that he drew most, and to whom his work on holiness was ultimately dedicated. His book, by the way, was the prescribed text for Wesleyan ministers on probation in Australia, as far as this doctrine was concerned, until Methodist Union.

Hunt's friendship for Hannah was maintained until his death, and what was probably the longest letter of his last year was written to Dr. Hannah in reply to one he had received from him. Historically it is an extremely important letter and deals with scripture translation, the Viwa Plan, catechism, and other literature being published. It reveals that Hunt was more than a little indebted to his tutor in his literary work as well as his theology. There are also some personal touches, appreciation of small gifts sent to Fiji, and the significant sentence: "I am trying to tell you how much we love you, and only tell that our love is untellable—if I may coin a word."

Two days before his departure for the mission field, Hunt wrote to Hannah, finishing his letter with these words: "Let me have your blessing, your paternal blessing. At your family altar, where your heart beats highest with fervent affection, there remember me and mine."

It was Dr. Hannah who, but a decade later, selected Hunt's name, from the seven missionaries who had laid down their lives in that connexional year, as the subject of his remarks at the annual meeting of the Wesleyan Methodist Missionary Society at Exeter Hall. He spoke first of his humble origin, and told of how grace had made him the man he became. "Grace," he said, "called forth mind. That mind discovered unexpected energies. These energies under the guidance and blessing of the Spirit yielded labours, the fruit of which shall not easily die." In the same touching obituary he said also, "I never knew a man more right-hearted with respect to the great work of our Lord and Saviour." Though to some extent we have anticipated the end of the story, it seems right in a way to deal at this juncture with some of those lasting friendships which Hunt formed in his Hoxton days.

Another was that he formed with James Calvert, his fellow student and fellow mission-ary. So different were these two men by nature that I have never been able to understand how they were so drawn together, unless like John the Beloved and the hot-headed Peter they found their unity in a strong love for their Lord. An anti-Wesleyan historian called one of them a "saint"; the other is best thought of as an aggressive Christian warrior. Their methods of evangelism were different. Calvert got many away from their heathen systems, but it was Hunt who got them to personal salvation. No doubt God had work for both men. It was the correspondence between these two men on their inner lives and striving for personal holiness in the light of the teachings of Scripture which led ultimately to the publication of the book already mentioned—one of the finest books of personal challenge that ever came out of the Pacific. Hunt wrote these letters to Calvert, who prepared them for publication after Hunt's death. As Hunt prepared himself to cross the last river, hav-ing commended his wife and children to the care of the Lord, it was from Calvert that he begged the last prayer, and it was in Calvert's arms he died.

II

We have already seen that as a local preacher Hunt had some ability to reason an argu-ment. His logical mind enabled him to make use of the theological institution in many ways, again, let it be noted, in development rather than change. Hoxton was no match factory.

No one can read his theological letters without appreciating how thoroughly he sifted out truth and arranged his facts. This is revealed beautifully in his *Sermons on the Evidences, Doctrines, Duties and Institutions of Christianity*, which he wrote in the Fijian language and for the Fijian scene; and also in his sermon outlines, many of which are still extant.

His systematic manner of presentation of an argument was but a reflection of his man-ner of life, for he had cultivated regular habits. In the early days as an exhorter, he formed the habit of meeting a fellow servant of the Word at 4 a.m. on Sunday mornings to pray for the day's programme. In Hoxton during his first year he planned his morning and evening devotions in the following manner.

Day:

(1) Commence the day with praising God for the mercies of the past night, and repeat the Lord's Prayer.

(2) As far as possible lay out the business of the day.

(3) Bring every part of this business before God in prayer, and ask His help against the probable dangers of the day.

(4) Read a portion of the New Testament on my knees.

(5) Read a portion of the Old Testament and pray for my friends, relatives, the Church and the world. Altogether this will occupy an hour.

Night:

(1) Commit to memory a passage of Scripture.

(2) Self-examination; Confession; Thanksgiving; Prayer.

Quite apart from the personal challenge such a programme should be to us, we see here a "method," which we shall continue to see running through the whole story to its end. Time after time, here in Fiji, those of us who follow ask how he was able to fit in all the things he accomplished. Clearly he did it by planning. He planned every moment of his day. When one thinks of the distances travelled, the translations and textbooks produced, the building, teaching, dispensing, the evangelistic work, its preaching and follow-up, one wonders how he found any time at all for study. Yet when he died he was theologically the freshest man on the field, and as a biblical expositor I doubt if our field has ever produced his equal.

Study in Hoxton had a peculiar effect on Hunt. He tells in his own private records how he would retire from Dr. Hannah's theological lectures with a deep sense of his own ignorance and need, yet at the same time he felt an appreciation of the truth and authority of the Bible, and this in itself provided a response to his own sense of ignorance and drove him forward in his Bible study. So great was his need and so great the supplies from which to draw that he wrote to Dr. Bunting and said that apart from his conversion, his coming to Hoxton was the most important event of his life. The purpose of the letter was to show it was his desire to continue studies for a second year, which was granted after the examination results came out.

I have said much of Hunt's debt to Hannah. It would not be fair for me to bypass Entwistle. Let Hunt speak for himself:

> From him I have received much Christian counsel and advice. He has endeavoured to correct my errors in reading and writing, and has given me much instruction concerning Methodism generally, and the duty of a Methodist preacher in particular.

In that, Hunt made not only a powerful evangelist but a devoted pastor, and became a real father to his people; we may safely say that Entwistle also left his mark on the Lincolnshire ploughboy.

The extension of Hunt's term in Hoxton enabled him to go more deeply into the study of biblical languages, and Greek in particular, in which he became an expert and continued with its study until his death. The Rev. Samuel Jones was his language tutor, and to him also Hunt was indeed a debtor, and thus indirectly played his part in giving Fiji a splendid translation of the New Testament, which, as I have already stated, was produced from the Greek, with the aid of the English, not vice versa.

John Hunt did not bottle himself up in Hoxton. He often went to town to do evangelistic work, taking with him a supply of tracts. Being thus brought into contact with the sins of others made him seek even more his own holiness. This was no conceit. He felt very humble about it all and earnest. He was not alone in this, for a wave of spiritual conviction passed through Hoxton at the time.

His second year ended and his results were brilliant. In the light of these he received a vacation appointment in Oxford where he ministered for a short term, learning much and much loved. He was permitted to return to Hoxton to await his missionary appointment, which he had never thought of being anything but Africa.

Among the highspots of the Hoxton days were the annual meetings of the Missionary Society, and Hunt had daily prayed for fitness for carrying the gospel overseas. Africa was in his heart.

Time drew near for the appointment. The vigour and spirituality of his character had impressed the congregations of Oxford, and many there were who tried to keep this man for the home service. Is it not always so? We who are missionaries know that full well.

Hunt was pained somewhat by all this and wrote to a friend:

> I give them credit for their affection and motives, but not for the simplicity of their religion. True religion is missionary and is glad for the heathen to have the gospel at any price. .

The extra months given him were specifically devoted to preparation for Africa. He felt his agricultural background might help raise the condition of the Kaffirs. His preaching at the time dwelt especially on missions and on holiness, and his advocacy had some considerable effect on his congregations. There was indeed a great interest in missions at that time.

The men selected were *selected* in every sense of the word—a point which most of our modern historians have missed. Hunt was every inch a man—"tall, well-built, broad-chested, a true type of the soul within," wrote one at the time; still perhaps something of the farmer, and with a little of the north still in his speech, but a steady eye that commanded respect; no coarseness, yet no dandyism—his was an honest, manly grace. Because he died at thirty-six, let us not imagine he was a weakling. We cannot say that of the man, who by the sheer magic of his personality could turn the heart of Cakobau from massacre to tolerance, but that is yet to come.

4

"PITY POOR FIJI!"

I

At about the same time as "Farmer Jack" was trying to make the personal adjustments required by his entry into Hoxton, two missionaries—Cross and Cargill—were preparing to board the *Blackbird*, which was to take them from Tonga to Fiji. This was a new project, an extension of the Tonga Mission, not, at this juncture, a new mission.

In Fiji they found cannibalism and more ingenious forms of human sacrifice than the civilised world had heard of. One of the missionaries serving in New Zealand, where he was transferred after eight years in Tonga, James Watkin, was commissioned to write an appeal for new missionaries. This he did under the title, "Pity Poor Fiji!"—a pamphlet which stirred British Methodism, and not in the least, Hoxton.

It has been stated that Hunt responded to the pamphlet and offered to go to Fiji. That is not so. His mind was still set on Africa, though he was naturally not unaffected by the pamphlet. When in February 1838 he was called to the mission house and asked whether or not he would go to Fiji, it came as a shock to him. To that we shall return in a moment. Meantime, let us consider why, when Hunt's mind was known to be on Africa and he had been accepted for this end and virtually designated for it, there is so sudden an attempt to deflect his interests to Fiji.

In the first place it was a dramatic change of policy on the part of the Committee. Men for the Pacific fields were sent to a more established post first. It was not customary to send an untried man into the very front line. Furthermore, there were men like Tucker, in Tonga, designated for Fiji. Again, Cross and Cargill had been prepared in Tonga before they moved into Fiji. Subsequently Lyth and Spinney were sent first to Tonga. Yet, though this policy was adhered to before and after, on this one particular occasion they sent three new men—none with any substantial circuit experience even in the home work—to the newest, least-known, and most dangerous field on their station-sheet. One can imagine it would not only be Hunt who received a shock at the news. Was it necessary?

What men were there still in the Pacific at the time who had experience in Tonga? I mention Tonga because it was the field with the greatest affinities with Fiji. Nathaniel

Turner was in Hobart Town, had begun his work in New South Wales, and had spent six years in Tonga. Hutchinson started in New South Wales and had returned there after two years in Tonga; Watkin, who wrote the appeal, was in New Zealand and had eight years Tongan experience behind him; Woon was also in New Zealand, after three years in Tonga. On the Tonga field itself was Thomas the chairman, who had been there thirteen years and stayed another twelve; Peter Turner, who went there in 1830; Charles Tucker, designated for Fiji and sent to Tonga in 1832; Rabone with four years experience; Brooks, Wilson, and Spinney with three; and Lyth with two.

While some of these were unlikely choices, the fact remains that there was no reason, as far as appointments were concerned, for the Committee's dramatic change of policy at this juncture. There were twelve men in the Pacific with experience in Tonga, and there were many others in Australia and New Zealand who might have been tried perhaps more reasonably than raw recruits without much circuit experience in England. The dozen men named had seen the nature of native conversions, had a knowledge of Tongan, which was known in many parts of Fiji, had some appreciation of the problems to be faced and some experience in handling them, and they knew the pitfalls awaiting the unwary.

Yet the London Committee sent three untried men, all in their twenties—young men and young wives also.

I have considered this at some length and can offer only the following possible solutions:

(1) The victory over darkness was virtually won in Tonga, and it was now a specific appeal from pagan Fiji which challenged British Methodism, and there was therefore reason why those who went because of this appeal should go to that particular field.

(2) There was something to be said for sending a team of men of one generation, who knew each other and could work as a team, perhaps for a long term.

(3) Watkin's appeal had been preceded by a strong appeal for a printing press and men to work it. Jaggar was a skilled printer and bookbinder, and so too was Calvert. So the pointer swung to a Hoxton team.   •

(4) Both Cross and Cargill were uncertain. Cross had been eleven years in the islands, and his health reports were bad. Cargill was brilliant but lonely, and not always at one with his brethren. With neither of these men certain, young men with strength, vision, and powers of leadership had to be found to draw from their resources before the inevitable break came, even if it did mean training a team in the front line.

(5) The Committee saw in Hunt the man they needed—but not the Committee alone. It was overburdened with debt and could not finance new fields. The appeal for men brought gifts also, and the authorities determined to send two men and transfer two from Tonga.

Hunt's admirers were not limited to Oxford and Hoxton. One from his home country, a Mrs. Brackenbury, offered to pay for Hunt's outfit and passage, and to contribute £50 per annum towards his expenses for three years if the Committee found a third man for the team. They rose to the occasion and Calvert went with Hunt and Jaggar. It was a strong team of England's best, and all three did yeoman service.

We may safely say that both the church leaders and people were satisfied that young Hunt was the man for the job. Another would be found for Africa, but Hunt almost seemed to be born for the task in Fiji.

There is often much detail that never comes out in public in these decisions, when policies are set aside. But reading the correspondence of Cargill over that period, one is struck by the sense of loneliness and depression. Cargill's lot was not nearly as difficult as some of the others who bore theirs more patiently. Although Cargill did splendid service in many ways, his heart was in the "braes of Tully-belton." The Committee could not fail to have observed this unrest, and Cargill was their linguist, and on the linguist depended the whole future of any mission, for without good scripture translation and teaching aids, where would any mission be? It is quite possible they visualised Hunt for this task before they sent him. It is not always easy to go back a century and discover motives, but one thing we must observe is that the appointment was not according to their regular policy. It was a shock.

II

But if the information Hunt got at the mission house that day was a shock because of its unexpectedness, it was a very much greater shock on quite a different score altogether.

Upon his return he dropped into the room of a fellow student and announced, "They have proposed that I go to Fiji!"

Watkin's appeal was in his friend's mind, and that appeal had given a picture of some of the vices that existed in Fiji. He expressed his sympathy.

"Oh, that's not it!" exclaimed Hunt, to explain his dejectedness.

"What is it then?" his friend asked.

"That poor girl in Lincolnshire will never go with me to Fiji; her mother will never consent."

So there we have it. For six years he and Hannah Summers had awaited each other. They had grown fond of each other in the Swinderby days, and to some extent had grown in grace together. She had agreed to share his missionary life with him, though she had not proved the regular correspondent he had hoped in his college days. And now the strong man who shrank at nothing on his own account was shocked at the Fiji proposal, which seemed to him to cut right across his plans for domestic bliss.

She was visiting Leeds at the time, and he set himself down to write plainly, hoping that he who gave the call would make the way plain. He wrote this:

> My Dear Hannah,
>
> I have some strange news to tell you and I am not able to use many words in making it known: you must, therefore, excuse my abruptness. I have been fixed on by the Missionary Committee to go to the South Seas. You must, therefore, immediately return home, and make preparations for becoming a Missionary's wife to a most remote Station, for 20 years. No one knows my feelings, dear, for our dear friends. I hope the Lord, who has led us hitherto, will still guide and help us. I never had such difficulty in seeing my way. I believe it is of God: it is entirely unsought for by me. I need say no more. May our God help us and bless us in this most important and distressing affair! I shall be at Newton, if possible, on Thursday. I hope to see my dear—my more than ever dear—Hannah at the same time. We have only a month or five weeks for everything. God bless my dear!
>
> J. Hunt.

Whatever doubts Hunt had about his prospective mother-in-law, he had none of her daughter. They had offered their lives to God, and if the opening had come in a way they had not expected, there was no suggestion of withdrawing the offer, and no doubt God would see them through. But it is clear that Hunt expected to have to deal with difficulties and obstructions. She had not the robustness of body that he had, and in her life she had known many more comforts. He doubted not her spirit or her call, but as to whether or not she could stand Fiji physically he was not so sure. Hunt was sorely tried on this point. Are not the eleventh-hour temptations often the grimmest? Fundamentally it was not that he was placing her in danger. They believed God meant them for each other. They offered themselves unreservedly to him. If his will was Fiji and not Africa, then that was an end to the matter. His was the service and he would keep his servants.

Hannah must have felt deeply for John when she read that letter, and for once she replied immediately. Hunt sneaked into the presence of his Hoxton friend again, his face all smiles. "It's alright," he said, "She'll go with me anywhere."

There was another on whose account Hunt was somewhat concerned. It was his mother. He had sent a special communication to her through a trusted friend who kept the tollgate at Balderton.

III

Departure from Hoxton was not easy. There "Farmer Jack" had been transformed into "John Hunt," developed rather than changed. He was impressed now with the responsibility and seriousness of preaching; he had a passion for souls, a deep respect for the Bible, its truth and authority, and within himself a deep desire to grow in grace and holiness.

None of these were new to him, but each had been developed in Hoxton. He had also been introduced to the correct methods of Bible study and now held in his hand that wonderful key, the biblical languages; his pastoral work had been enriched by his experiences at Oxford—and now life lay before him, life more mysterious, more unknown, more dangerous than any of his father's tales of his army adventures.

Hoxton had given him fellowship and comradeship, he had drawn freely from devoted tutors, and the time had come to go.

His fellow students gave him a copy of Bloomfield's *Notes on the New Testament* and Robinson's *Lexicon*. What great use he was to make, especially of the former, in years to come! They parted with prayer—"a melting time" was the phrase Hunt himself used of the departure.

IV

On 6 March 1838, John Hunt and Hannah Summers became man and wife at Newton-on-Trent, and after a few days departed for London.

On 27 March the young missionaries were ordained at Wesley Chapel, Hackney, and the congregation wished them Godspeed. Four weeks later the General Secretaries accompanied them to Gravesend and said goodbye.

The 29th of April 1838 was a great day in some ways, when the young men and their wives departed for Sydney—for it may be taken to represent a very great venture of faith and experimental Christianity. I don't think this has ever been thoroughly evaluated—it was, of course, quite impossible at the time. Only in time can such things be seen in perspective. It represented the culmination of a series of significant facts.

Hoxton, though an old institution, was as a Wesleyan Methodist theological institution, quite a new affair. Many considered it an intellectual venture, pure and simple, and therefore more likely to be injurious to the plain evangelism of young ministers. Not everyone was selected, and many viewed Hunt's selection with fear. That their fears were quite groundless has been indicated by subsequent events—the immediate event, the revival in which the Hoxton students played so great a part in Hunt's own day, and the more distant results as seen in the witness, service, and literature of the Hoxton men during the midcentury period.

There was a mighty power in that Hoxton revival. It needed harnessing in some way or other, and applying to specific fields of service. Surely it was no mere chance that the intense missionary enthusiasm of the period coincided with that revival, and that the young ministerial trainees figured so prominently in it. Most great missionary ventures have begun in some religious movement or revival at home—and Fiji was no exception.

That such a revival should come from within Hoxton, a theological institution, where men are sent to do spade work, to dig out facts and assemble them for future work and use, to be trained in method and discipline—that the revival should begin there, speaks volumes for the spirit and devotion of its leaders. These were wise men, and as I have said before, Hoxton was no match factory. Calvert was Calvert, and Hunt was Hunt, each his own unique self, but each cultivated, with the roughness smoothed out, and the true features drawn out in bolder relief.

So before we leave England in our journey—never to return, for Hunt never again saw these people from whom he was now departing—we pay this last tribute to the men who led him through those formative years between candidature and ordination.

There was Entwistle, the pastor and father to them all, who saw their training was not purely academic, but that opportunities for pastoral work were provided, and wherein they tested whether their theological experiences were practical or not. Hunt learned much from Entwistle, and we may truly say his fruit was found being cultivated in the nursery in antipodean Viwa.

Then there was Dr. Hannah, who realised the potentialities Hunt had as a theologian. I can well imagine that if there was one man who would have liked to keep Hunt in England it would have been Hannah, but I have never found the slightest suggestion to that effect. For Hannah, like Hunt, believed in a man being what God wanted him to be; and though there may be a thousand places where a man can greatly serve God, there is only one place where he can give his very best—the place for which he was born. Hannah had seen in Hunt the tender flower of holiness. He had seen that Hunt's evangelical power came from his deep humility and his intense desire to be a holier man. He loved the young man for this and encouraged him to talk about it, to preach of it, and to write. It is fitting that when Hunt's *Entire Sanctification* (1849) became a book it should have been dedicated to Dr. Hannah. When Hunt saw a man in sin, it gave him pain; not because he was angry, but because it made him feel his own frailty and his need for deeper sanctification. The sin of the other man always led Hunt to deeper prayer, to personal confession, and to intenser love. When the great and terrible cannibal king, Cakobau, heard of Hunt's death, he hurried to gaze for a last time on the lifeless form. He was told of Hunt's last message for him. The man who had devoured a thousand bodies in his lifetime could not speak. He was greatly moved, moved as he had never been moved before. Here was a man who had loved him greatly—loved him despite his sin. The flower was Hunt himself, but Hannah had brought it through its most formative years.

And let us not forget the Rev. Samuel Jones, tutor in the classics and mathematics. He too saw in the work of John Hunt in Fiji the full fruit of the seeds he had planted, and more particularly does this apply to Hunt's appreciation of the Greek New Testament, which made him so ably qualified for translating the Scripture into a foreign language.

Whatever Hunt's conception of his life work may have been when he went in to Hoxton he came out and turned to face Fiji with a definite threefold programme, to which he gave his all. Firstly, there was the conversion of the Fijian people, a programme of evangelism and pastoral follow-up. Entwistle helped prepare him for that. Secondly, there was his desire to put the Scripture into Fijian. Through Samuel Jones that was made possible to him. Thirdly, he longed to spread the doctrine of scriptural holiness, and here we see the hand of Dr. Hannah.

I cannot leave these names from my record, for they were surely the understanding gardeners whom God used to take these tender tips and tendrils and set them on the trelliswork of Hoxton that they should themselves reach out to the sun. I have no doubt whatever in my mind that it was God himself who sent Hunt to Hoxton into the care of those understanding gardeners.

And then the Missionary Committee did an unprecedented thing. It determined to send an untried Hoxton team into the heart of paganism for the move from Polynesia into Melanesia, when there were a dozen experienced men already in the Pacific who could have been transferred with little difficulty. Theirs was, for once, the inspiration to abandon their set policy, and to throw the young revivalists into the hottest spot on God's earth. It was one of those desperate acts of faith which inevitably leads to two things—costly sacrifice and glory.

V

The voyage was in some ways an extension of life in Hoxton, except that they worked on their own now without tutors, and that their wives were with them. Fellowship and study continued; prayer meetings, classes, and Sunday services were held.

The journey to Sydney occupied four months, and for a period of two months the party was detained in Australia, which was all very much to their advantage, for they moved about and did a good deal of preaching. Here again, however, they met the same tempting offers—opportunities for good service without going any further. Here also they heard more of Fiji—things more terrible than they had heard in England, and they had now reached the far edge of civilisation. There are similarities with the story of Augustine's band journeying to pagan England. There were certainly many good openings in Australia, but the party had faced this issue long before—the orders came from above.

Among those with whom they fraternised in Sydney were the members of another missionary band under John Williams—whose boat, the *Camden*, was in port—en route to the Navigator Islands, and thence on its fatal voyage to Erromanga.

The Wesleyan party was to sail on the *Letitia* for Lakeba. A farewell service for the two parties, London Missionary Society (L.M.S.) and Wesleyan Missionary Society (W.M.S.), was held strangely enough in a Baptist chapel.

Sydney in 1838 was the edge of civilisation. Out beyond, the Pacific was blue enough, but on the maps of the day the islands were coloured black, and the young adventurers had no doubts about the grim possibilities that awaited them behind the palm-fringed beaches, and the fearful rites that were performed in the groves of *vesi* and *ivi* trees that stood on the outskirts of every Fijian village.

The *Letitia* was a miserable craft, a schooner of seventy-three tons, quite inadequate for the goods and passengers she carried; and what can now be flown in a single day took them twenty-six for the first stage and then, after a ten-day break in Tonga, three more days to Lakeba.

There was something to be said for going to Fiji via Tonga. They had a chance to look about and get something of the feel of the Pacific. Then after another three days they reached Lakeba. Joeli Bulu had made that same journey a few months before in a native canoe and cut a day off the time.

So actually the whole journey from England had taken them 228 days and had run into the eighth month. It was bad enough, but not by any means as bad as it might have been. Ford, appointed eight or nine years later to one of the new Vanua Levu stations, spent a full year on the journey, and was so painfully sick for the whole journey that he was quite unfit for service when he arrived, and after trying in vain, had to return home in his second year.

When the Hunts, Jaggars, and Calverts landed in Lakeba in December 1838, they brought with them not only the promised printing press but also the intimation that a new Fiji District was now constituted under Cargill's leadership, instead of functioning, as hitherto, as part of the Tonga District. The Committee in London had approved expansion in Fiji, and this set its seal on the move into Melanesia, which had actually been anticipated by the removal of Cross to Rewa, without Committee approval, earlier in the year.

It is hard to feel that British Wesleyanism really knew what a momentous decision had been made with that step. It was something of a counterpart of Paul's decision to go from Asia into Macedonia. It is true that the mission to Lakeba had made the move inevitable sooner or later, but the move from Lakeba to Rewa was in many ways bigger than that from Tonga to Lakeba. Lakeba was very Polynesian, and there were many Tongans there. The first preaching was done in Tongan. True, there was also a group of Tongans at Rewa, but the setup there was manifestly Melanesian. It is 1838; that represents the biggest jump in the forward move in the missionary attack on Fiji. Cross' transfer to Viti Levu was a feeler—a successful feeler. Hunt was sent to join him, Calvert and Jaggar remaining with Cargill to strengthen the Lakeba base, behind the spearhead of the attack. This was the church militant.

If the generals on the field had acted on their own initiative, it must have been most encouraging to them to know the Committee in London (which had been very obstinate in stopping similar advances from Tonga into Samoa) supported the Melanesian scheme and now sent reinforcements and equipment. But at the same time it must have been quite a mystery to Cargill, the new chairman, to know why the new men had not been dropped for trial in Tonga, and experienced men brought on to Fiji, especially as the vessel had spent some ten days in that group.

The situation could not have been easy for Cargill, who, by having been made chairman, now had to take the initiative. Cross was in a very serious state of health and had permission to remove to Australia. He had met with sufficient success in Rewa to warrant the continuation of the project. There was a small Tongan group there, and Cross knew their language well and was getting a grasp of the peculiarities of Rewan with their aid. Cargill, it must be admitted, had an unusual team. Cross, with whom he was prone to quarrel anyway, was his only other man who could speak the language of the mainland, and he was seriously ill. The rest of his team was new, inexperienced, and knew neither Tongan nor any Fijian dialect. Two native teachers he had sent to stand by Cross.

So Cargill began the first Fijian district meeting with Cross absent and three new men before him. Someone had to go to relieve Cross. Calvert and Jaggar were wanted for printing. The lot fell on Hunt, who agreed readily—so with no knowledge of the people, and no knowledge of any Pacific language, Hunt went to Rewa, believing he was to free Cross to return to the colonies to recover his health, and he, a stranger in a strange land, was to carry on alone. Only Cargill can have known what this meant, and one can well imagine what he thought of the London Committee's decision to send new men to Fiji.

The plan as originally envisaged was to open up several new stations in Fiji, under the Tongan District, with experienced men. The newly constituted Fiji District drew in its horns. Two stations were quite enough for the present. This was the first decision made. Cargill could help the two in Lakeba, but what was in store for Hunt, only God himself knew.

Meantime, they all spent Christmas together. I note the Hunts spent three weeks in Lakeba—one can well imagine how that three weeks was spent, knowing Hunt's habits of study, and knowing Cargill's responsibility for sending him out unprepared into the darkness. Hunt is not likely to have been idle. Cargill had prepared a useful vocabulary of some three thousand words, exclusive of proper names, and had compiled a simple grammar. As a Master of Arts in languages, he was well fitted to do this. Each new missionary for years made himself a copy. Naturally Hunt had first claim.

5
INTO THE DARKNESS

I

"Jan. 7th 1839. This morning we came in sight of Rewa," Hunt wrote in his journal, "and in the afternoon anchored safely in 'our desired haven.' We have long and anxiously looked for it, as those that watch for the morning and now see it, and for apparent wretchedness it comes up to all our preconceived notions . . .

"We anchored about five or six miles from the Mission Station. Our way to it was up a most beautiful river, which is said to be more than a hundred miles long. In the wet seasons this river is very useful to the inhabitants, the water being fresh and very good.

"The island looked very beautiful as we sailed along the winding stream. The island is low, but still the beautiful coconut trees and bread-fruit trees, and various others which bloom with perpetual spring give it a richness and beauty to an eye accustomed to sights much less beautiful. Nature all appeared charming until we saw her masterpiece—man— and a sight, especially the first sight, of a Fiji man is very appalling . . ."

So it goes on, but let us note in passing that Hunt considers he has his first sight of a Fiji man in Rewa. He has been three weeks in Lakeba and has, of course, seen plenty of Fijians. That bears out what I have already said, that the advance from Lakeba to Rewa was as great a move as that from Tonga to Lakeba. Our hero has now arrived in Melanesia.

The heart of William Cross was greatly cheered by the arrival of his young brother and, his health being at that moment slightly improved, he most vigorously declined to leave the young couple alone on the station. True, they had come in faith not knowing what to expect but believing that God was leading them, and they accepted the restoration of Cross' health as the Lord's doing, and that was the end of the matter. It was marvellous in their eyes and the name of the Lord was praised, for they thought and lived in the terminology of Scripture. Nor can I myself believe that it was anything other than the work of God, for Hunt had yet to draw from Cross as he had from Hannah, Entwistle, and Jones. A good observer, he now witnessed a missionary technique which was Cross' own.

Stores for food and barter, and a few meagre comforts for the mission house, were brought in the *Letitia* by Hunt, and the chief of Rewa gave them help on the following day to land their goods. Hunt had also brought a Fijian from Lakeba, one who had been converted in Tonga, and a most valuable addition to their team.

The Christian cause in Rewa when Hunt arrived was small—about 140 in all, mostly just nominal Christians, for though they were sincere enough in their rejection of heathenism, their form of Christianity was rudimentary on the whole. They were concentrated in two centres, one at Rewa and the other at Viwa, an island not very far distant, of which we shall hear more later on. The majority of the Rewan congregation were Tongans, and their steadiness may be accounted for by the presence among them of a strong Christian chief. Cross made fortnightly visits to Viwa and occasionally to Bau.

II

William Cross was nearly forty-two years of age when the Hunts came to live with him at Rewa. Hunt was fifteen years his junior. The old, well-tried warhorse was not born a Wesleyan, and his youthful years had been somewhat unregenerate. It was a funeral sermon on the death of a young lady which convicted him of sin and led him to join up with the folk for whom, up to that point, he had a great aversion—the Methodists. He was zealous in his search for the light and soon afterwards married a godly woman, and through her began attending class. In this way he came to understand the doctrine which meant so much to the Wesleyans—the forgiveness of sins and assurance of life everlasting. He advanced along the normal course of development—prayer leader, exhorter, and preacher. As his Christian experience grew, his mind turned to missionary work. For this he offered, was accepted, ordained, and sent to New Zealand. Though appointed to Hokiauga, he was turned aside to accompany Nathaniel Turner of Tonga. He was there by 2 November 1827.

So Cross had been over eleven years in the Pacific Islands when he met Hunt—and what an eventful eleven years it had been; years of long journeys in all forms of native craft; pioneering years; years of patient, fruitless labour followed by a period of rapid breakdown in pagan resistance, and glorious harvest; years of storms, exposure, food shortage, sickness, and shipwreck; years of teaching, preaching, chapel-building, and of attending to the means of grace. His first wife was drowned in a shipwreck in Tonga, and he himself well-nigh lost his own life trying to save her. Fourteen adults and five children died on that occasion, and strangely enough it was a Fijian who saved Cross' life and thus spared him to take the gospel to Fiji. He lost his books, furniture, and wearing apparel. Then there had been the mission to Lakeba, and after a time he had launched out alone into Great Fiji.

For some reason or other he and Cargill did not always agree. They were both strong-minded men, but Cross had seen much more of life than Cargill, and much more of the Pacific, but Cargill had scholarship as Cross never had. It wasn't the first time that age and experience has crossed with youth and learning, nor was it the last. They were better working apart—in fact, apart they were both, in their own ways, good missionaries.

Cross came from no particular school of thought. His methods were his own, methods he had thrashed out the hard way by trial and error on the field itself, but for all that they were effective. Cargill was a purist when it came to the language. It had to be got down and systematised according to the rules. Translation had to be accurate. Cross cared nothing for literal accuracy as long as he could get it across into the pagan heart, that he was a sinner and needed a Saviour, and Jesus Christ provided that salvation he needed. Cargill wanted to build for years to come a literature and means of worship that would stand the test of time, and even if all the ideas of Scripture were without meaning to the Fijian at the time, they would, as time went on, assume meaning if correctly translated and recorded. Cross saw nothing about him but the people with whom he was then dealing, their need, and the truth he had to offer. What was to happen in twenty, thirty, or fifty years to come did not concern him. No doubt God would send other men to work among them. His concern was that which lay about him now.

It is not at all difficult to see how these two worthy brothers could both quickly get impatient with each other. For the time being Hunt was living with Cross and was observing the practical man of experience, not the academic linguist, and I have no doubt at all that, if God moves in history at all, it was is will that the Hunts should commence their ministry with the Cross family at Rewa.

Cross, I have said, had evolved his own methods of work. This was now the third time he had commenced on completely virgin soil, and in no case was it long before results began to come. The fifteen years' difference between them might well have seemed more to the youngsters, for a decade and a half in the tropics on a pioneering job can age a man terribly. Hunt thereafter thought of Cross as his "father."

Then how was young Hunt, fresh from Hoxton, impressed by Cross' idea? Cross took terrific risks. He never counted the cost if he felt there was something he could do. He took risks, but trusted as he took them. He felt his life was in God's hands to take or spare, to use as he desired. "The doctrine of a superintending and ever-watchful Providence, as taught by our Lord (Matt 6:25–34)" wrote Hunt, "was inscribed on the heart of Mr. Cross, and manifested itself in all his spirit and conduct." Then he quoted the passage, "Thou wilt keep him in perfect peace, whose mind is stayed on Thee: because he trusteth in Thee."

Was there a better old warrior in the Pacific to take the young couple, so alive, so intense, so devoted, and teach them to apply this faith to the Fijian scene?

Though there is much in Cross that reminds us of an Old Testament character, whereas Hunt belonged to the New—and I think the differences of their preaching also corresponded to that definition—yet it was the penitent psalmist of the Old Testament I see in Cross, and he was not so far distant really from the New. How often were the psalmist and prophet in the thoughts of our Lord himself. So Hunt found in Cross both a fatherliness and a solidarity of faith and experience, and the two developed a strong affection for each other.

Six years afterwards Cross, having repeatedly declined to take the break in the colonies, paid the supreme price, and it fell to Hunt to take his place as chairman. And Hunt also it was who wrote his memoir, and he did not fail to state therein how many and inspiring were the memories of the few months they lived under his roof. It must have been very satisfying to Hunt to see that, after eleven years of eventful buffeting in these islands, the older man was still firmly established in the faith that God was himself living and active in the group, and that no trial or danger or loss had shaken his belief that God was still watching over him. Nor do we wonder that in time Hunt was to make the same impression on those who followed.

III

Fiji at the time had no paramount chief. She comprised a number of kingdoms of roughly equal strength. The greatest of these were Bau, Hewa, and Somosomo, with Verata fast on the wane; and these mainly by the accurate and ruthless marksmanship of degenerate white men (shipwrecked sailors and escaped convicts) with an abundant supply of Western firearms and ammunition (which could be easily had from traders and whalers for women, sandalwood, or *beche de mer*) had established their power over all maritime Fiji.

Somosomo was sufficiently far distant in the north to live in comparative isolation, but Bau, which ruled the central and eastern part of the group, and Rewa, which ruled the south, were so close to each other that the dominant political factor over the years of pioneer missionary activity was the hostility of these two kingdoms. They were in a continual state of warfare, and pagan warfare made evangelism difficult.

William Cross had endeavoured to establish his station at Bau but had failed. He was accepted at Rewa. Yet although the paramount chief had given him a dwelling site, the chief war lord was hotly opposed to the new religion. A Christian station was established across the river from the pagan town. The advantages of being across the river will be seen when we come to deal with Hunt's days at Somosomo, when he was not so fortunate. The site was, and still is, called Nasali, but the missionaries inspired by Joeli Bulu called it Zoar (Gen 19:22). Originally it had been the site of a heathen temple that had been neglected and fallen into disrepair.

The establishment of a mission in Rewa had been made possible because of the existence there of a party of Tongan workmen, a number of whom had married Fijian women—and this gave rise to a class of persons known as Tonga-Fiji. Cross had also brought Christian Tongans with him from Lakeba. There were a number of Tongans who soon became Christian under the influence of Cross' preaching, among them a chief of some importance, Fatafehe. Actually, though he did often use Tongan, Cross conducted his first service in the dialect of Lakeba. He immediately set about to adjust himself to the Rewan dialect, and after eight days hard work tried preaching in it.

Among the teachers Cross had brought from Lakeba was a Fijian, Aisake Bukavesi. He it was who succeeded in getting a message through to Namosimalua of Viwa concerning the value of the Christian religion. Namosimalua was at the time smarting under the punishment brought upon his town by the French reprisals on account of the massacre effected by his nephew, as told in the first chapter of this book; and so disgusted he was at the inability of his gods to protect his town and property that he willingly agreed to give Cross a hearing.

Cross convinced him of the truth of Christianity, and he asked for a teacher to be stationed at Viwa. Thus there began a small Christian cause in Viwa—two miles over the water from Bau. Cross visited the place fortnightly.

The strain of exposure, long journeying, and unhealthy living conditions had worn down Cross' health—and for six weeks he lay seriously ill. The house was unhealthy, and had but a single room, was built on damp ground, and almost surrounded by a moat of stagnant water. In wet weather it emitted an intolerable stench. The doors were only three feet in height and there were no windows. Here Cross suffered from cholera and then from typhus. Lest the reader should wonder why he didn't adjust these matters himself, it should perhaps be explained that the whole matter of house-building was subject to the will of the chief. The missionaries had to go where they were put, and rebuilding, removal, and alterations were subject to his consent. It was easy to offend a chief, and it might lead to the expulsion of the mission from the place. The missionaries tried always to abide by the social laws of the people.

Eventually the chief had a better house built, larger and stronger and drier—with doors, windows, and apartments. Then H.B.M. *Conway* arrived with stores and Cross' lot was greatly improved. The health of the missionary also improved, and by the time Hunt arrived he was up and about again. He now established a third preaching place and a school where some thirty-five scholars were learning to read and write. There was a small Society meeting, and a converted chief offered his house for public worship. Though the king did not become a Christian, he protected Cross.

Life in the district was unsettled. There had been several attempts to burn the town, partly successful.

Hunt said that one of the objects of Christian biography is to show that the religion of the Bible is, when tested by experiment, all that it professes to be. It boasts of being able to support the mind under all circumstances of life, however trying. He goes on to say it effected all this for Mr. Cross during his afflictions at Rewa.

That was the impression it all left on Hunt's mind. It was one of the first impressions he formed as he pieced together the story of the weeks before his arrival. It was an impression that lasted. So if Hunt was praising God for the recovery of Cross' health to such an extent that he did not have to face his first station alone, there is also no doubt that Cross was giving thanks for the arrival of the young man and woman who had, as it were, drifted into his life from out of the blue.

IV

Cross had already witnessed a number of conversions, and all had been stories worth telling. There were two brothers who determined to burn the household god, which comprised some oil and turmeric which hung in a basket, saying that if the god was true he would put out the fire. The basket blazed well enough and the brothers turned to the Christian faith. Their friends however were angry at this destruction of the sacred basket and there was trouble. One of them went to dwell on the Christian side of the river and eventually became a personal servant of the Hunts.

Another there was whom the priests gave only two days to live, but turning to God, he prayed—and lived.

There was a Fijian woman, whose temper was so vile that her Tongan husband had beaten all the teeth out of her head. She became ill and returned to her Fijian relations, who determined to put an end to the trouble by burying her alive. However, when the burial began, she resisted and escaped back to her husband. Eventually both of them were converted, and religion, we are told, produced a really remarkable change in her.

So it went on. It was very encouraging, although some of the motives for conversions were not particularly logical according to our way of thinking. Yet there was another side to the story—anxieties and disturbances, plundering of the mission stores, and petty persecution of one form and another.

The Hunts were awakened often at night by the sound of a musket and would wonder if it was the signal for an attack; but Cross, who had been kept through long years of such experiences, would sleep on peacefully through it all. The young couple accepted it all as a useful lesson to them in resignation to the divine will.

One day a member of the Christian party informed Hunt that a woman had been abandoned by her friends to die in an uninhabited house. When he found her, a number of boys had dragged her out and were trying to kill her with sticks and stones and intended to throw her into the river. Seeing the Christian, she called to him that she was hungry. He rescued her and fed her, but despite his help, she died. The Christians buried her decently. This was typical of many acts of cruelty they witnessed in those days and typical also of the changed outlook of converted Fijians.

A good example of this came from Viwa, where we have already seen there was a small Christian party. A man of some rank had sought permission from the king of Bau to kill Namosimalua, the Christian. The king not only refused but also informed Namosimalua and advised him to club the man and his family—a form of punishment Namosimalua had previously delighted in for much smaller offences. He now replied, however, that it was hardly right to punish the innocent with the guilty, so the family was spared. He even spared the life of his disloyal subject who pleaded for mercy. And with what result? The traitor himself became Christian.

V

Cross and Hunt, in addition to their fortnightly visits to Viwa, also called on Tanoa at Bau, and were even permitted to preach there if I read Hunt's journal correctly. Tanoa often promised to build them a mission house at Bau, but never did so, and Hunt firmly believed that this was because of Cakobau's influence against it.

Bau also permitted preaching on the mainland opposite, and there were converts as a direct result of preaching, despite what Henderson (1931) says to the contrary. More often, however, the converts were won by personal work, and the services were considered the place for making public testimony of the decision, often previously made in private.

Hunt was not slow in learning the language, which he realised from the start was his primary point of contact with the natives. The daily proofs of cruelty and degradation he witnessed stirred him on in his study, and we find that within about a month of his arrival in Rewa, Cross having gone to Bau, he tried taking the Rewa service himself. He had composed his first sermon in Fijian, most of which he read, but finding the people attentive, he felt that, for the first time, it was "a comfortable time." A week later he preached in Fijian again, trying here and there without notes, and before long he was preaching two or three times a week, and three and a half months after his arrival in Rewa he was able to preach a fluent sermon in Fijian without the use of notes—a truly remarkable performance.

John Hunt found favour with some of the lesser chiefs, one of whom put the question to the king of Rewa that it might be to their advantage if they all embraced Christianity. The king replied that he could become a Christian if he so desired, but that he (the king) would look after the land. This is an interesting episode as it throws light on the chief's view of Christianity as being contrary to the things of the land. When, some years later, Cakobau became Christian, he set the church fair and square in the heart of the Fijian social system, for the possible cleavage of church and state was almost beyond a Fijian's comprehension. The second point raised by the king's remark was the obvious reluctance of a lesser chief to become Christian before his superior. In some ways this was a great hindrance to conversions, and yet there were hundreds who became Christian despite it. In all probability it was not a bad thing. It meant a man had to be fairly certain of the truth of Christianity before he risked the anger of his chief. If it slowed up the numbers of converts, it also improved the quality. The missionaries did not take long to realise this, and that accounts for the manner in which they launched their evangelistic attacks in this way on the ruling chiefs, and why they sought to establish themselves at the chiefly centres. From the very first year of the Mission, when Tui Nayau, the chief of Lakeba had made the excuse that it would be difficult for him to *lotu* (i.e., become Christian) before the paramount chief of Bau, the missionaries had been trying to establish a foot in Bau itself. The "Road to Bau" was the vision behind the departure of Cross from Lakeba, and though he had failed to effect his purpose, he had gone to Rewa to be near at hand. The conversion of Namosimalua was a step nearer. While it is quite true that in most places—Lau, Vanua Levu, Rewa, Kadavu, and even Bau itself—there were scores of converts before the chief, the missionaries knew that there could never be peace or freedom from persecution until the paramount chief of the area was numbered among them.

Hunt himself felt the Fijian people feared for the safety of their gods, and many who were not Christians felt that Christianity would ultimately prevail. In Lakeba it was already said that their god had actually left the island—beaten up and sore, by the God of the Christians. The Viwa priest had dreamed that his god was leaving Viwa in fear of Hunt. I doubt if the missionaries really understood that in the Fijian mind their religion was social, and the acceptance of Christianity really had to be the substituting of it for their ancient ritual in the social system itself. They would most willingly have accepted Christianity as a new form of worship beside the old—but the missionaries would have none of that. The new faith they brought was exclusive, and that to the polytheistic Fijians was a major problem. Becoming a Christian meant not just accepting Christ, but also rejecting the tribal deities, and as they deified their highest chiefs after death, there were many who considered it treason to become a Christian.

To what extent the missionaries appreciated the full significance of this Fijian point of view I cannot say. It is easier for us who look back from a distance. Some of them certainly did not—one or two; among them, John Hunt may have done so. As time went on and Christianity grew in strength, and the anti-Christian party became hostile and persecuted bitterly, more than one Fijian chief was in a serious dilemma. How could he maintain the unity of his people? They found the Christians by far the better citizens, working harder, fulfilling their obligations, and loyal; yet if he did not persecute them, the anti-Christian party wanted to assassinate him. The most significant series of events in midcentury is really the behaviour of Cakobau in 1854 at the time of his conversion—the series of conferences he called, which determined, not that he should become a Christian (he had already decided that himself), but that Christianity should be substituted for the ancient religion of their fathers. It was Cakobau who destroyed the thirty temples of Bau and put in their place one church. That, of course, is the end of the story and happened six years after Hunt's death, and the student of history has the advantage over the actors of the drama in that he looks back and sees the whole picture. Cross and Hunt were moving slowly forward, believing God was with them, but not at all certain at this stage just where they were going. Somehow they felt that their direction should be heading for Bau.

Shortly afterwards, Messrs. Cargill, Jaggar, Lyth, and Spinney arrived at Rewa, and six missionaries and their wives assembled together—a rare sight—for a district meeting which determined that another attempt should be made to move into Bau. Lyth and Spinney had come from Tonga, but the latter was medically unfit and removed to the colony where he died the following year.

Tanoa raised objections—the smallness of the island, lack of firewood, shortage of water—all true enough, but they did not really worry Cross, and so the chief was obliged to say outright "No!"

Cross has been criticised by several writers for turning away from Bau, first to Rewa and then to Viwa—but, I feel, unjustly so. Hunt, who knew him best, said, "Though courageous, he was judicious and never offended a heathen." It is difficult to see what else he could have done under the circumstances, and if the same men were standing looking back on the scene today, I feel sure they would say that after all the Lord knew best.

So as Cross had previously turned to Rewa, he now turned to Viwa. This was a definite advance nearer the metropolis, and there were good reasons why the missionaries should not yet be admitted to Bau. They had still much to learn about Fijian customs and language and politics. Viwa was a first-class observation post, from which Bau could be studied with profit. The Bau dialect was used in Viwa. A Christian settlement there had the protection of being insular; at the same time it was near enough to Bau to attract the attention of her thousands of annual visitors from all parts of maritime Fiji. The island was certainly on the road to Bau, and it would certainly have been hard to find a better place for the dissemination of Christian truth.

Again, there were certain political issues in a highly unsettled state at the time. Tanoa was ruling in Bau, but his star was setting and Cakobau's rising. Tui Dreketi ruled in Rewa, but his rule was not complete. His two younger brothers, Qaraniqio and Cokonauto, were both restless and had parties of followers. This threefold division of Rewa ultimately brought about its downfall. The relationships of Tanoa and Cakobau were repeated in Somosomo with Tui Cakau and Tui Kilakila. In each case the old man was inclined to be sympathetic, but the rising warrior adamant in his opposition. However, let us note what a suitable time it was for big events—the three great kingdoms were facing crises, with their old chiefs' powers waning and those of the younger waxing. Sooner or later the changes would come. Was it not an excellent time for missionaries to be on the spot, observing, learning, preparing for the crises?

Does that mean then that Bau was not ripe for conquest at the time? It could mean that the missionaries were not ripe for the task. It is significant that when the time did come both were ready together.

On the other hand, much had already been achieved. If the triumphs at Rewa were limited, they were not limited to Rewa. Viwa itself was an offshoot, and it had given them a chapel, a congregation, and a chief's protection, right under the shadow of Bau. This was now constituted a mission station—a cell had divided into two. Let us not fail to note that this was in itself quite an achievement. Cross moved into Viwa in August. No one appreciates better than I do the strategic importance of this move, for as I write these lines at the present moment I look from the window of my house on the hilltop at Bau, and Viwa is there before my eyes, so near and clear that I can distinguish the kind of trees which form its vegetation.

We leave Cross there. This is Cross the pioneer, of whom Hunt said, "Diligent, never unemployed, ashamed of nothing but sin."

Hunt had learned much from Cross, and afterwards spoke of him as his "father." Among the things which had impressed him were his methods of evangelism, and among these was the habit of composing brief paraphrases, not actual translations, of scripture episodes—short accounts of a Bible narrative as one would tell it to a child. These he worked out carefully, paying more attention to the rhythm and assonance of his Fijian than to the literal detail. Then he would make many copies of his final draft and distribute these among the natives who could read. They, in their turn, would go from house to house reading these paraphrases, until eventually they would give away their copies and go back for another.

Cross did very little real translation work as Hunt and Hazlewood did later, and that which he did attempt was far too free to be of much use to the young linguists who followed him and set out to give the Fijians an accurate translation of the Bible, but it was good evangelistic method, and Hunt learned much from it, and he did not forget it later when he had the training of exhorters in his hands at Viwa.

Cargill's vision of an accurate Bible was undoubtedly sound, but Cross' method of work was certainly the best way of getting a knowledge of the use of Fijian idiom, which was itself necessary for the achievement of Cargill's ideal. Hunt followed the method of Cross until he was ready to attend to the task of which Cargill dreamed.

VI

It would not be fair to Cargill to say Hunt was not indebted to him. The three weeks Hunt had spent in Lakeba, working on Cargill's grammar and dictionary, had made a profound impression upon him. The speed with which he advanced in preaching is evidence of this. Though Hunt was never attracted to Cargill as he was to Cross, he firmly believed that each missionary had a task on the field and gifts commensurate to that task, and therefore he drew from all men and, like Paul, was debtor to both Greek and barbarian. He actually set the idea in writing in these words: "The gifts bestowed on the Apostles and first Christians were exactly adapted to their circumstances and the work they were called to perform."

But Hunt carried this doctrine a stage further, not being merely content to develop his own abilities, but to draw for himself from the virtues of others and thus increase his own abilities. We have already seen his intense search for knowledge and improvement, and his drawing from Entwistle, Hannah, Jones, and Cross. We have yet to see what he learned from Lyth, and I must admit, that though Hunt and Cargill were never drawn to each other as deeply as the others, yet it was Cargill who formed the link between the linguistic groundwork Hunt had from Jones and the glorious vernacular library he left in Fiji.

For six months Hunt worked systematically at the language, trying to master the peculiarities of its construction and grammar, pondering its highly complex system of pronouns, trying to clarify the differences between the three dialects he had met already, getting his vocabulary classified according to its dialect. As I have myself ministered in areas where upwards of a dozen different dialects are used, I can imagine something of the nature of his six months at it. Then—it was on 18 June—he turned in earnest to a systematic project of translation work. He began on the Gospels. He had some of Cross' paraphrases before him, and some of Cargill's translation into the dialect of Lakeba. Cargill had to this point translated into Lakeban all of Mark, sixteen chapters of Matthew, the Epistles of John, and a part of Genesis.

So Hunt set to work, intending, as he wrote in his private record, to call no man master and to do his own thinking. As we have grown now to expect, he began by planning a method of work:

(1) To take a chapter of the Greek New Testament and read it through, noting in particular any word about which he had any doubt. Read Bloomfield's *Notes* and Campbell's *Translation*, and any other books on the subject he had to assist in ascertaining the true meaning of the text (he mentions the use of Blakestone's *Commentaries* from time to time).

(2) After mastering the chapter, commence translating, using the Greek text as the standard, together with the English version, and for the translation, himself, with references to any made translations and the assistance of all natives to whom he had access.

Whence learned the Lincolnshire ploughboy these scientific methods of translation work? Though neither Jones nor Cargill was his master, he certainly drew heavily from them both.

VII

Although Hunt's private reading was heavily biblical and theological, he did not neglect other fields. We often find references in his journal to works he has been reading. He seems to have had a fondness for biography—I have noted Byron, John Smith, and Swift mentioned.

There is in Fiji a rather dilapidated book in which Hunt had kept note of certain business transactions, among them one concerning books. The Rev. Francis Wilson died at Vavau, Tonga, in 1846. Partly to relieve the widow of an unwanted library and to provide her with ready money upon her return to England, and partly for the value of the books on the field, Hunt bought them, sharing the purchase with the men in Fiji. It must have been a considerable library, for the price over all came to about £70, and Hunt's own share, £20.8.10, was by far the biggest. Every book was individually priced, and apart from an encyclopedia and Watson's *Works* and a few dictionaries and lexicons, most of them were low-priced, so the library must have been considerable for those days.

It is with no little degree of interest that we note Hunt acquired for himself some texts and a Latin dictionary, so I think we may assume that either he knew a little or was about to take it up. The number of Greek works he acquired leaves us no room for doubt—he must have been quite at home in the language.

However, also among the names, we find works on Napoleon, also poetry and fiction, for example Cowper is there, and Goldsmith also. There is a book on chemistry and a *Cabinet Lawyer.*

During the last year or so of his life, as the pressure increased and he pressed on more and more with his translation, his general reading seems to have decreased. It was a race with death. One can understand it.

VIII

The special district meeting of 10 May, which determined on the removal of Cross to Viwa, also determined on several other moves, which indicates that a strong feeling existed among them that the time had come for a bold advance into Melanesia proper.

Cargill and Jaggar, with the printing press moved into Rewa, brought the chairmanship and publishing into the front line, a bit risky in the latter connexion as events were to prove. Hunt, who had now quite a grasp of the language, was to pioneer the new field at Somosomo.

When Hunt agreed to undertake this responsibility, it was thought that he and his wife would be going alone. Though he was quite willing, his mind was not quite at rest about that decision in the district meeting; and the native folk of Rewa did not approve at all. There is a sentence in his journal which suggests the team still had some adjustments to make in their relations with one another. As to its precise nature, we are left guessing, but clearly the academic man of Aberdeen and the scholar of Hoxton had different ideas on applied Christianity, and Hunt felt some of the matters were not quite straightforward. He did not flinch at going alone to Somosomo, but was pleased, two months later when the boat came to take him, to discover that Lyth was to accompany him.

The Lyths were on board the *Letitia* on 15 July when she brought Cargill and Jaggar and the printing press for the Rewa station. The Hunts now prepared to advance a step further into the darkness. True, it was further away from chiefly Bau, but the move left three missionaries near the centre, and the move into Somosomo was the greatest trial of faith yet to be faced. During their term in Rewa they had witnessed about one hundred conversions. Relationship with Cross had been most cordial, and they had made great strides with the language. A little persecution served to prepare them for Somosomo.

6

THE CRUCIBLE OF GOD

I

It is with some degree of trepidation that I attempt to evaluate the Somosomo experience of John Hunt. There were four men whom God turned over in that crucible. They all came out refined—the finest gold. But it must have been a costly experience. I have spent the last fourteen years reading missionary reports, documents, correspondence, journals, and biographies, but I have yet to find a finer team of workmen anywhere than John Hunt, Richard Bursdall Lyth, David Hazlewood, and Thomas Williams. These were all men clearly divinely selected for their respective tasks. One cannot read the history of the early church in Fiji without seeing that God was himself an active factor behind it all, making use even of the tragedy and persecution with which these men and their amazing wives were faced. This was surely the same God of whom it was written as having "spake in time past unto the fathers by the prophets"—the God who selects, prepares, and uses men to achieve his purpose.

Each of the men I have mentioned lived to see a little of the fruit of his labour—an earnest, an ἀρραβών,[2] as it were. Yet none saw the full result of his accomplishment.

But before there were any results at all, these men had to pass through the test of fire. They were tested in every conceivable way. They were thrust away beyond the reach of their brethren. There was here far more isolation, far more danger than they had met hitherto, and a far greater arrogance and tyranny in the despotism of the chief. But these men and women had already proved they did not fear these things. Ships did go to Lakeba and Bau, but Somosomo was still more or less shut off by its completely pagan night. Very few vessels they saw, save the mission craft, and that not often. Once there was a pirate, once an exploration expedition, whose captain tried to encourage them to leave the place with him—but God had set them there and there they would stay. In the very centre of sin, they had to live and witness it daily—not on the other side of the river, but in the house wherein the chief set them beside the cannibal ovens. Whenever these men resisted the sin about them, their lives were in jeopardy, and not theirs only but also their wives. They had to see their little ones lain on the altar of submission to the divine will. It is not every

---

2   The word really means a portion or foretaste now, which is a promise and pledge of more to come.

person who can maintain a holy warfare at the same time as he sees his children laid cold in the grave, especially when the heathen cry, "Now, where is thy God?" Somosomo meant all this—and more.

Somosomo, from a point of view of the expansion of the Mission, its converts, and statistics, meant failure—absolute failure as the world measures it.

There were converts among the Tongans and Wallis Islanders, but these converts moved on, leaving what? Nothing!

Had they come to Fiji for this? Had they left their homes in England, their people, their occupations—Hunt his farming, Lyth his medicine—for this? For this, had they set themselves aside for special training? For this, had they rejected offers of great service for God, both in Oxford and in Australia? For this had they suffered and endured much; the long journey by sea; their shortage of food; the loss of their loved ones; the loss of home, of comfort, of companionship? For this they endured their present plight, the horrors of cannibal feasting, the stench of the bodies baking in the ovens. Day after day, week after week they endured, they suffered, they prayed—for what? For converts! And there were none. After seven years Somosomo had eleven members, ten of them the staff, the other a stranger. Here was failure, utter failure. For this they had given their love—their life. Yet when they had the chance to go, they elected to remain.

He is a great man who can endure failure and still go on in faith, especially when the price paid has been great, and more especially still when he had previously enjoyed the fruit of success. The Somosomo experience was an acceptance of the divine will—the absolute surrender of the human will to God's, irrespective of results. As Hunt himself put it so often: "Duties are ours, events are God's." The men were clearly mystified by their failure, but it never occurred to them to doubt—they believed the end was in God's hand.

Yet to those of us who look back now and have the advantage of seeing events in perspective, clearly *there had to be a Somosomo*. There had to be a place where men like Hunt and Hazlewood could do their literary and linguistic groundwork. There had to be a multiplication of Dr. Lyth's medical knowledge, and a transference to others. In the economics of the kingdom of God in Fiji, Somosomo had its place—God knew best. Evangelical success in Somosomo would have sent the men out on long treks, on preaching, teaching, ministering, and consolidating, for which they were not ready—and furthermore it would have made their literary and medical groundwork impossible. How often, when the waves of conversion did come in Fiji, they came in mighty floods, and the missionary reserves, supplies of alphabets, Scriptures, and native teachers who were available, were sadly inadequate for the task. On these occasions there was time for nothing but pushing ahead. Such success before the machinery of the Mission was ready for it would have been fraught with dangers. Again it was Hunt who prepared the basic theological work for publication, and on this work the Mission built for years to come. His own personal experience, "perfected through suffering" like his Master's, has been written over the church in Fiji, its hymns, its catechism, its preaching, right down to the present day. I myself, a present-day missionary, acknowledge my personal debt to the man, and I have heard older Fijian ministers speak of other missionaries who have made the same acknowledgement—several of them chairmen after him.

We may perhaps compare the Somosomo experience with that of Paul in the street called Straight, and the wilderness of Arabia. There was this stage—a meditative, submissive, deeply religious stage—needed before the cultured, selected, and prepared Roman citizen, Greek-speaking student of Gamaliel could become the Christian missionary God wanted to send over into Europe. The difference between the man who was led blind to the house of Judas, and the author of the famous chapter on love, is something like the difference between the men who went into and came out of Somosomo. To say that the John Hunt who came out of Somosomo was a more mature man would be to put it mildly. Pain, sacrifice, long hours of prayer and meditation had aged him—and had aged Hannah too. Once he got to Viwa again, the difference was apparent. There was a desperateness now about his pleading. He had a new sense of time—not of the clock but eschatological. Suffering and sin has not made him quiet, for he is still the man of fire and a vigorous personality. If possible his passionate love for the sinner is greater. He is more intense. There is a desperateness about his evangelism, a pleading, a suffering with the sinner. He had learned to weep for the sinner as the Master himself had done.

Somosomo taught Hunt that a missionary's days were numbered, and from this time on he radiated with energy. The hours he worked, the sermons he preached, his writing, his translating, his travelling—it was an endless stream of energy, sweeping on like a river in flood. Six years he had still to live, and it was as if he knew, and determined to take no rest until he rested with God. How he put so much into those six years is a complete mystery to all of us who have tried working overtime in Fiji. But I am pushing too far ahead. If Somosomo meant all this, we must then take a good look at what happened there before we move on to Viwa.

II

The Somosomo mission was established because of the desire of the Somosomo chief.

Somosomo was the centre of a powerful kingdom which reached far away into the north and towards the sundown. It included many small islands and Taveuni, where it was situated, and stretched along the long coastline of the Great Land, where lay a large gulf that was almost like a sea in itself. It was Thomas Williams, one of the Somosomo prophets, who first put the true depth of that gulf on the map (though the geographers have given him no credit for it), and another missionary, who subsequently gave his life among the hillmen of Great Fiji, who made the first census of the villages along the coastline of the gulf.

The extensive and populous kingdom came under the iron heel of Tui Cakau and Tui Kilakila, his son. They were absolute dictators in a truer sense than any other chief of the time. But the kingdom was so extensive that during the forties the Somosomo people were having some trouble maintaining their authority. First there had been the rebellion of Vuna, and then of Natewa, the people of the great gulf. There was fairly good evidence that Bau had had a finger in the pie in each case, and perhaps not without reason, for with Bau and Rewa engaged in a life-and-death struggle in Great Fiji, it was safer to see Somosomo had problems in the north to keep her mind occupied.

The forties was a period of war. At one stage there were seven wars being waged at once. Then suddenly there shot forth into the darkness a ray of light. It shot right across the heart of pagan Fiji. Had it not been for this light, those three kingdoms would undoubtedly had finished by exterminating each other. Meantime, for the purpose only of this record, it must be apparent that the missionaries had to consider the strategic, political, and military importance of Somosomo. So fearlessly they turned to this place, beyond the white man's influence, the place considered at the time as the very home of cannibalism, the place beyond the horizon, beyond the last reach of the highway where the white men's ships sailed, unknown save by stories—they turned to this place because it seemed to be the key to the Great Land as Bau was to Great Fiji.

Here went the Hunts and the Lyths, all still more or less in the fair bloom of youth, with the grand willingness to make sacrifices which youth seem sometimes willing to make with seeming abandon. One can well imagine the mixed feelings with which they left Rewa and headed into the unknown.

Yet behind the venture there were two facts which seemed to them good signs. It was the chief who had invited them, and a Fijian scout had gone ahead and reported there was a Tongan settlement there. These two matters must be examined briefly, for they have important bearing on the missionary methods.

The canoes of Somosomo had visited Lakeba not long before, and these voyagers were astonished at the difference Christianity had made to the place since their last visit. On that occasion they had been asked to establish a station at Somosomo. Yet they had few illusions about it. They fully realised that the attractions Christianity had to Tui Cakau and Tui Kilakila were no more than the regular and apparently unlimited supply of knives, fishhooks, and axes which went with it. Cargill put it down to pride and ambition. A chief with a missionary must have been a man with considerable prestige in the eyes of the other chiefs. Tui Kilakila had said on that occasion at Lakeba, "*Sa turaga levu sara o Tui Nayau. Sa luvu koi au*" ("Tui Nayau is a very big chief, but I sink"). Furthermore, places where missionaries were stationed were more frequently visited by overseas ships, and this also offered chiefs some opportunity for acquiring wealth. So Cargill reasoned at the time, and as chairman he promised to do something about it as soon as he had men free for the appointment.

There is another record, a letter written by Cargill 23 May 1837, when the cause at Lakeba comprised 138 full members, 76 on trial as members, and many more adherents, which states that the visits of these people were frequent, and they urgently requested the appointment of a missionary to Somosomo, and argued in this fashion (the actual words I quote from Cargill's letter):

> The Chief of Lakeba is not powerful. His people are very few and poor, and he cannot practise what you teach, without the consent of his superiors. If you come to us we will allow our children to be taught to read on your first arrival, and we will listen to your doctrine, that we may know if it is true or false, beneficial or useless.

On one occasion Tui Kilakila kept Cargill answering questions for two hours, and later upon their departures he and his father pressed Tui Nayau to use his influence with the missionaries to procure a mission station for Somosomo. It was partly in response to such appeals that the extra staff was sent out, as we have seen, in 1838.

Eventually, when Tanoa of Bau was in exile under the protection of Somosomo, and Lajike, the royal Tongan, was gathering his forces there to aid Tanoa, the faithful Josua Mateinaniu (a Fijian of Vulaga, who had been converted in Tonga and had come back with Cross and Cargill to preach to his own people) was sent to these Tongans under the protection of a chief. Many abandoned heathenism through his preaching, so that he was able to establish a class meeting, and ultimately a party of these young Christians went to Lakeba for the express purpose of receiving Christian instruction. These were Tongans, but one needs to remember that in Somosomo, as in Lakeba itself and Rewa, Tongans had formed the original nucleus of the Christian cause. This same Josua Mateinaniu, who had already proved himself a first-class advocate, was yet to demonstrate his ability in the spearhead of evangelism among his own people in as yet untouched areas. This man, Joeli Bulu, and Paula Vea stand out as three of the great pioneer evangelists of Pacific church history—they were more than pioneers, they were advance agents. But at this stage they had still to win their spurs. However, Mateinaniu's immediate success at Somosomo, together with the fact that the missionaries knew they had been invited by the chief, inspired them with some hope in their project as they turned their backs on Rewa in the *Letitia*, which headed north on 22 July 1839.

III

The *Letitia* was a wretched little schooner, with cramped and ill-ventilated sleeping quarters. No attempt was made to keep the craft clean. Its one steward was as dirty as the vessel, and half the time the captain was drunk. The two families tried to sleep on top of chests and boxes, but without success, and Hunt was frightfully seasick. Everything was open to the fumes and odours of the hold.

The hope they had when they left Rewa was dashed soon after their arrival, for there was no enthusiasm at their coming. The internal political balance had changed at Somosomo. Tui Cakau, the old man now over seventy, was no longer an actor in public events. His gigantic son was regent.

A temporary house was prepared for Hunt and Lyth—quite a good house as Fijian buildings were. Actually it was one of the chief's own houses, and Cargill, who had escorted them to the new station, had the ship's carpenter set to work with their packing cases trying to make a few adjustments inside the house to suit it to European requirements. Rooms, windows, and large doorways are features of modern house-building, and two families, it must be remembered, had to live in this house.

The captain and the crew were thoroughly scared of everything during the unloading. The Fijians on the canoes that surrounded the *Letitia* seemed to verify everything they had heard about the terrifying nature of the Somosomo people. The boarding nets were up and the crew sat on deck with loaded muskets and fixed bayonets while the mission party went overboard into a large canoe. They were not the only Europeans who said it was all sheer madness.

Then the *Letitia*, with the chairman on board, sailed away into the south. Hunt and Lyth with their truly noble wives remained and lived in that house for two years.

Somosomo was indeed a prison. They were not received as they had been promised. The people did not give them a hearing as had been promised also. They were forbidden from going from town to town preaching, and the people were prohibited from becoming Christian by the threat of the same chief who had invited them and assured them of a hearing. They were forbidden permission to build a house of their own. They were mere puppets, dolls, playthings of the chief—his white novelties like monkeys or birds to entertain him and make him famous and provide him with hardware from overseas.

IV

There had been a white man, a Scotsman, who passed through those waters, making from the windward to the leeward islands and chanced to touch on one of these islands. It seemed to the inhabitants that he had a little property, so they clubbed him and ate his body and made off with his frugal possessions. About the same time as this was happening, Hunt and Lyth arrived at Somosomo. Life counted for very little—and still less if its owner had possessions.

V

Ra Bici, one of the chief's sons was lost at sea and, as was their custom, his wives must needs be strangled to accompany his spirit into the next world and serve him there. There was nothing unusual about that, and Somosomo proceeded to attend to its normal responsibilities to the dead, but it has bearing on this chronicle of events because it brought Hunt and Lyth up against Tui Cakau in their first clash—and a mighty shock it was to each of them.

Hunt went to the chief to beg the lives of the women, and the man flew into a rage—not on account of the women (what were they anyway?), but because the stranger should dare to express an opinion, should seek to interfere with his tribal authority. Actually Hunt had made no active interference; he had but presented a request, and had presented it in the correct way. Possibly this very fact added fuel to his anger. Had it been wrongly done, it would have been put down to ignorance, but a correctly made request put the chief in an awkward position, and being a very big man he did not like people trying to change his decisions.

If Hunt and Lyth now realised how fine were the threads by which their lives were held in Somosomo, the chief was no less shocked to realise the fearlessness and independent spirit of his "playthings."

However, in the hope that the lost canoe might be sheltering somewhere among the islands, the missionaries persuaded the chief to delay the strangling, and an agreement was made with the captain of the *Letitia* to go to the islands to seek the lost chief. The agreement was that five thousand yams be the payment for the voyage and that the captain be allowed to trade for any more the people should bring. He went as he was instructed to Koro and Nairai, and discovered only that part of the canoe house of Ra Bici's craft had been washed up at Batiki. He returned with this information and asked for payment. It was refused, and when he complained, the people were told not to trade. The actions of Tui Cakau and Tui Kilakila were determined not by their promises but by their moods and the profit that could be made by them.

Sixteen of Ra Bici's wives were strangled that day, and the deed was done in front of the missionaries' house, and night after night they witnessed the pagan death festivities which accompanied this event. At midnight they would be startled by the melancholy wail of conch shells and the terrifying yells of pagan dancers. In respect for the dead, men and women amputated their fingers at the joints, fastening the pieces of finger on reeds in rows along the wall of the house. A hundred pigs were baked to conclude the ceremony. One of these was sent to the missionaries. This they knew was an act of friendship. Although they were subjected to insult and humiliation in many ways, they were never regarded as enemies. It was a peculiar form of friendship, and it came as a rather terrible realisation to them that fellowship with the people of Somosomo meant that they should have to witness all sorts of pagan festivals, cannibal feasts, lewd war dances, widow strangling, body mutilation, and countless other things—not only to witness them, but to witness them more or less in silence.

It was a dilemma of the first magnitude. On these people they depended for food. But what was the price of the food? The future looked grim.

VI

A month later an epidemic of influenza broke out. It was the occasion of a visit of some Tongan canoes, and it was noised about that this was a disease of the *lotu*. Then Mrs. Hunt sickened of it and dysentery followed quickly, and being with child she became very sick indeed, and at one stage Dr. Lyth feared for her life.   .

Yet this sort of thing was all in a way part of the training of John Hunt. On occasions like this he acquired his nursing experience under the guidance of Lyth—experience which stood by him in Viwa later. Hunt grew a little despondent at the thought that sooner or later he might find himself on a station alone, and from that moment he made it his business to draw from Lyth's medical knowledge and experience as he had drawn from Hannah and Jones and Entwistle. He did it effectively—witness the fame of the Viwa dispensary later on.

Mrs. Hunt recovered after her son was born, but Dr. Lyth's journal records simply, "after a painful and exhausting labour on her own birthday." But alas, the child lived but a short time, dying after an ailment from which he suffered for twelve days—aged three weeks. To his great personal friend Calvert, Hunt wrote:

> Here then we are, my dear brother, in the furnace of affliction. But what? Has God forsaken us? Oh no! Glory be to Him, He is with us in all our afflictions, and will, in His own time and way, deliver us out of them all . . . I had long had an impression on my mind that some great trial awaited me, but I looked for it from without. In this I was wrong. My mind, however, was somewhat prepared by such impressions, and the prayer to which they led, and for what may yet come. "It is the Lord; let Him do what seemeth good."

In that this statement comes from a private letter and shows something of the mental attitude of Hunt to his afflictions, we may perhaps pause with it for a moment. It is easy for Hunt's biographer to produce a great deal of highly introspective material, and to do so at the expense of the living personality ever active in the Fijian scene. Rowe did that in his biography of Hunt. Yet it is inevitable that we do study the mind of the man. In the first place, we cannot deal with his important theological book on *Entire Sanctification* unless we do; and for our more immediate attention at this juncture, the affliction and failure of Somosomo represent the last formative stage in the development of John Hunt of Viwa.

In this letter Hunt shows himself steeled for facing trial. He expected it from without. His mental readiness has enabled him to endure the family trial. The phrase "what may yet come" indicates he has no illusions about the perilous position they are in at Somosomo. We also see that he considers his responsibility to face what comes, giving thanks to God that he can be commissioned in his service. There is an absoluteness about his obedience. It is in this that we may trace the tremendous powers of endurance in Hunt and his devoted wife.

At the same time, he wrote to Cargill the chairman, reporting the event. It is a more matter-of-fact letter, more about the mother, the birth, and the death and burial than about his own mind.

Baby John was the first missionary burial in Fiji. The following twenty years saw the burial of four children and the missionary William Cross on that Somosomo station; Mrs. Cargill and three children at Nasali (Rewa); Mrs. Samuel Waterhouse and Mrs. Hazlewood died at Nadi (Vanua Levu); and Mrs. Wilson at Bua; Moore, Watsford, and others buried their children in Vanua Levu; Hunt another at Viwa, where he himself also lies buried; Crawford died at Levuka; and Polglase at Bau. Several of the men were returned home or to the colonies to die prematurely as a result of their Fijian experiences, among them Spinner and Hazlewood. Every person in that tragic list, with the exception of William Cross, was under the age of forty years at death—but none of them died in vain. Somewhere in this record the reader has to be confronted with this aspect of missionary trial, and what better place is there than with the account of the first burial. John and Hannah Hunt were the first to take this cup.

Rewa, Somosomo, and Nadi were three stations with tragic medical records for the mission staff. And they were three mission ventures which perished within a few years— Rewa because of the wars with Bau, Somosomo because of the refusal of the chief to allow his people to become Christian, and Nadi because the Christian town was wiped out by heathen treachery of Tui Levuka, whose promises were on a par with those of Tui Kilakila. Yet from these stations the missionaries found their experiences so widened that they were able to turn their hands to new forms of service; in particular, medical work, in which they had received no previous training. Sooner or later the place of medicine in old Fiji will have to be the subject for a whole volume, and when that book is written the name of Dr. Lyth will shine as the stars, and it will be seen that men like John Hunt and Thomas Williams, who lived with him, drew tremendously from his knowledge and resources. The journals of Richard Bursdall Lyth in the Mitchell Library, Sydney, must be the basic primary source for such a work, but the writer of that book will also have to study the journals of the other missionaries, and he will be surprised at the number of medical references and the extent of the medical knowledge of these ministerial missionaries.

Hunt and Lyth were together for three years at Somosomo, but their contacts were not terminated with their separation. For instance, there is a reference in Lyth's fifth journal to the fact that Hunt at Viwa is somewhat baffled by some of the symptoms of a sickness with which Jaggar (at Rewa) is afflicted. Hunt, doing all he can for the patient, has also written to Lyth for advice, and keeps in touch with him, reporting recovery a month later.

There were times at Somosomo when the whole party was sick at once, when both women were confined at the same time. Elsewhere in his journal Lyth records that the whole party was suffering from "severe colick fever." Hunt was learning his medicine in the "University of Hard Knocks." The Lyths lost a child with croup, and Hannah Hunt was again brought low with dysentery which lasted for several months. Later on in that same year one may read in Lyth's beautiful handwriting this brief but significant record:

> Wed, Dec 1841 Mrs Hunt, after a long and anxious labour—still-born child.

Poor Hannah!

VII

Dr. Lyth sailed into Fiji from Tonga on the crest of a wave which had carried him in one swift action from a place where considerable response to evangelism was being consolidated into an organised religion to the very spearhead of missionary attack in the darker part of Fiji.

He sighted Fiji on Sunday, 30 June 1830, and in less than a month he had been introduced to the work in Lakeba, and had seen the uprooting of the printing establishment there and its transfer to Rewa. This station too he had seen as Cargill took over. Under Cargill he had been a member of the district meeting which had given him his first appointment. It had been intended to let him start at Lakeba, which had many affinities with Tonga and where he would have been of immediate service in every way; but the health of Spinney, who had accompanied him, demanded his return to the colony, and therefore his inability of going with Hunt to Somosomo as planned. So Lyth took his place, leaving Calvert at Lakeba.

On 19 July he had witnessed the first meeting of the Language and Translation Committee, and by 27 July, less than a month after his sighting Fiji, he was in Somosomo paying his respects to the chief. Things could happen quickly in Fiji, even though it might take a missionary a whole twelve months to get there from England (as it did, for instance, in the case of Ford, who was seasick all the way, and so suffered from aftereffects that he had to return almost at once to England).

There were times when the missionaries on the field had to act without reference to the London Committee.[3] There were also certain matters best left to them. One of these in which there had been speedy and definite action was the matter of grasping the Fijian language and getting out literature for anyone who would learn to read. Cross and Cargill pioneered this field with the assistance at first of Josua Mateinaniu. The orthography was Cross' and the grammar Cargill's. The latter had done definite scripture translation in the Lakeban dialect; and though Cross' work was more paraphrase than literal translation, he had done some specific work on the Psalms and certain passages from the Epistles. They had agreed on the orthography before their separation at Lakeba. It was a good system and presents no difficulty to the people who use it, though some foreigners and present-day Europeans

---

3   The English authorities of the Wesleyan Missionary Society (W.M.S.), sometimes confused by journalists with L.M.S. [London Missionary Society].

who are not prepared to take the pains needed to master the language, and especially the ten-day tourist journalists, are critical of it. Yet the men who created it and worked with it—translating, teaching, and preaching—found it excellent, as do we who follow.

John Hunt sang its praises on several occasions and wrote at length about it in his "Memoir of William Cross":

> It has a letter for every elementary sound in the language, and—none useless.

And again:

> The eye and ear are not at variance as in reading English, but in general you
> know how a word should be pronounced the moment you see it, though you
> have never heard it uttered . . . The advantage of such an alphabet to the native
> is great.

Hunt points out that this was Cross' genius, and though Cargill was his superior as a man of letters, he was convinced at once of the value of such an alphabet. Its advantages in printing were tremendous.

The reader will readily understand how, with men like Cross and Cargill in charge, there was going to be nothing slapdash about translation work. All the missionaries were expected to do translation work, but there had to be some kind of a common working basis. Hunt, Watsford, Lyth, Williams, and Hazlewood fell in so naturally with this scheme that I am unable to say whether they were of this opinion beforehand, or whether they were themselves the fruit of the system of Cross and Cargill. Jaggar and Calvert were printers rather than translators, although much printed material was revised subsequently by Calvert, including Scriptures and textbooks.

We are therefore not surprised to find this early record of 19 July 1839 of the functioning of a Language and Translation Committee, meeting while the men were gathered for that district meeting. That committee determined on the following plan of action:

> Work with definite projects in mind.
>
> Two dictionaries—one of Scripture and proper names, another of all Scripture
> words, so to be arranged to get opinion of all members, and settle on a firm basis.
>
> (1) Orthography of proper names.
>
> (2) Adoption of best words in Fijian language for purposes of translation.
>
> (3) Introduction of suitable foreign words where required. These works to be
> ultimately enlarged and adapted to suit different dialects.

Now that is an extremely important historical record, preserved by Dr. Lyth, only so many days freshly arrived in Fiji. It is one of a number of statements which he alone seems to have kept, for there is no other trace of this in the Mission archives. Yet consider for a moment just what it implies.

It reveals a clear and definite policy from the very start. There was direction and motive in their decisions. The primary motive was the evangelisation of Fiji, and it was their firm belief that to accomplish this the Scriptures would be the principal instrument. They must then get the Scriptures into the Fijian language as soon as possible, but the translation had to be good, because it had to endure. "The Word of God" was a tenet of their creed. Here is an aspect which seems to have been missed by students. Christianity had a great advantage over paganism in this respect. The Christian God not only spoke to his people, but he gave them a written record and put it into the hands of the people, who could read it for themselves and obtain guidance thereby. The pagan religion of Fiji had no counterpart of that—temples, priests, prayer, worship, sacrifice, inspiration, and other things she had—but the printed word of God was something entirely new. And it was tremendously important, yet no Pacific historian has yet attempted to evaluate its importance, as far as the writer is aware.

The Scriptures were not only required quickly, but they had to be in the best possible translation. The time had not yet come for the selection of the best man for the job, and for the time being every man was asked to do his part, and they pooled their work, testing and criticising in order to find the very best. One doesn't need to go beyond the journal of Thomas Williams (which, having been published, is available to the public) to see that this method was carried on for years, even with works other than the Scriptures.

Again, it was quite apparent to the Committee that there were many complicating factors. Translation involved new ideas, and new ideas often meant new words. The introduction of foreign words required careful thought, likewise the transliteration of proper names. A standard of some sort was required. Then there were words that, though similar in meaning, varied in tone, intensity, or occasion of use. Every speaker of Fijian knows that these words just do not follow the brain tracks of the English mind. The right word has to be found for the particular situation. Such investigations held up the speed of translation work, and the new men on the staff at the time appreciated this difficulty. In some cases the Fijian language is rich in vocabulary, and the meaning of the Greek or Hebrew is more simply brought out than in the English; but in other cases, and especially in those relative to virtue and morality, there was a tragic shortage of essential vocabulary, and it had to be determined whether or not the new words to be created should be of foreign origin or created from existing Fijian roots. There had to be a great deal of research and then a central clearinghouse for this sort of thing, and well they all knew it.

All this pointed to the need of an approved vocabulary, and the Committee, as we have seen, went the whole way and determined on two dictionaries, whereupon the staff as a whole turned to systematic language research with continual experimental translation in the dialects for the time being.

Cargill, the best linguist, had spent most of his time in Lakeba, and Calvert and Jaggar also. Cross had only been about a year in Viti Levu, and Hunt about half that time. They ministered at Rewa and Viwa, where different dialects were spoken. They had no illusions about their experience and considered their translation work purely experimental. Their experiences revealed the need of constructive and coordinated research as a team rather than as individuals. By far the best linguistic research was done in the years that followed at Somosomo.

Within less than a month of their arrival in Somosomo, Hunt was adapting the catechism to the Somosomo dialect and using it in his preaching, whenever he got a chance to preach. In passing, it should be mentioned that they had a good team of native evangelists with them. I find references to Joni Mahe, Ilaija Taaga, Josua Mateinaniu, and Joni Kami. Others came from Tonga, en route to Rewa. There is a record in Lyth's journal to Joni Mahe preaching in Somosomoan, and this was two months after their arrival. A week later Ilaija was explaining the catechism in that dialect, and Hunt said it was the best spoken sermon he had heard up to that date from a Tongan native in a Fijian language. It must be remembered that the missionaries always had the help of natives in their linguistic studies—and a very considerable help it was.

As yet no one dialect had been selected as the *lingua franca*. Hunt prepared himself a manuscript polyglot dictionary for use in translation work. I often wondered what happened to that document—how valuable it would be now!

Strangely enough it was in the dialect of Somosomo that the first really constructive attempt was made at preparing a collection of Wesley's hymns. It was the cooperative work of Hunt and Lyth (who were constituted the Language and Translation Committee in June 1840), and comprised forty-eight hymns, Lyth having composed a few more of them than Hunt. The hymns were all (with one exception taken from Watts) selected from the Wesley Collection and, according to a fellow missionary, were a good representation of Wesley's doctrine. They began with *Me udolu a yameda*—Hunt's version of "Oh for a Thousand Tongues to Sing." This hymn has remained No. 1 right through to the present day, though with each new edition the series has increased. Yet the hymn itself has changed considerably. Hunt's translation still appeared in the 1877 edition of the hymnbook, but subsequently its place was taken by a new translation by S. J. Gibson, which was itself drastically revised in the 1938 edition, with only the opening line unchanged. Undoubtedly the present form has slightly better rhythm and fits the English music; but that does not mean the natives handle it better, though in this particular case they sing it well. In the original Wesley Collection this hymn had ten verses, of which 6, 7, 9, and 10 have now been dropped in the English hymnbook. The hymn is common metre, but Hunt getting it down into Bauan found it fell more naturally into long metre, and so for half a century it was sung as a long-metre hymn, and undoubtedly this was the reason for its ultimate rejection.

But Hunt's hymn, though but four verses, did captivate the real spirit of the Wesley original, and was one of a number of hymns used in the spearhead of the evangelisation of Fiji. The hymnbooks of the midcentury used Wesley's system of indicating metre so no difficulty was experienced in use.

It is important to note that the collection of Fijian hymns was arranged in a similar sequence to the Wesley Collection—and the theological significance and teaching value is immediately apparent. These men used Bible, catechism, and hymnbook, and they used them to a single end.

As to the nature of their evangelism, the early hymnbook is a good indicator. One does not find there the *hellfire evangelism by fear* we have heard so much about. This was more common later on in the century. The Wesley Collection contains twelve hymns on "Death" (funeral hymns), twelve on "Judgement," twelve on "Heaven," and one on "Hell," and the last two verses of this hymn are of "grace"—in a collection of 769 hymns. The Fijian hymnbook of Hunt and Lyth had one funeral hymn, one on judgement, and one on heaven. It opened with five on the gospel call, three on the goodness of God, two on praying for blessing (one for use after reading Scripture), a holiness hymn on perfect love, several repentance hymns, a couple for backsliders, a few for believers rejoicing; others on personal prayer, the Christian task, seeking full experience, intercession, the promise of the Spirit, the Lord's Day, worship, opening and closing meetings, praise, and thanksgiving. The instructional value of such a collection of hymns is manifest. It was in use early in 1840.

From my reading of the records, I imagine the staff at Somosomo had each member make himself a manuscript copy of the collection. I can find no record of this Somosomo collection ever having been actually printed. However, the hymns supplied so great a need that early in 1843 it was determined to prepare translations of the Somosomo hymns in Rewan, Lakeban, and Bauan, and to print them. By this time Hunt had removed to Viwa, and he prepared the Bauan edition with the help of Jaggar and Mrs. Hunt, and this was printed before the end of the year—printed at Rewa, the first actual printed hymnbook in Fijian, as far as I know. The Lakeban edition appeared in 1846 and was the work of Lyth. The Bauan hymnbook was the basis for future building. It has been revised many times and much added to, and today the collection includes over four hundred hymns, classified according to Methodist doctrine. The names of Hunt and Lyth have practically disappeared from the book, but many of the unsigned hymns are theirs, and theirs was the foundation on which all subsequent editions were made. Perhaps the new book is better geared to the new day, but that is not to say it still has the magical rhythm of old Fiji. Over forty Lyth and twenty-five Hunt hymns were in common use throughout Fiji prior to the death of Hunt in 1848.

On Monday, 24 May 1841, so Lyth's journal informs us, he and Hunt completed their portion of the dictionary of proper names. Their main purpose was to have as few alterations as possible to the English form, especially to the middle of the names, and in the pronunciation. They worked out a system in the following manner:

(1) Words ending in a vowel in English need no change.

(2) Words taken direct from the Hebrew, not forming their oblique cases by any alteration in the end of the word, it would be difficult to retain the identity of a Hebrew name if the closing consonant was cut off. Though a vowel must be added to make the name Fijian, it was thought best not to be confined to one vowel. Therefore, when a word ends in a consonant and cannot lose final consonant without losing identity, the rule is followed thus:

- The letters *r, l, n* take *i* (e.g., Esri, Samueli, Kenani).
- The letters *t, c, s, m, f* take *a* (e.g., Kata, Seca, Mosesa, Jerusalema).
- The letters *k, p* take *e* (e.g., Lemeke, Nope). (The vowels were not placed at random, but were so arranged to form sounds which were familiar to their ears as *ri, li, ni, ca, sa, ma,* and so on.)

(3) Names taken from the Greek. Cut off final consonant in about one hundred cases. Sometimes altered vowel before final consonant, thus:

us becomes *o, as* becomes *a, es* into *i* (e.g., Theophilus = Ciofilo, Aretas = Areta, Zelotes = Siloti).

(The identity of words in the Greek language was thus preserved. Words ending in Latin nominative *us* and transcribed into this form into English, generally have nominative *os* in Greek, and their dative in ω, so that "Ponitos" would be recognised in a moment as the name of the Roman governor, which in English is Pontius and in Fijian Pontiusi, which no person could prove to be the same name as the Greek Pontios or Pontio, etc., as they stand in the Greek Testament. Words ending in *as* have their dative in *a*, and those in *es* have their vocative in *e*.)

Thus Hunt and Lyth planned to shorten words and preserve their identity at the same time.

For our present purpose, the interest in that somewhat academic quotation lies in the thoroughly rational manner in which Hunt and Lyth got down to the task they had been set. It was, as has been pointed out, still in the experimental stage, and though there were a few changes later, its basic rationale stood the test on quite a number of points like the retention of familiar Fijian sounds, and the dropping of final consonants in the Greek. Some slight variation was made in the manner of selecting a final vowel for the Hebrew names, but I regret I am unable to trace the reasoning for the same, and Langham made further alterations at the end of the century, e.g., Samueli did not become Samuela until his revision.

Having settled upon a written form for proper names, Hunt got to work on Luke's Gospel, twelve pages of which were prepared and printed in the Somosomo dialect. As few Fijians in Somosomo had yet learned to read, the value of the script was mainly confined to the Mission staff—but to them it had the dual value as preaching material and as experimental translation. It is sometimes supposed that the work of John Hunt was confined to the New Testament. This is not so. He did regular Old Testament study from the Hebrew and New Testament from the Greek. It was all a useful preparation for the still greater translation task he was to face later at Viwa. Nor do we wonder that before long Lyth determined that he would have to take up the study of the Old Testament language, which he began under Hunt's influence at Somosomo in mid-1842.

VIII

The two families had commenced living together under the same roof at Nasima when they arrived there in July 1839. Two years later they were still there in the same house. It was not until 14 September 1841 that they were permitted separate homes. Their work was at all times restricted by the active opposition of the ruling family, and their limited successes had been among the strangers in the land, not the Somosomo people themselves. Their few converts were Tongans and Wallis Islanders, and though a few Fijians did worship, they were compelled to remain mere onlookers. Everything militated against the comfort of the missionaries. Tui Kilakila had a violent temper. Once this giant of a man burst unexpectedly into the house and seized Hunt and Lyth, one in each hand, and dragged them to the door where he had thrown down his club, offensively declaring his anger, as if it wasn't quite apparent enough. He intended to club them, but mystified by their apparent lack of fear, he satisfied himself with smiting Lyth across the face. These furious demonstrations of anger were not rare, and the two Englishmen never knew quite what to expect next. Then sometimes his friendliness was as embarrassing as his anger, and he would thrust his cannibal face right into theirs to scrutinise their manner of eating, and in the same action sweep their plates with his beard.

At times they were forced to witness the most revolting spectacles and forbidden to shut doors or windows when human bodies were cut up and baked beside their house, and there were episodes without number when dark faces at the window laughed at their discomfort. This happened once when Mrs. Hunt was bending over her dying child. One can only think of the patience and meekness of these folk with the greatest admiration.

Their preaching was faithfully done, but the fruit was small. Sometimes the services were in Tongan, and sometimes in English among themselves, and sometimes in Fijian. There is entry after entry in Lyth's journal with reference to the quality of Hunt's preaching.

> "a searching sermon from a solemn text"
> "an excellent sermon on the excellency of a good conscience"
> "a comforting sermon"
> "a good practical sermon"

They are a few of the comments taken at random during his Somosomo days.

In order to improve his Fijian, Hunt employed an instructor, one O Mai Na'eli, but his message was plain enough. It was not the quality of his Fijian which held them back—it was fear of the chief.

And then there was war also—for much of this period it was war with Vuna (of which Hunt's journal has preserved some valuable details), and this also militated against evangelistic success.

All these hindrances were a sore trial to Hunt, who wrote of it at the time:

> Our prospects are rather mysterious. The work of God is going on, I doubt not, but we have not much appearance of good.

Yet his faith and courage continued an inspiration to the little mission group, and his colleague said of him:

> The want of direct fruit of our labours, of a spiritual kind, was greatly calculated to discourage and retard effort. But it had no such effect on my friend's mind. His motto was, "Onward"; he looked for the promise of God, and believed that depending on Him, we should not labour in vain . . . He pleaded with God in holy boldness, and "against hope believed in hope." The result was that, while all around us was wilderness, our own little enclosure was as a "field which the Lord had blessed." I can never forget the happy seasons we enjoyed together in our social means of grace.

It says much for Hunt and Lyth also, and their wives as well, after living for two years together in a one-roomed Fijian house under the conditions I have described, that such a judgement could be expressed by Lyth, who also said:

> Such faith and patience, perseverance and equanimity, under circumstances so difficult, were highly characteristic of the man, and inspired all the rest with courage.

The more one reads the records left by John Hunt and considers them in the light of the judgement of the men who worked with him and under him, the more one is forced to say that here was a real man, a man chosen and called, a man where God wanted him to be and doing the task for which he was remarkably prepared. Here at Nasima we see his powers of leadership about to blossom forth. He is the comforter and inspiration of the little group which is faced with the bitter truth that it has failed.

The elements of faith and belief with which he inspired the little mission domestic group were essentially the same as those which very shortly were to inspire the whole mission during what was without doubt the most remarkable chairmanship in the whole history of Fijian Methodism. Lyth's estimate of Hunt of Somosomo is essentially the same as that given later by the General Secretary (Walter Lawry) of Hunt of Viwa, except that it covered a wider field.

And so when on Saturday, 27 August 1842, the time came for Hunt and Lyth to separate, the latter took his pen and wrote in his private journal a few simple but significant sentences:

> We parted this morning with our dear friends Bro. and Sister Hunt, with whom we have spent three profitable and happy years. We prayed together before we separated and the Lord gave us a parting blessing. Ours has been a truly Christian friendship. God has made us of one heart and of one mind and I doubt not that it will prove to be a lasting friendship. To God through Christ be all the glory.

Hunt had drawn much from the medical knowledge of Lyth, and Lyth had learned much from the patient faith of Hunt and his industrious and systematic methods of biblical, theological, and linguistic study. Together they had thrashed out the foundation work for theological training in Fiji, and Fijian hymnody which is the forte of the people to this day, and they had applied the language theory of Cross and Cargill to a practical end and developed it. If Cross and Cargill laid the linguistic foundations, Hunt and Lyth laid the foundations of the big publishing programme which played so important a part in the mission's first period of real crisis. But it was *their* project, and in honour their names should remain joined together.

IX

William Cross was an extremely sick man. His race had been run. He was relieved of the burden of chairmanship, which was his own desire, and removed to Somosomo to be near the doctor; and Hunt was now to move into Viwa, where there were already signs of spiritual awakening and where a vigorous man was needed. Hunt was the obvious choice for the task.

He had previously visited Viwa from Rewa and knew its background and its strategic importance. But it was a different Hunt who came now to Viwa. The rough ore which had been cast into the crucible of God three years earlier was very different from the refined metal which came out, and the impact the new Hunt made on Viwa was immediate and electric, as we shall see shortly.

In the interim, Mrs. Cargill had died at Rewa and also her child (she had previously buried one at Vavau, Tonga), and Cargill returned to England, to be subsequently reappointed not to Fiji but to Tonga. Cross had become chairman upon his departure, but his removal to Somosomo was to relieve him of this responsibility in the hope that it might help him to recover. Though the oldest of the team, he was by no means an old man. He died there, aged forty-five years, having served Christ in Tonga and Fiji for fifteen years. We may truly say he died of exhaustion.

Hunt was the obvious choice for the chairmanship, but his appointment came to him as a shock. It would be wrong to use any milder term, and it was some time before he could mentally adjust himself to the truth, that the mantle of Cargill and Cross had fallen on his shoulders. Almost in bewilderment, he accepted the truth. He was so affected that Lyth had to help him through his first meeting. He broke down before them and could not go on. That is not difficult in Fiji when the strain is on. There are times when a strong man can want to go away and hide himself and cry like a baby. There is no doubt about the fact that Hunt faced the emotional crisis of his life at the district meeting that year, when almost in fear and trembling the ploughboy of Lincolnshire put his hands to the plough as chairman of the Mission in Fiji, and turned the truest, deepest furrow that has ever been turned in these sunny isles. But I am jumping ahead too fast.

X

Before we leave Somosomo, there is a question to be asked and answered. It has been said that as an experiment in evangelism Somosomo was an utter failure. For the purpose of this account which purports to be a study of the life and work of John Hunt, we make no attempt to pursue the issue of the Somosomo experiment to its conclusion and abandonment in 1847, when the staff was withdrawn from the station and transferred to a more responsive and more strategic centre. Were that my purpose, a long page of further tragedy would need to be written, and this record would become but a miserable catalogue of calamity and disappointment. But the question must be applied to Hunt at the time he left the station. Was the project a failure? I mean, was it a failure as far as the Somosomo people themselves were concerned? For among them we are told there were practically no converts at all.

We remember the anger of the chief when the missionaries suggested saving the lives of the widows from strangling. We remember the peril with which they were faced when they desired to change any pagan custom. We remember the atrocities they were literally compelled to witness and the cannibal ovens beside their house. Were these things endured in vain?

For example, early in 1840 the bodies of eleven men killed in war were dragged to the door of the missionaries' house. The body of the chief among them was ceremonially set aside for the god after skilful dissection. The others were cooked and eaten beside their house, the smell of the ovens pouring in upon them. Time after time this happened, and they were forbidden to shut the doors and windows. This particular event followed a period of food shortage when the missionaries had been deliberately deprived of food by word of the chief, a typical event of the period, and they had the choice of watching it or being killed themselves.

Yet Hunt could write:

> We feel our trials and we feel them deeply, but the Lord is with us in this lion's
> den, and we know He who hath delivered us can still deliver. I thank God specially

that I can love these my enemies most cordially and heartily, so that if only they will allow me to live I will spend my strength for their welfare.

Was there anything gained by it? Was it mere sentimentalism? Or was he right?

Then there was the occasion when the American scientists of Wilkes Exploring Expedition arrived and the captain, observing the absolute hopelessness of everything, did his best to persuade the missionaries to leave the place and offered to take them away in safety.

They remained. It was not for them to reason why. They had been given a post to guard, and guard it they would, no matter how grim things were. That was in 1840. Eighteen-forty one came and went, and half of 1842. There was no improvement on the surface. There were no conversions. They were faced with failure, as the world sees it, and Hunt is now appointed to Viwa, and the time of departure has come. How does he sum up the situation himself? Then let him speak:

> Somosomo has been a place where every feeling of our nature and every principle of our religion has been tested. We believe that we have been made a great blessing at Somosomo, though the fruits of our labours do not yet fully appear, nor perhaps will at present.

Elsewhere he pointed out that changes really had taken place. Remembering the reception their first suggestions to save the widows of Ra Bici had got, he pointed out that a town had been taken in war without bodies afterwards for the oven, that a large canoe had been launched and had gone on her maiden voyage without the use of human rollers, and that the Somosomo people had feasted the Bauans for several weeks without offering a single dead body. Hunt himself felt that in this way their presence had been felt, even if there had been no converts.

But was this enough?

There were people in Britain who felt the Somosomo experiment was a waste of men and money. The London Missionary Society had met the same criticism after sixteen years of apparent failure in Tahiti and Tonga. And to those churchmen who cannot see beyond statistics and balance sheets, these enterprises were foolish and misdirected. Others said the Somosomo advance had been premature, that the work at Lakeba should have been more consolidated, and then a full effort be launched on Viwa and Rewa. There was something to be said for such a policy, yet for eight years the Somosomo experiment was continued. For a couple of years prior to its closing, the men on the field, led by Hunt the chairman, had pressed for a rearrangement of stations in more strategic positions—but no approval came from the London Committee. When eventually the withdrawal was approved, it was not because of failure, but a strategic move as Hunt had advocated, because of the growth of the cause in Bua and Nadi in Vanua Levu. The removal of the men from Somosomo to Vanua Levu drove a ray of Christian light right through the dark heart of Fiji and certainly shifted the centre of the struggle to a more promising field, where a body of local Christians had already been won and had proved their ability to resist persecution. At the same time, Somosomo was not abandoned in the real true sense of the word. It was worked from Vanua Levu, and this hurt the pride of Tui Kilakila, but he had none but himself to blame. Before long he sent to Vanua Levu seeking the reopening of the Somosomo station, but he had to be satisfied now with Christian teachers, not white missionaries. He had got the first station under false pretences and had not honoured his promises. For eight years they had endured much, and when they had gone, he realised what he had lost, but life for him went from bad to worse, and eventually he ended his life a leper, isolated from his people and possessions and kept at a distance by those who served him.

Looking back from the present time, we have the benefit of seeing things more in perspective; and in the same way as Paul's imprisonment, which must have been a mystery to him at times, did really work out for the furtherance of the gospel, so the church in Fiji did benefit tremendously from the Somosomo experiment. The way was hard, but clearly behind it all was an acting, directing Factor, which can hardly be mistaken for mere accident.

There is (or was) a certain professor who did much research on this Somosomo experiment, who points out the difficulty the men faced in withdrawing in failure, because they had gone there in the first place believing it was God's will. Yet doing God's will they had failed, and he throws it back almost as a jibe. It was an admission that it was all a mistake. A sort of glorious mistake maybe, but a Gallipoli that achieved nothing.

The theological weakness is not in their minds but in the professor's, for these men specifically stated time after time that their afflictions and apparent failures might even work out in the end to the glory of his name whom they served.

Gallipoli wove a pattern and strength into the Australasian national fabric and personality. This, as Pericles said in his great panegyric, was "woven into the stuff of other man's lives." Is this then failure or a mistake? Affliction and even death may mean victory in the end. Was the cross Christ's only, or are his servants expected to take up their crosses and follow him?

Then what did come out of Somosomo? Well, first of all there was the groundwork of Hunt's Fijian New Testament, of Hazlewood's Old Testament and dictionary and grammar; the hymns of Hunt and Lyth; the Viwa Plan (of which we shall hear more in chapter 8); the groundwork of Mission medicine, language, translation, preaching, education policy, and method—all these things grew out of the experiences of the four men who came out of that station of affliction. Quite apart from the dynamic personalities that were forged there, these things made an impact on all Fiji that determined the shape of the Fijian church unto this day. We still sing their hymns, we still follow their devotional methods and the religious exercises they prepared there, and we build our sermons today on the translations they carved out. These things are as much Fiji today as her language itself. So we cannot agree with the historian who was better at collecting historical data than at evaluating the theological experience of the actors of the drama.

And then quite apart from all these things there is another we must not overlook. Fiji was almost ripe for (to use a term from the war) the "big push," and Cross and Cargill had run their courses almost. These men of Somosomo had patience and courage, but beyond this at Somosomo there was testing of their complete submission to the will of God, even when they could not see the way. We, who look back now, can see they came out of that crucible of God with so much material ready for use, that had been crude material before, with a superb grasp of the language and a deeper knowledge of the people, not to mention the pent-up feelings that charged them with a holy fire. Well, it seems to one who reads the ancient records they left that we have here a veritable college of prophets.

Therefore I have no hesitation in saying that, looking back from a distance, if there was to be a Christian conquest of Fiji, there had to be a Somosomo first, just as truly as the gospel had to have its cross.

7

"TOO DISGUSTING TO MENTION"

The realist of the sex novel is no match for the old sailors who left us some of the narratives of plain facts as they saw them in Fiji a century or more ago. The missionaries have often been blamed—quite wrongly—for overpainting the picture for propaganda purposes. Their Victorian ways usually demanded that much be covered by some proper phrase like "too disgusting to mention" for some very improper subject. They might have printed much more than they did, judging by some of the things one finds in their journals.

Lorimer Fison, who was in Fiji three years before the murder of Thomas Baker, the missionary who was eaten by cannibals, has left a manuscript entitled, *The Fijian: Judged by His Words*. Many of the words he mentions are not used today, and a few have been completely forgotten, and others have changed their meanings. Thus when I say harmlessly today that I have "a strong desire to eat fish," what I am saying would have meant that I had "a passion for human flesh" a century ago. So as life changes, words too change their meanings, and each age adds a new coat of paint as it were; but beneath it all lies the gruesome past, and to get its real horror one would normally go to the mariners rather than the missionaries.

However, it seems to be the time now for us to scrape off some of this veneer of the first Christian century in Fiji and see if we can reconstruct something of the religio-social scene against which men like John Hunt laboured. To look back and see it only in the light of our own times is in some ways a highly perilous course, which may lead us to quite wrong conclusions. As we proceed we shall discover that most of the critics have but displayed the superficiality of their research. Of course, on the other hand, we must not be blind to the shortcomings of the missionaries. Like other human beings, most of them had their share of faults; but one charge I will not countenance is that of insincerity. No issue brings this out better than the matter of native dancing, and what better subject to start our glimpse at the Fijian scene of the time?

So with an air of authority Henderson writes:

> The records of the missionaries in the middle of the last century fail to convey
> any adequate impression of the part played by the *meke* in sustaining the joy-

ousness of the people and making the wheels of government run smoothly. The
missionaries looked upon it with no favourable eye: it excited lustful feeling, and
sometimes ended in scenes of debauchery. Instead of preserving it and trying to
purge it gradually of its grosser elements, they adopted the usual policy of sup-
pression. (1931, 70–72)

That statement is absolutely untrue—it was as untrue then as it is today, as we shall
see in a moment. It is not the purpose of this book to write an apology, but rather to consider the scene against which background the missionaries worked. But in doing this I fear
one shall have to somewhat undermine the authority of Professor Henderson. So too does
Eason, under a Fiji Government Department imprint, writing on Rotuma, but tarred with
the same brush, write:

It may be noted here that it then became customary for the Wesleyans to allow
their adherents to take part in songs and dances, but only at a time when a
Church collection was being made. (1951)

This seems to me to be a rather nasty insinuation, which the Fiji government should
never have published.

Sometimes even mission historians have accepted the jibe without investigation and
put it down to some of their predecessors having been of "the narrow type and unduly
censorious," or "of narrow and Puritanical aspects," or "of over-zealous and not sufficiently intelligent missionaries who were inclined to be narrow and prejudiced." These quoted
phrases refer to *kava*, tobacco, Sunday, and native dances. Now surely the rational attitude
to take is that if a *tabu* was placed on some particular thing like this at a particular time,
but not on others, then there must have been some particular circumstances which called
for it. These men were not "insufficiently intelligent." No one can read their journals and
say that.

The anthropologists also have sometimes had a smack at the missionaries on the same
count but for a different reason—viz., for establishing English culture at the expense of
Fijian. But their anthropology is better than their history.

In Fiji it is a present-day characteristic of the church (i.e., the Methodist Church to
which almost 90 percent of the Fijians belong) that it is indigenous. It is certainly neither
English nor Australian. It maintains enough of the ancient system of controls to be a natural thing in the local environment. It retained the religious terminology of the pagan cults
for the new religion, transformed pagan chants into Christian devotional exercises, and
developed existing oral tradition, adding accounts of biblical heroes and creating religious
mekes about them. It established a class of native preachers to substitute the old priesthood
and, strangely enough, many of the pagan priests joined its ranks. Social life and tribal
security was built on a system of *tabu*, and a *tabu* on Sunday was no more than a procedure
with which they were quite familiar. In fact a religion without some *tabu* would have been

incomprehensible to the first Fijian Christians. The war against *kava* and tobacco was certainly not pressed at the start, nor within the first thirty or forty years, and when it did come it came for a reason which made it imperative at the time, and the missionaries of the period have stated their reasons in black and white. It is not a bit fair to pass these things off as puritan narrowness or as insufficient intelligence. A fair critic may differ with their opinion, but he must admit that they had a case before putting a *tabu* on anything.

Now Hunt was a strong supporter of the holiness of the Lord's Day, but he certainly predates any *kava* or tobacco controversy. But one issue did concern him—namely, that of native dances. It concerned all the staff of the time, and they were all of one mind on the matter as far as I can discover. Let us remember that they were formative days and the men knew it. They knew that those who came after would have to build on their foundations. They observed that, like the custom of *tabu*, native dancing was part of the religio-social system, and therefore they must retain as much as possible. They did nothing until they were sufficiently familiar with the language and custom to acquire the true meanings of the dances, their words and actions. They were determined to preserve the forms of dance—the *wesi*, the *meke wau*, the *vakamalolo*, the *seasea*, and many others. They not only approved them, but they had them taught in the schools, and they even provided them with new ballads to accompany them. They encouraged their agents to use these dances for teaching mathematical tables, history, geography, and scripture knowledge, and I can prove this by producing the words of the *mekes* and the times of their composition, and in many cases the name of the composer. They particularly encouraged the preservation of the historical ballads of the tribe, and dozens of these they wrote down in their journals with descriptions of the actions and meanings, occasions of use, symbolism, and so on. One type of *meke* they particularly desired to preserve was the *lele* or dirge. It was composed after the death of a hero, and was to them what the lament over Absalom was to David. This particular lament, by the way, is still chanted by the old women of Fiji as if it was one of their very own laments—I heard it chanted just a couple of weeks ago by some Koro visitors at a Bauan *solevu* (festival).

In the face of those facts, the reader may well wonder where the professor got his ideas. The fact of the matter is that there was a sifting and a testing, and there were *mekes* which the missionaries set their faces firmly against. These were of several types.

The sexual practises of the Fijian people varied considerably. It is quite apparent that the culture of the hill tribes, for example, is more overtly sexual than that of the outer islands. Even to this day the unwary traveller who chances to mention the totem animal (or tree in some places) will be violently treated, stripped, and thrown into the river by the women of the tribe; or if he is in good clothes, thoroughly saturated with water and subjected to other remarkable treatment, because this is the name they use for their private organs. In some parts, the dances, like the people, were highly sexual. The words at first might seem harmless enough:

Sausau na taba ni vivili,	Cockleshells are clapping,
Sa ua levu no na bai tiri.	High tide on the mangrove fish fence.
Edaru sa biu 'ani.	And we two are left behind.
Edaru sa biu 'ani.	We two are left behind.

But this song is an invitation from one young person to another of the opposite sex that they may go away alone together, like the two shells of the bivalve. Not only were these "invitation *mekes*" a regular feature, especially for visitors to the village, but they were part of the regular facilities provided for what was considered really good pre-Christian Fijian entertainment, and there were women kept in every village of importance for the very purpose of exciting the visitors with these invitation songs. We may say they were born to this as a chief is born to rule. These were the women sold to white men for a musket a piece, and if too few in number, some village would be attacked, the men massacred and the women carried off as slaves—i.e., to fulfill this function. This was a regular means of keeping the warrior clans satisfied while awaiting departure for war, and for paying them upon their return. Thus Batinamu promised these things on a grand scale to his warriors and said he would take Mrs. Williams for himself after he had defeated Ritova. However, he was murdered before the design was achieved, and so Mrs. Williams was saved from this unhappy fate. Others were less fortunate. This was the fate of a wholly Christian village wiped out by the pagans in the same area about the same time, and some of the young captives refused to sing the "invitation songs" and were forthwith clubbed.

Lorimer Fison, who came to Fiji long before the end of these customs, wrote in a private record, "Nothing can be more abominable than the heathen songs, nothing more indecent than the heathen dances." He goes on to explain how in any dance there would be a chorus or couplet repeated here and there. It might have no bearing whatever on the *meke* itself,[4] but it is in that couplet that one usually finds the filth, and the people await the repeat of this and greet it with raucous laughter. "Filth," he says, "is the Fijian's ideal of wit." I think it may be true that one of the hardest battles the Fijian has had in becoming Christian is to rid himself of this.

Then in addition to these, there were the war dances—various forms, some preceding and others following war—and these are the dances to which the missionaries took most violent exception. There was no hidden meaning here—in word and gesture they were "too disgusting to mention," as the missionaries put it, and because they recorded no printed facts their statements have been devalued. But what they said was true. Each tribe had its own lewd way of having the young women of the village performing a dance round the na-

---

4   The literary technique (though not the content) may be compared with the Hebrew construction found in the Song of Solomon.

ked bodies of the captive warriors accompanied with some form of abuse. In one place they poked the male organs with sticks as they danced; in another these were cut off and removed to adorn a sacred tree as fruit; and in one outback place I know myself, a pot known as the *kuro ni soresore* is preserved still. All these things concentrated on the sex organs, and the young women were instructed to perform these dances to make the end of their enemies as ignominious as possible—and this was truly part of the life of the people when the missionaries came to Fiji. Nor was this all. Immediately prior to this ceremony, when the warriors returned with much noise and the shout of victory, the women went out to meet them with songs and dances as the Hebrew women did—but as Williams noted, very different in character. These songs were sexual songs. They sang the praise and conquests, not of the warriors themselves, but of their male organs.

The early missionaries witnessed these things, and though they described in their letters home the tragedy of cannibalism, patricide, and widow-strangling, they could never quite bring themselves to describe the place of sex in the social life of entertainment and war. But even the saintly Hunt has left a page or two of such description. It brings the reader of his journal up with a jolt. But he never put it into printer's ink. And of course there was war somewhere almost all the time, and there were always visitors to be entertained in the big and chiefly villages—so was there ever an end to it? I wonder if Henderson really knew what he was saying when he spoke of "the part played by the *meke* in sustaining the joyousness of the people and making the wheels of government run smoothly" (1931, 70–72).

I must leave it for the reader to judge for himself. When Hunt and his colleagues set their hearts against these *mekes*, they also increased their efforts to preserve a good type of *meke*, for no people can safely be left without entertainment or cultural exercise. Were they not right in directing Christian Fijians towards the lament over Absalom, the building of the temple at Jerusalem, the struggle between Baal and Elijah, and the picture of the New Jerusalem? The people took these to their hearts and use them still.

II

Life in Fiji had little value. Take a run quickly through the occasions which demanded human sacrifice—quite apart from cannibal feasting—and the reader will understand this at once. There is some evidence to the effect that the heavy cannibal feasting for the sheer love of it had grown during the last fifty years prior to the invasion of the white man, but these customs to which I now refer were the older and traditional ways of the pre-Christian Fijian race.

Human sacrifice was required for the building of temples and chiefs' houses, for the launching of new canoes, and on the lowering of the mast upon the occasion of the delivery of a canoe to its owners after its maiden voyage, and also for welcome ceremonies for chiefly visitors. It can be seen then to have been part of the social structure, and at the same time it was a religious requirement (though it should be remembered that the social/religious cleavage is a white man's differentiation, and the Fijian never thought of them as two things). A feast presented to the chiefs always included a sacrifice to the gods. Human bodies were offered to Degei and other high gods (gods of a former culture taken over by later migrations) and to the fish shrines of deities (e.g., the shark and king eel), also with thank offerings, offerings of the firstfruits, requests for success in war, and so on *ad infinitum*, each of these having its own special ritual including the presentation of human offerings, sometimes dead and sometimes alive.

Bodies taken in war were considered gifts from the gods, and the victim of highest rank would be offered to the god, and part of this body would usually be devoured by the victorious chief. In many parts these bodies were eaten as part of the ritual of victory, and the strength of the slain was supposed to increase the strength of the victors who devoured them. In Lau the captor had the right to sacrifice or enslave. Shipwrecked people were also considered the gift of the gods for feasting after sacrifice.

At the same time there were local rules in most places about the eating of human flesh—it was considered food for chiefs, and common people had to make ritual application and presentations to deity and chiefs for the right to eat it. In times of war these restrictions were lifted, as everybody eaten was supposed to add strength to the eater.

Mothers rubbed raw human flesh on the lips of their children; later it was said to give them a taste for it, but the original significance of this act was to act as a preventative against a disease thought to be caused by a shortage of flesh.

So it is quite apparent that the whole religio-social structure of old Fijian life involved murder, offerings, and cannibal feasting. During the war period which began a few decades before the arrival of the white man (and was speeded up by him), there were so many bodies available that *tabus* were not enforced, and often the warriors were paid in human coin—men to eat and women to eat or enslave. So the period when the missionaries arrived was one of excesses. The ritual and *tabus* of ancient tradition were already breaking down, and things were generally out of hand and the population was being reduced at a rapid and tragic rate.

Lest the reader should still have some doubt about the religious significance of this, let me turn to the nature of human sacrifice—remembering that Hunt and his fellow missionaries were endeavouring to substitute Christianity for this.

Cross and Cargill described in 1837 how human beings were selected from a tribe other than their own and often kept for a time, until they were sufficiently well fed and fat to be worthy offerings to the god. Eventually the victim was made to sit with his feet under his thighs, and hands placed before him, and was so bound as to be unable to shift from that position, in which posture he was placed on the hot oven stones and covered with leaves and earth to be roasted alive. Then removed from the oven, the face and body were painted as a man ready for war, and still in the same sitting position he was carried to the temple and offered as a sacrifice. After this act the deity was supposed to use the spirit part of the offering, and the body was removed elsewhere for dissection and distribution among those whose rank was sufficiently high to enable them to eat the offering body.

Canoe launching was another occasion for human sacrifice on a large scale. In Lau ten bodies comprised the minimum sacrifice, but big war canoes demanded a heavier penalty. I have a record of one occasion when forty bodies were used, each lain straight between two banana tree stems, and these being softer than the bodies would allow the weight of the canoe to ensure the maximum amount of pain and suffering and blood for the sacrifice, for the bodies were used alive as rollers, and the more bloodshed in the launching of the canoe the more the blood that would flow in its war exploits. The cries of the unwilling victims were heard for half a mile, but to all nearby they were drowned by the demon-like hauling song of those who performed the ceremony.

When the famous canoe of Cakobau, known as Ramarama, had made its first voyage and was lowering its mast for the first time, Cakobau enquired as to what sacrifices had been made by the builders when it was launched—as he put it, to ensure its sailing, durability, and success in war. It had taken seven years to build, and from time to time sacrifices had been made on the spot, and there eaten. But Cakobau pressed his point (this was twelve years prior to his conversion)—what about the launching? Had Tui Kilakila (under whose eye the canoe had been built) no slaves to serve as rollers for its launching, or was this the result of missionary influence? There was far more truth in the jibe than was at first apparent, for Hunt had only just written home from Somosomo describing how this canoe had been launched without the customary sacrifice, partly as the result of their efforts.

In the ceremony of the lowering of the mast, the heel slipped and caught one of the sailors and killed him. Immediately Gavidi was dispatched for human offerings to correct the error of the Somosomo chief. As an addition to the normal sacrifices of the occasion, for which he had already provided ten bodies, he acquired a further eleven so that twenty-one in all were offered on this occasion. The accident had been taken as a warning not to neglect the sacred rites of human sacrifices associated with canoe launching.

All these occasions had their peculiar and appropriate ritual, and after the deity had received his spiritual part of the offering, the bodily portion was for the chiefs and priests of the tribe. Yet all these acts were, in a way, quite rational, and the reader will have noted that I give reasons for the various acts or sacrifices of which I tell.

Just as rollers were needed for canoe launching, so men were needed to hold up the posts of temples and buildings of great importance. How could a temple or chiefly house stand for long without men holding up its posts? And as for those buried as sacrifices for the occasion, had they not given their lives to sit there in the correct position buried with their arms round the posts, and on account of this sacrifice been strengthened by the god to continue upholding the house after they had expired by suffocation in their burial? And wasn't it an honour to be selected for such a sacred task? (These were not the only cases where live burials were performed in Fiji.)

David Cargill has left the account of the establishment of a temple to the Bauan war god Cagawalu. They captured enemies to bury with the posts because he was a war god. Because of the death of these men, their relatives strangled their wives and retaliated against Bau, whereupon Bau took revenge, and so the building of this temple accounted for over three hundred deaths in all.

There were also occasions of child sacrifices. An enemy child taken in the capture of a town was suspended from the masthead of the conquering canoe as a thanksgiving trophy in honour of their war god, for the capturing of a child today deprived the enemy of a warrior tomorrow. But quite apart from this sort of thing, there were deities in old Fiji who demanded child offerings. There was the deity of Vusaratu, whose animal shrine was the sacred eel, which lived in a freshwater hole beside the temple—a creature of immense size, as big round as a man's thigh (said seaman Jackson, who saw it)—and after success in war an infant was taken from among the captives and offered there as a sacrifice.

The question will naturally arise as to whether the human sacrifice, and the cannibalism which invariably followed, were the result of a need or an excuse for finding a need. There is no doubt that both were true. We have already seen that Gavidi had to be on hand in Bau to go for sacrifices whenever needed, but there were other occasions when the supply of flesh was abundant; and on examination of the details of such accounts, I have been impressed with the ease with which excuses would be found for sacrifice and cannibal feasting. Even then it could be argued that their gods having provided the bodies, there must be a reason, even if not apparent, so the sacrifices and feasting would go on.

A minor dispute might lead to an attack and a massacre—quite regardless of rank, age, or sex; a brutal and unjust retribution might be made on some other village, allied perhaps in some way to the perpetrators of the original attack, but themselves quite harmless. Even if an attack was simply through the whim of some aggressive chief, with no reason at all, there would never be a feasting on bodies without a prior offering being made at a local temple, and invariably some favour would be requested of the deity as the sacrifice was presented.

Hunt witnessed such an event beside his house at Somosomo, when eleven bodies were devoured. But although the massacre had been quite unexpected and with little, if any, sound reason, yet its follow-up was perfectly orderly and ritualistic. The people approached the residence of the chief with reverence and the beating of the drum. He spoke to them and demanded the religious observances before any feasting began. The offering was presented and accepted in the ceremonial way, and everything was subsequently divided by the officer of the tribe whose hereditary duty this was. The body of the murdered chief was taken to the temple, and at the request of the local chief the deity was propitiated that there might be rain in the land. On other occasions it might have been sunshine or favourable winds, atonements, thanksgivings, success of social events, house-building, canoe-building, or war. There had to be a reason for the offering and the feasting. For any of these reasons human bodies were worthy offerings. Even apart from war, Fijian life was saturated with blood.

These customs never sprang up overnight. They predate the war period, which had commenced some decades before the arrival of the white convicts and sandalwood traders. What did happen with the appearance of these renegades was that flesh for cannibal feasts became so abundant that *tabus* were overlooked, and desire for revenge increased. Tribal intercommunications became more and more difficult, and when the missionaries arrived the native society was in a state of decadence, and in many parts anarchy. Native society as it had been known for generations was breaking down within itself. Everywhere there was religious and social decay, which was only accelerated by the influx of muskets and white marksmen. In the eyes of the poets and storytellers of the period, it was alas the end of the age. Nor were they wrong in their judgement.

III

The title "Too Disgusting to Mention" should have warned the reader of this chapter,[5] but all has not yet been told. The human sacrifices described were mainly forced on unwilling victims. We pass on now to a completely different kind, in which, more often than not, the victims were willing. Voluntary sacrifices were not associated with cannibalism, but

---

5   There are many who think that much has been written about these things and it is now time they were forgotten, and yet I have deliberately included them for the following reasons:

(1)   Much opinion has been expressed in writing, without sufficiently concentrated research having been done. So many wrong ideas have been accepted in certain quarters that some such statement seems necessary in the interests of truth. The writer has put thirteen years of research behind the writing of this unit.

(2)   I don't see how I can evaluate the views and actions of John Hunt unless we take a peep at the elements of the life he witnessed day by day in Fiji, and which he was himself sifting very carefully, noting all the time what had to go and what could be preserved. During those formative Somosomo years, he lived square in the centre of the village life, and the dissection of bodies described above took place but a few yards from him.

(3)   Though it was manifestly impossible for Christianity to be anything but hostile to many of these social horrors described, it is not generally realised that Christianity did retain a tremendous amount of the ancient social system, and that this in itself was one of the driving forces behind the missionary—determination to capture the chiefly system itself for the *lotu*, with all necessary modifications but no more.

(4)   The biographer has to find his way between two extremes. He may, by overpainting his background, make his character a mere child of his environment. Or on the other hand, he may overpaint his character, showing him purely as a moulder of events and devoid of environment. Neither is satisfactory. Yet biographies, and especially missionary biographies, often fall into one of these groups. Invariably the secular historian puts the missionary in the first extreme, and the missionary historian usually swings to the latter bias. In order to see the whole picture of Hunt in action then, we must see first those forces with which he was dealing—quite apart from their nature, whether gruesome or otherwise; we have no other alternative. Just as the stark reality of the cross stands out in the record of the loveliest Life, so the grim sufferings of His servants must be faced up to with honesty.

rather concerned friends and relations—widows and the sick. This reflects still another aspect of the religio-social atmosphere in which Hunt laboured.

These two forms of sacrifice had three points in common: (1) they were usually voluntary, (2) they were respectable and honourable acts, and (3) the mode of dispatch was usually by strangling.

On the other hand, there were important differences, especially in the matter of motive.

In the cases of the aged and infirm, and even of younger persons if seriously ill, it was considered the proper thing for an invalid, whose sickness was prolonged, to ask his friends to terminate his life and thus reduce their burden in caring for him, for nursing and feeding required time which might well be otherwise spent. Although this involved personal sacrifice, it was not a sacrifice in the normal ritual sense, though ritual acts were associated with the event. Everard Im Thurn (1925) says the custom is new—but whatever he means by "new," it predates the white man's period. At any rate the Fijian considered it an act of piety, and a noble mode of death.

Widow-strangling, though equally honourable, was quite another matter, and involved a number of religious ideas. It was a sign of a wife's love and respect for her late husband. Nor was it unknown also for a daughter to follow her father, though society did not demand this. The whole idea of widow-strangling was tied up with the pre-Christian conception of life after death, which varied considerably in different parts of Fiji. How could an important chief go on into the next world without someone to serve him? And furthermore, if a wife did not submit willingly to the strangling cord, was it not then clear that she was not a faithful wife, and unfaithfulness to the chief during her lifetime had other and less honourable penalties. Better to die with honour and a name for virtue than to pay the price for one's lack of virtue. They died willingly enough!

Once again there was a set ceremony for the event—the victim being prepared by the women, oiled, garlanded, decked in her best finery, and with turmeric in her hair. It was a gala day, and after the general kissing goodbye, after the Fijian fashion, the strangling cord was placed round her neck and pulled by two men of rank, and so the widow followed her lord. The custom died hard in Fiji. After a time the number of women strangled was greatly reduced, and this as a direct result of missionary effort, but there was strong opposition from outside Christian circles to any chief being allowed to go into the next world unattended, and more than once Christians were massacred for refusing to participate in the pagan rites associated with this particular ceremony. As already pointed out, the ritual varied, but the general belief was widespread throughout Fiji.

I know one record of a number of wives of one chief having been spared because they were childless, but it stands alone. It is however an interesting reference and rather suggests that the service rendered to the deceased chief was not wholly out of their devotion to him, but that if not properly attended he might work ill on his son in the days to follow.

If a high enough chief, he himself might be deified later, and this would not go well with a negligent son. If, however, there were no children, then this fear did not exist.

This treatment of the widow and the infirm was not always (though it usually was) done by strangling. Sometimes the victim was buried alive with all due pomp and ceremony. Accounts of such dispatches are preserved in the missionary literature of the period, and much also is narrated of their gallant efforts to terminate these customs. When attempting to prevent such an event, the missionaries themselves performed the accepted Fijian ceremony of presentation of a whale's tooth and making their request in the traditional manner. Usually they got a hearing; sometimes the number killed was reduced; sometimes the business was speeded up in another house so the request would be too late. Meantime, let us note they were not mere iconoclasts, these missionaries; they followed the proper native procedure of petition, and were usually respected for doing so.

IV

What then was the nature of the religion which accompanied such social institutions?

The religion of that day was a complicated syncretism derived from various migrations to the group prior to the coming of Christianity, and is not without some evidence of remote contacts with some aspects of early Babylonian thought, but very rudimentary. Most early writers described it conveniently as polytheistic. It is true they served many gods (there were some thirty temples in Bau alone), and they were gods of great variety and suggestive of vastly different origins. I can see no other interpretation than that they represented survivals of various strata of pre-Christian group migrations. Several missionaries tried to work out a classificatory system of some sort, and these vary considerably, though much of their detail is the same.

Undoubtedly the most recent and powerful stratum was a form of ancestor worship, the deities approached being of two forms, often confused by students today: (1) the deities of the tribe, god also of their founder and perhaps also of other tribes of common origin; and (2) the deified ancestor, founder of the clan or tribe. This, being more or less common to the whole group, may be taken perhaps as the top layer. Fairly common also is the totemic system which ties up with this ancestor worship. Mainly there are three tribal totems—a land creature, a water creature, and a tree. In some places there is only one animal form, and in some places there is a food totem quite apart from these others. But allowing for such variations, which may be accounted for perhaps by environmental factors, there seems to have been a fairly common basic totemic system accepted by the Nakauvadra people, who represent the last big migration (except for the slow Tongan movements into the group in very recent times) and the topmost veneer of religio-social thought.

When we come to compare and contrast the totemism of the hill tribes and island peoples, however, we find that there are bigger differences. For instance, ritual heavily charged with war significance among the latter is heavily sexually oriented with the former. This may probably be accounted for by the fact that the aboriginal people of the mountains were dominantly a phallic people in their religion, and while accepting a layer of the totemic religion of the invaders, adapted it to their own religious ideas which they still retained.

Besides the totem there is also a "shrine" in which the deity or ancestor manifests himself; this may be an animal (either land or sea), a tree, or even some inanimate thing like a stone. The Fijian never confuses this shrine with the totem, though many students do so. Terminology varies a great deal in different parts of Fiji, but nowhere is there confusion in the native mind. The existence of totem and shrine side by side itself suggests syncretism of religion of invader and aboriginal people. In addition to these, there were sacred animals (especially birds, e.g., the kingfisher), which were considered "messengers" for disclosing the mind of the deity relative to projects in hand. There were also sacred trees and sacred stones, which had become sacred because of some manifestation or revelation at that particular spot on some specific occasion. It is essential therefore for students of these things to discover the exact nature of these forms and the function they perform before attempting to evaluate them—something which has been most indifferently done in the case of Fiji. The very complicated nature of it all indicates how Fiji has been a meeting place of religious ideas in the past.

Beyond all this lay a completely different system of gods of wider powers and range of influence, and these were graded into district, national, and universal gods. These were high gods and some of them were greatly feared, but remote and far above the ordinary people of the tribe. Little was known of them, save their greatness, and offerings were presented in the hope that they would remain remote. Most of the religious exercises were directed to the clan gods, who were much less remote, and who were more interested with tribal wars, crops, and small things. The high gods seem to have no natural place in the Fijian religious system the missionaries found at work. They appear as respected strangers; possibly they came from one of the earlier of the aboriginal peoples, whom the Nakauvadra people took over as gods of the land rather than give them offence. These universal gods were Degei, the creator; Ratumaibulu, god of the harvest; and Daucina, god of light, whom Waterhouse thought had wider worship than Degei (1866, 256–58). Degei and Ratumaibulu both had the snake as their shrine, and survivals of ancient snake cults have been found in Taveuni, the Yasawas, Kadavu, Bau, and Viwa—and are, I believe, very old.

Hunt spoke of the creator god as Ovē, who lived in the heavens. This suggests a ray of Christian influence as the sound of this name is very similar to the Fijian Jiova (Jehovah), although strange as it may seem there is a tribe in the mountains whose tribal deity was Jehovah, although in every other respect he is a perfectly normal tribal god. Ovē, on the other hand, is, I feel sure, a recent drift from Tonga. There is a great deal about Degei which compares with Jehovah—is more abstract; is creator; is eternal; controls earth movements, rains, and seasons. These deities, though still respected and given worship in Fiji when the missionaries came, are hard to fit into the religious system of the people, and are often actually in conflict with it, and we do not wonder that Williams, for instance, can write that the priest of Degei complained that his god was being tragically neglected.[6]

Beneath these were the national gods—Cagawalu, Betaniqori, and Dakuwaqa (the shark god), who were the children of the high gods.

The gods of Fiji were anthropomorphic, but their passions and vices were much stronger than those of human beings, so it was therefore dangerous to rouse the anger of a god, and any mistake or accident which could do so was quickly covered by an atonement.

There were also tutelar deities and, especially in connexion with carpenters and fishermen, their ritual of worship was elaborate and detailed.

The Fijians did not worship idols. Only one early missionary claimed they did, but the evidence and other missionaries are against him. They did set up stones in sacred places, and offerings were presented to deities who enshrined themselves in stones for purpose of worship or approach, but they were not idols. I have in front of my house in Bau one such stone where Digo was presented offerings with request for rain or sunshine, but there are three places within a radius of three miles where similar ritual may be undertaken for the same purpose of the same deity; the stones are shrines only, not the god himself.

There was common belief that a spirit could inhabit a tree or a rock (especially a rock of peculiar appearance), and to this day there are many stones which have their simple ritualistic acts connected with superstitions—placing a spray of leaves thereon as one passes, or decorating it with a garland, for instance. The meanings vary. One will assure the person of a safe return journey, and another of the capture of a wild pig on the journey, and so on.

The spirits of departed friends were beaten off by noise, and ritualistic tricks were employed to deceive ghosts as to the whereabouts and names of tiny children. There was great fear of apparitions, especially of the spirit of a slain, unchaste woman, and also of those who died in childbirth, who were thought to be very revengeful. Malignant spirits were said to go to and fro on the earth doing mischief, seducing, tormenting, and killing mankind. An individual in Lakeba, Matakalou, could see them and detect their design and thwart their efforts, and made much profit by his arts.

So Fijian religion was a complicated affair, though not all its ideas were of equal antiquity. Each deity had its ritual and its advocate to perform the rites. Every corner of the forest and coastline had its lurking dangers waiting to do harm to the poor mortal, and those who say the heathen was really happy in his heathenism make a gross misstatement.

---

6   Williams, *Fiji and the Fijians*, 217.

He spent much of his time performing his sacrifices and paying his dues to his priests, knowing that otherwise terrible things awaited him, and finding little comfort also in knowing that should his offerings be incorrectly presented his fate would be no better.

The primitive Fijian contemplated the possibility of life beyond the grave. Was there some glimmering of truth that drifted down from Cathay or India some centuries before and came with one of his ancestor strains to Fiji? At any rate there was a general belief in something beyond, but his expectations were as varied as the nature of his gods. In different parts the missionaries obtained quite different pictures. Cross and Cargill told of Bulu, the underworld where human souls ultimately resort. Its tyrant king was Lothia, whose colleague was Samui'alo (Beater of Souls), who sat on the bank of a deep cavern of fire into which he precipitated human souls. The souls of Lakeba people were said to go to Namokalevu, a waiting place near the sea, where for a time they engaged in life similar to that which they had known on earth. Eventually they had to appear in Bulu before Samui'alo, who examined them and, if he took a dislike to them, hurled them into his fire, which meant annihilation. Such a fate was inevitable to any who disobeyed the gods. Some spirits wandered in Bulu till they decayed and were then burnt to form manure for Lothia's gardens, and there existence for them ended.

Another missionary spoke of a long journey with many trials, judgement, and an intermediate state, life in Bulu, as on earth, comprising the raising of families, planting, and war. Actually very few reached Bulu. One could be deified, punished, or suffer annihilation, as pleased the gods. The long journey was a frightful experience. The soul of a bachelor, after many vain privations, is certain to be dashed to pieces on a large, black stone by one Naganaga. The traveller had to meet the Beater of Souls. If wounded, he was doomed to wander the mountains; if killed, he was cooked and eaten; if victorious, he faced judgement. Many other forms of destruction he had to face before reaching Bulu, and even there, if his life didn't please the gods, there were various punishments to be inflicted. There also, any whose ears had not been bored on earth would be subjected to certain painful and humiliating penalties for this neglect. There were similar punishments for women who had not been tattooed, and such might even be ground as flour to make the bread of the gods. And there was a defiling punishment for the man who had never killed an enemy.

Therefore we may judge that life after death wasn't really so bright a prospect for the old Fijian. Yet Professor Henderson writes of "the measure of success which the missionaries achieved by the use of extraneous aids such as the threat of hell-fire" (1931, 110). What had this doctrine in it to terrify them that wasn't in their own conception of life after death? The early missionaries did not preach hellfire as an isolated element of theology but, as was stated by Paul in Romans 6:23, as a plain alternative. There was far more heaven preaching than hell preaching, and far more converts from it as the early records show.[7]

However, before we leave the Fijian ideas of life after death, it should be pointed out that here also there is much evidence of various strata of religious ideas. Quite apart from the general ideas of the journey to Bulu, there were also local places where the souls of the dead resided, and these were connected with the independent tribes, were purely local, and represent ideas often in conflict with the picture given above. Clearly two of the migrations to Fiji had completely different ideas on life after death.

In this chapter, and in particular, in this section of the chapter we have endeavoured to answer a question: what was the nature of the religion which was associated with the social institutions described above—human sacrifice, war ritual, and so on? We have observed a multiplicity of anthropomorphic wonder gods, scores of malignant spirits waiting to do mischief to the unwary, high gods who were the subject of worship but somewhat remotely removed from the people (no doubt a survival of an earlier culture), complicated and constant worship of tribal deities and often of deified ancestors, social life built up round a multitude of *tabus*, a grim prospect for the soul after death, with hope only for those who had shed much blood, and the possibility of deification if they also had chiefly rank.

Undoubtedly the greatest ambition of a Fijian chief was power and glory on earth and deification in the life to come. This required continual warfare, which alone offered opportunity for glory. The doctrine of the deification of heroes, the doctrine of Bulu, the neglect of the universal gods at the expense of the tribal deities, human sacrifices and cannibalism, strangling of widows, and the lewd dances in which the women debased the bodies of their male enemies, the bathing of new canoes in blood, were all elements of tradition which stood together—and they were interdependent. The loss of any one weakened the whole.

But on the other hand, once a chief saw himself as a sinner in need of a Saviour (which was the drive of missionary preaching), the whole religious and social structure came tumbling about him as a pack of cards. This is just what was happening. Isireli Takai of Oneata, Josua Mateinaniu of Vulaga, Raitono and Ra Esekaia of Bua, Ratu George of Dama, Lua of Nadroga, and Ilaija Varani of Viwa were men of high rank who had passed through this experience by 1845. Although we can never sufficiently praise the spirit and courage and zeal of the early missionaries to Fiji, it was on these men that they most depended. They used Tongan evangelists, in some cases with great power, but that was not enough. The greatest attention was paid to the Fijian chiefs, because the whole structure of old Fijian paganism was built round them and their ambitions on earth and in the life beyond.

A Christian chief had no easy task before him. He had to build up a new society, without disloyalty to his superior chief. This meant social reconstruction, cleaner villages, better

---

7   I have dealt at greater length with this matter in a monograph (Tippett 1954).

buildings, improved cultivation. Thus, for example, Tiliva and Viwa became model villages, and scores of heathen determined to hear more of Christianity on this account. One of the things that rather unsettled Cakobau was the fact that his Christian subjects, though subjected to all forms of persecution, were the first to send in their tribute and provided in property and service more than they had previously done as heathen. Christian Tiliva under Ra Esekaia and heathen Bua under his brother were on opposite sides of the river, a living parable of the difference Christianity made.

Cakobau, after a period of absence, had visited Lakeba. The transformation of the place astonished him. Again he was unsettled. The institutions of Viwa had a similar effect.

Varani, upon his conversion, might well have been persuaded to become a preacher, but Hunt valued him more as a Christian chief, and as a chief of his people Varani did his great service for the kingdom of God in Fiji.

So the missionaries prayed and worked for the winning of the greatest of all the Fijian chiefs—Ratu Cakobau of Bau.

V

But the chief was only one of the mainstays of this system. When seaman Jackson, disgusted after witnessing the burial of men alive to hold up the posts of a large building, summed up the picture as he saw it, he used the phrase "degraded by priest-craft." He lived by his wits sufficiently long among them to form an opinion. It seems right then that we should turn for a moment to these people against whom Hunt and his colleagues had pitted their efforts.

Captain Siddons, who was in Fiji 1809–15, made four points about these priests which may help us to visualise their function in Fijian society. Primarily they were preservers of the law, and they were the officials in charge of many public ceremonies from sacrifices to burials. Sometimes they were called upon to foretell events (though as with Israel, this was normally the job of seers), and if they thought fit they could withhold certain kinds of information from the tribe. Essentially they were to preserve the law and society in the best interests of the tribe or, as it had become when the missionaries arrived, in the best interests of the chiefs.[8]

The gods were not directly approached by the people (an element which helped Roman Catholic priests rather than Protestant missionaries), so that a priest was always employed and duly rewarded for his services. A private person could cast lots to determine his course of action, but this was as far as he could go without the help of a priest, according to Cross and Cargill. The office was usually hereditary, but Thomas Williams said that it was not always so.[9] There was a priestly division of Fijian society, but not all members were

---

8   Thurn, *The Journal of William Lockerby*, 1925, 163-76.
9   Williams, *Fiji and the Fijians*, 227.

invested into office. Fison provides us with detail of such an investiture ceremony. Priestesses were known, but were few. A break in a priestly line was a major tragedy, and Hunt tells of an occasion when the priest line in Viwa had no member (both living sons of the deceased priests having previously become Christian), and so another was appointed, but his election led to neither enthusiasm nor response. Here is a mariner's description of what he saw in a temple in pre-Christian days:

> It was at the back of the town, where a very high *bure kalou* (temple) stood, entirely enveloped in trees, mostly ironwood; and in front was a heap of human bones whitened by the weather. Inside the priest was sitting with his long beard hanging down on the little table constructed of human bones, and his chopsticks of the same material in his fingers, the nails of which were an inch and a half long. On the table lay two skulls, used for drinking *agona*, several more lying about the floor. At the further end, inside, were placed several muskets with which men had been killed, dedicated to the god, and a great many clubs of different sorts; the short round-headed ones, I observed, had men's teeth sticking in them, where they had been clubbed in their mouths. Overhead where the priest was sitting was a lattice-work, used to put the leg or arm of a man upon, for the god to eat at his leisure, as he said; and the bones of such parts were lying there, which were left from time to time, no-one thinking of disturbing them or anything else belonging to this sacred place. On each side hung long pieces of broad *tapa* of different colours, suspended from the very top of the ridge poles and reaching down to the floor, which assisted very much in giving it a serious or sacred aspect. They were hung very thickly so as to form a kind of graceful veil, and seemed to convey the supposition, that, although black deeds were worked outside, blacker were concealed behind these dismal looking curtains.

The priest would become "possessed" by the deity when about to make a pronouncement. This could happen in an ordinary house, and I have read of it happening on a canoe at sea, but the usual place for inspiration was in the temple.

Thomas Williams described the mode of approach in this way:

> The principal person presents a whale's tooth, states the purpose of the visit, and expresses the hope that the god will regard him with favour. Sometimes there is placed before the priest a dish of scented oil, with which he anoints himself, and then receives the tooth, regarding it with deep and serious attention. Unbroken silence follows. The priest becomes absorbed in thought, and all eyes watch him with unblinking steadiness. In a few minutes he trembles; slight distortions are seen in his face, and twitching movements in his limbs. These increase to a violent muscular action, which spreads until the whole frame is strongly convulsed, and the man shivers as with a strong ague fit. In some

instances this is accompanied with murmurs and sobs, the veins are greatly enlarged, and the circulation of blood quickened. The priest is now possessed by his god, and all his words and actions are considered as no longer his own, but those of the deity who has entered him. Shrill cries of "It is I! It is I!" fill the air, and the god is supposed thus to notify his approach. While giving the answer, the priest's eyes stand out and roll as in a frenzy; his voice is unnatural; his face pale, his lips livid, his breathing depressed, and his entire appearance like that of a furious madman. The sweat runs from every pore, and tears start from his strained eyes; after which the symptoms gradually disappear. The priest looks round with a vacant stare, and, as the god says, "I depart," announces his actual departure by violently flinging himself down on the mat, or by suddenly strik-ing the ground with a club, when those at a distance are informed by blasts on the conch, or the firing of a musket, that the deity has returned into the world of spirits. The convulsive movements do not entirely disappear for some time; they are not, however, so violent as to prevent the priest from enjoying a hearty meal, or a draught of *yaqona*, or a whiff of tobacco, as either may happen to be at hand. (1858, 224–25)

This is the man through whom the tribe has its dealings with its god. Through him are presented thank offerings after success in fishing or war, or recovery from sickness; the firstfruits and other food offerings (*dalo*, yams, pigs, human bodies, etc.), offerings of native property (*tapa* cloth, pig's tusks, whale's teeth, mats, fans, pottery, and many other articles), human fingers as mourning for the dead are presented through him. Requests for fair weather for sailing, foul weather for the approaching enemy, favourable winds, rain, sunshine, fruitful seasons, and good health are made on their god by this person, and so too atonements for calamities, mistakes, and defilement, for he alone can approach the mysterious deity who holds in his hands the fortunes of the tribe for good or evil, and he has been set aside for this special task, and none but the priest is certain of the particular ritual required for each special occasion.

Yet long before the missionary came, and before the sandalwood trader, the priest knew he was slipping; his power was declining.

Before the white man had said anything about the falsehood of his priest-craft, the first signs of disbelief had appeared among his fellow countrymen, and especially among the chiefs themselves. There were already strong chiefs who would stand no nonsense from any priest; who maintained the priests only existed to do the will of the chiefs. In Hunt's day there had been several episodes between priests and chiefs which left no doubt about the matter. Qaraniqio had silenced the high priest of Beqa in the midst of his convul-sions, as the utterances of the god did not please him, adding that it was only for fashion sake that the whole class of priests hadn't been exterminated long ago. On another occa-sion Cakobau did the same thing at Bau. It is not difficult to assemble evidence to this effect—that the chiefs themselves were partly responsible for the decline of the power of the priest class, and by their own arrogance, without their realising it, they were undermining the whole fabric of their religio-social system.

However they were not alone in this undermining of the prestige of the priest clans. There was another class of individual at work long before the missionary arrived—namely, the sorcerer.

Perhaps the reader will have noticed that all the tasks attributed hitherto to the priest have been sympathetic to the tribe; I have mentioned no black arts. It is essential now that this truth be grasped by the reader. The priest and the sorcerer were not the same person. A priest-sorcerer was exceptional—and he was a corruption of old Fijian religion. They were enemies. The priest was part and parcel of tribal life, and his magic was communal and sympathetic. The sorcerer was individualist and hostile. The priest represented the personal interests of the individuals who comprised the tribe, the sorcerer operated for one against another; so the former was an instrument for unity, the latter for division. The conflict between these two characters continues to this present day, for often when black magic is applied against a man, his friends go, not to the Fijian minister, but to the tribal medicine man; for the old belief still prevails that it requires the white arts of the tribe to counter the black arts of the sorcerer.

When the missionaries arrived, the sorcerer was rising to the height of his power, and the inability of the priests to deal with this power was one of the major elements of discontent among both chiefs and people. As these individualist opportunists gained strength by the success of their magic, that of the priest grew less and less. Even at the time there were chiefs who would not hesitate for a moment to give a priest a thorough thrashing in public, even during his "inspiration," but who would tremble at the very mention of *draunikau* or *yalovaki* (black magic and sorcery). Even down into Christian times it is tragic to contemplate the number of strong chiefs who have perished through black magic: a foreign enemy which came into Fiji about the same time probably as firearms, and worked as much havoc.

Occasionally, but not often, a priest in despair would become a sorcerer, feeling his existence was otherwise threatened. On the other hand, it is interesting to note how many priests, realising they had little power against the sorcerer, determined to become Christian. Some of these, whatever their original motive for this act, later on came to a great appreciation of the Christian faith, and not a few who had been pagan priests became Christian teachers and did worthy service as such in the end.

Although the heathen priest still had power in Hunt's day, and was the organiser of most of the hostility to the growing church, yet we note his decline had already begun, and the breakup of the religio-social structure of Fijian society had already commenced when the missionaries arrived. What the end would have been had the church not come at that juncture can never be really determined, but I myself have no doubts in my mind that tribal wars, white man's disease, grog, muskets, debauchery, and sorcery would have exterminated the Fijian race before the end of the century—and what a ghastly extermination it would have been!

For all the evils of priest-craft, the priest did preserve law and order. But against disease and alcohol and muskets and sorcery the priest had a hopeless task. And it was there at that point that Fijian society was breaking up. Theocratic historians will ask, was it by accident then that at this particular moment of Pacific history a new kind of religion arrived in Fiji?

VI

One more question remains to be considered before we leave this attempt to reconstruct the religio-social background of John Hunt's Fiji. What was there in this society that was worth saving, and to what extent were the missionaries (including Hunt) iconoclasts (as some critics say)?

Now any conscientious student of this subject must sooner or later realise that, despite the gruesome and gory associations of Fijian daily life, which the missionaries often just passed by with the phrase "too disgusting to mention," that the people were not entirely dark. They had their arts and crafts for instance, and their pots, fans, houses, ornaments, canoes, and mats were of very fine and skilful workmanship. Even their instruments of war and cannibalism, their clubs and spears, their cannibal forks and the bowls from which they ate their horrid food, were objects of delicate carving and craftsmanship. Every possible example of workmanship which could be used in a Christian home or in a Christian way was preserved, and though they introduced new elements into house-building, they absorbed all the native elements. The church at Tiliva, which was the finest church in the Pacific at midcentury, though English in design was of Fijian craftsmanship. The artisan side of Fijian life was certainly accepted by the missionary as it was, and new ideas (e.g., coral-lime houses) were given to the native as optional.

The missionaries improved their cultivation of crops and their construction of pathways—they inspired emulation by offering prizes for the best banana gardens and so on. They improved sanitation and drainage. None of these things destroyed native culture, but rather opened up the way for natural development. They encouraged the use of their own musical instruments and taught new tunes to widen their range. They taught the women new crafts, some of which have been handed down to this day and which could well be taught back to us again—they have become their own because they were so very like their own.

In the arts of fishing and the search for food, the missionaries made no changes except to provide them with fishhooks, pots, bottles, and axes to simplify their labour. These articles were only Western counterparts of less efficient instruments and utensils they already had. In other words, in the normal round of daily work they made no material changes at all, but accepted life as they found it and opened the way for healthy development. In navigation also they maintained the existing methods. Fijian canoes were used in the mission work for many decades—and in some of the outer parts are still used. I used the sea-going canoe quite a lot myself during my term in Kadavu. The missionaries acquired canoes of their own and sailed hundreds of miles in them. They accepted the Fijian world of navigation as they found it.

In three aspects of life they made changes—war, entertainment, and religion.

They opposed wars of aggression, and as peacemakers they rendered a useful contribution towards saving the Fijian race from extermination.

Entertainment they sifted carefully. That which was wholesome or harmless they preserved, and through their schools they introduced new games, which are still played by the children of today. On that which was lewd or immoral, they placed *tabus* (itself a Fijian device). This applied to songs and dances and games. But nothing was banned without something being given in its place. No iconoclasm there!

In matters of religion there had to be changes, and they did set their heart firmly against much of the custom of the people. But let it not be forgotten that it was Ratu Cakobau himself who ultimately determined what was to be the final form of the Fijian church. When he accepted Christianity, he did it with a ceremonial rejection of the religion of his fathers and took the church as it was (i.e., as he saw it at Viwa) and set it in the heart of the Fijian social system. The old religion had failed him time after time. It called for rejection. He saw that the breaking-up point of Fijian society was primarily at the religious level, and he took the new religion as it was. To this end the missionaries had worked and prayed. This is what I call "The Road to Bau." It is true that in Viwa and Bau sacred groves and temples were destroyed, but in each case it was by order of the converted chief, not the white missionary. In each case it was a symbolic act of rejection of the old and acceptance of the new, and in each case the materials from the destruction were used for the building of a Christian church. I leave that statement of facts to the reader to interpret himself.

Actually I do not know of a case where a missionary destroyed a temple or a sacred grove or an idol (for there were no idols). Many of these places remain to this day for the archaeologist. Heathen temples were often offered to missionaries for use in preaching. This alone should serve to show how the old religion had lost its punch.

The festivals of the religious year—planting, firstfruit, and harvesting—were all incorporated into the Christian year and in the social system. This was aided by the fact that the Jews, like the Fijians, combined their working of the land and their worship of God.

In tribal, ceremonial customs of the land, there were many ceremonies which were used under the old dispensation (and religious at that) which are still maintained today as customs of the land, and though the old religious meaning has gone, the social bond is maintained. Thus the ceremonial welcome of the land may be given at an administrative or a church gathering. In the same way, when a minister goes to a new appointment, he presents his compliments to the chiefs of the people he goes to serve in the customs of the land, and is ceremonially received by them. The only change then that has taken place is that an itinerant ministry has replaced a resident priesthood. Cakobau had the insight to see that he could take over Christianity with very little dislocation to the social structure, and indeed there is a touch of genius in the way in which it was done.

The biggest social problem or adjustment demanded by the acceptance of Christianity was the change from a polygamous to a monogamous culture. And the critics of Christianity have had plenty to say about this, but not one has thought to point out the change from pagan wars of aggression and plunder to the view of war only for the maintaining of defence and the establishment of law and order (which was the attitude of the Christians to war afterwards); and the rejection of the system of paying warriors and others with female bodies from the slave group made monogamy an absolute necessity for purely physical reasons. For no society could completely deny its common people any satisfaction of its natural instincts. Ancient society had a way of providing for this—viz., by war and other forms of service; thus, for instance, the slave women of Bau went to Viwa and earned their supplies of firewood by offering their bodies in payment. After Viwa became Christian, they had to go elsewhere, and they called Viwa "a town of women." All these things went when Christianity became the religion of Fiji, and the commoners had to be given the right to marry. So it was quite hopeless to imagine that there could be this changed attitude to morals and to war under a polygamous system. They were all bound up together, and polygamy had to go when the pillars on which it rested went.

On the other hand, no person was forced to reject his many wives. He was free to worship regularly and enjoy all the forms of public worship provided and their fellowship. He was so classed as an adherent. He could, however, not become a member or hold office without accepting the full Christian position and limiting himself to one wife.[10]

Monogamy had perhaps one problem—I mean to us who look at it today—sometimes women suffer from too rapid a succession of children. The critics have hammered away at this point, but they have never stopped to think of the lot of the poor women of the slave class, who were nothing but animals, and who for some trivial offence or sometimes for no offence at all were just sent to the men's house, and often so abused that in the end there was nothing left but for to kill them and eat their bodies. But with the coming of the church that slave class passed away, and the commoner found a wife, made a home, and raised children in love and tenderness. Furthermore, very few of the rejected wives had

---

10   For a fuller treatment see ibid.

any difficulty in finding husbands, and I know no documentary record of one claiming to be worse off afterwards, but many to the contrary.

The remarkable thing about it all is that the changeover was achieved with so little dislocation. Cannibalism, widow-strangling, patricide, infanticide, human sacrifice, body abuse, and polygamy went when a man or a chief or a town turned to Christianity. Clearly they were tied up, and it was right that they all go together.

I remarked above that old Fiji was not entirely dark, and mentioned handicraft, navigation, and other arts they had acquired. But even in religion itself, there was not complete darkness. In some ways—primitive certainly, but still true—there had been a preparation for Christianity. Had they been devoid of religious impulse, how could the gospel have been presented to them in the first place?

Observe that the temple has been mentioned from time to time. Here was a sacred place where a deity could be approached. Was it not the heathen temple that was so often offered to the preacher to proclaim his message? Thus the building of a Christian chapel was not an absolutely incomprehensible event to them. Here was a holy place where some deity could be approached with some act of devotion. It was at least a starting point.

And likewise, we have already met the priest, the individual set aside for sacred duties, for seeing the religious exercises performed in his building were in order. There was then a known category for the missionary—another starting point.

And we've mentioned sacrifices and ritual acts, and even the pagan, if he saw a baptism, a marriage, or some other Christian rite, would recognise it as a ceremony of religious significance. If I know anything of Fijians, those who saw it would soon enquire of that significance—another starting point.

They also had their conception of revelation and inspiration. Nor was the idea of a religious service or gathering strange to them. Quite apart from ritual associated with specific events like the consecration of knights, presentation of firstfruits, dedication of a building, and so on, there were occasions of community acts of devotion, and I know a pre-Christian record of a solemn religious service to which the tribe retired every morning led by the priest.

Nor should we overlook the people's familiarity with the act of prayer—vocal prayer—led by a priest with various observances making requests known to the deity. Adoration and confession were also known.

Chanting was associated with ritual acts. All these things the missionaries capitalised on, taking over the native forms, developing them; and so the pre-Christian religious terminology was taken into Christianity and slowly charged with new meaning as the converts grew in experience. One might well say that the faith had come, as Christ Himself came, in the fullness of time.

Well, were they iconoclasts? The missionaries varied as their personalities varied, and some were more aggressive than others. I am not prepared to go beyond that. But there is one thing of which I am certain—they had thought out their position very carefully and had a definite idea of what parts of Fijian culture had to go, and apart from this they retained everything else. And after all, as we say today, they were not there just for the good of their health; they were missionaries of the gospel, and they believed God had called them, and they were willing to give themselves unreservedly to the task.

8

"TREAD SOFTLY HERE!"

I

In much the same way as the long thirty years of the earthly life of preparation of Jesus of Nazareth came to a dramatic activity in three powerful years of public ministry, the forces we have already observed at work in the formation of the character and personality of John Hunt emerged, as it were, into visibility at Viwa.

There is a sacred moment in the life of every man who throws himself unreservedly upon God and accepts His guidance in nothing but a blind faith, wheresoever it leads, however dark and mysterious its ways, but going on because of a sure conviction that the impulse is of God. Let me repeat—there comes in the life of every such person, sooner or later, a sacred moment, a golden opportunity, a time indeed and a task for which he was surely born. It may be a short moment of time, even a single act, a sacrifice, a word, or it may be a longer term of service, a ministry, a published book. But whatever it is, however long or short, these great occasions are not lightly given, and they invariably demand their price. But if the price be paid and the moment accepted, the blessing is not his only but the world's. "To this end was I born," said Jesus to Pilate, "and for this cause came I into the world" (John 18:37 KJV). He knew Himself rejected—condemned. It all led to a cross, but in that cruel death there is life for every true believer. His was the price, ours the blessing:

> Mine the life won
> Thine the life laid down.

I have called the Somosomo experiences the "crucible of God" for there souls were strained and characters tested; there failure had to be faced, and men had to learn to go on trusting still despite failure. There they had to face things utterly revolting to them, and witness them knowing all the time they were powerless to stop them. There their beloved children were given and taken, and the heathen cried, "Where is thy God?"

Perhaps hardest of all, they would think of their successes in England and in the colonies, of the friends who had tried to convince them that their job was there, where they would certainly have served effective ministries—but only this blind faith urged them on, calling them like Abraham into the unknown, and a willingness to go, to suffer, to toil, and even to fail. This is the kind of person who sooner or later, like Kipling's "Explorer," discovers the new land which brings blessing to generations yet unborn. In the spiritual realm this unreserved obedience to the divine urge brings that discovery of the sacred moment. Each man who came out of that tragic experience of Somosomo discovered his sacred opportunity.

John Hunt was born for the Viwa ministry, 1842–48, as sure as the sparks fly upwards.

Let us observe here and now that this brief period was the psychological moment, the critical point of all Fijian history. True, Cakobau did not become a Christian until 1854, but it was in 1848 that he knew he would—on his own admission.

In that brief period the forces of the Western world, both good and bad, the primitive forces of Fiji itself, the pantheon of Fijian religion, the metropolis of the group, the centre of the greatest maritime power Fiji had hitherto known, and the activity of the greatest military leaders of these islands were all concentrated on Bau and Viwa. Bau was fighting with Rewa a grim and devastating war. Politically there was foment everywhere. Seven wars were being waged at the one time in various parts of the group. The old religion was crumbling. New ideas were being accepted almost without testing.

"Is it the end of the age? Alas! Alas!" sang the minstrels. This was 1842 to 1848.

John Hunt moved into Viwa. He was a magnetic personality in the prime of life—thirty years of age, as pure a speaker of idiomatic Fijian as the mission ever produced, a keen observer of native politics and customs, a clear thinker, and a man who made the heathen cannibal Cakobau feel he really loved him. This is the man who established the Viwa Plan for schools in Fiji. His dispensary was famed to the extremities of the group, and he built Viwa into a Christian stronghold and a city of refuge—and all just two miles from Bau itself. Political events demanded the removal of the printing press from Rewa, and it also came to Viwa where it remained the publishing house of Fiji for years.

Here we have a great psychological moment—a concentration of Christian witness onto every thread of the whole fabric of island life and the Fijian chiefly society. If God ever acts in human history, that moment and John Hunt were surely made for each other. The God who brought Israel out of Egypt and the house of bondage also brought Hunt into Viwa in the forties.

Walter Lawry visited Fiji during the days of Hunt's chairmanship. "Everything," he wrote afterwards, "takes from the Chairman, not a sombre hue, but a tinge of evergreen, a glow of life; and giant strides are being made in every part of the Fijian work." "He is," he went on, "an extraordinary man, both in body and mind."

This radiant man came to Viwa, and there he gave his all, and six years later they laid him to rest beside the Christian chapel there. He had died utterly exhausted. When his work was done God took him, in his thirty-sixth year, or as Dr. Hannah put it in his obituary, he "fell in his armour, gloriously."

It was a triumphant death and has never been forgotten in Fiji—not to this day. Many a time have I heard a Fijian speaker refer to it. It is the classic sermon illustration of how a holy man should die. Later on, after his conversion, Cakobau admitted that it all began with the dying, and the dying prayers, of John Hunt. Here was the supreme moment in all his life and work—to give his life, and in his last breath whisper the words which took root as a seed and eventually gave Fiji the Christian who did for the native church what no white man could ever have done.

II

Whenever I go to Viwa, it seems to me I tread on sacred earth; and I never go there but I look at the grave and say a prayer in my heart. From my house on Bau I often look over to his island stronghold and gain inspiration from his memory, for he has become so real a personality to me that I remember him as I do my father, though he predates me by nearly a century. The Viwa people do not use the normal word for "tread" when they welcome you at Mataidigo, where Hunt is buried, but a less common word that I have never met elsewhere in a speech of welcome. It means "tread softly" or "tread respectfully."

On this piece of land, where pagan forms of worship were originally practised, is found today a strange little Christian cemetery, where Hunt was buried in 1848. Beside him lie others who also died in armour. There is John Polglase, who came in response to Hunt's dream for theological training in Fiji. And there is Joeli Bulu, the Pacific Islander who was tried in a circuit because of the staff shortage that year of Hunt's death, and who two years later was the first of his race to be ordained in Fiji. Others lie beside them—children of white missionaries, Fijian ministers and their wives, and a Fijian missionary who spent many years among another Pacific Island people. They represent a solid unity—a true church.

And when you visit the place, the Viwans say they are so glad to see you, but they courteously suggest you "tread softly."

III

I have already said that the settlement at Viwa was given its character by Hunt. As long as there were Fijians alive who remembered the man, it retained that character. They remembered how often in times of trial or failure he had said:

> The future is with Him. On Him we rely.
> We thank God and take courage.

And so they endured persecution.

Before he had been long at Viwa, he was able to write, "Fiji is not what it once was—there is a Church in Fiji today."

One of the most amazing things about the whole story is that Viwa was built whilst surrounded by one of the most desperate wars of Fijian history—a war of extermination. There was no mere skirmish about the First Bau-Rewa Var of 1843–45, and yet it was during that war that Viwa was baptised in a great wave of religious enthusiasm, which was the Fijian counterpart of the English Evangelical Revival.

In Viwa some six hundred Christians gathered for worship and religious instruction long before the conversion of Cakobau, and gathered, what is more, despite his persecution of them. Here was a Christian city of refuge, a stronghold, and a society which had taken root in the heart of Fiji proper—Melanesia as distinct from Polynesia.

It does not require much imagination to see how useful a haven of rest like Viwa could be to a persecuted person from some village where a heathen chief persistently plundered his simple possessions and gardens. So, as would be expected, there was a steady drift of persecuted persons to Viwa for protection sake, in the same way as the Nadi and Bua Christians had to take possession of an old fortress and unite themselves there for self-preservation during what was probably the most bitter of all the persecutions of Fiji. Thus Viwa received isolated Christians from all parts of the Rewa delta and the Tailevu coastline.

But in the wisdom of John Hunt, Viwa was never allowed to become just a city of refuge, as an end in itself. As soon as he discovered in these people a sufficient degree of faith and religious experience, he sent them back into the pagan world again to carry the truth and to be its advocates. Many of them went, to their death, but many also lived to be instrumental in the spread of the gospel in their villages.

Most craft which came to Bau, both native and foreign, visited Viwa also. No better place could have been found, or none so near to the crossroads of Fiji, for the dissemination of Christian truth.

The chief of Viwa was Namosimalua, whose conversion, though rational rather than spiritual, had nevertheless represented a real change of life. He still retained much of his island outlook in his religious concepts, and many of his subsequent claims for Christianity were fantastic. Even so, he became a more steady person and abandoned much of the "animal" in his old religion and in a primitive way was quite loyal to Jehovah. The missionaries never counted him a great success as a convert, but at least his conversion had involved him in a courageous act of faith and placed Viwa at the disposal of the church—and, what is more, did this *in spite of* Cakobau.

He is much more kindly remembered by the Fijian people, and perhaps, after all, they were better able than the white men to judge the truly remarkable change Christianity had effected in his life. He presented the church with land on which to build and destroyed his pagan temple, using its stone foundations to make foundations for a Christian place of worship, and cutting down his grove of sacred ironwoods to make posts for the chapel.

To this place, then, the Hunts came, and with this material they began to build.

IV

The labours of Somosomo had not been in vain. The foundations of church music had been well and truly laid, and Hunt now had a congregation to use the religious aids that had been so carefully prepared. William Cross had not been without some success at Viwa and Levuka, where Christians numbered ninety-five and sixty-five respectively when Hunt arrived. In addition to this, Cross had managed to get six schools established in different places, and some 275 scholars were under instruction. Hunt began, aided by his capable wife, to teach these people the place of hymn singing in Christian worship—an aspect of religion the Fijians accepted, as a duck takes to water—and though as time went on they learned many Western tunes, Hebrew parallelism was more commonly used at first, as being itself so similar to Fiji rhythm and chanting. So as they learned to read, they learned to use the hymnbook and also the catechism.

Viwa now began to assume a character of its own—and a form of worship was established which retained all that was possible of the ancient traditional rhythm, but now Christian instead of pagan. Much of this character is still retained in the Fijian village church to this day. The strange intonations and rhythm of Fijian traditional chanting is often laughed at today by the young Fijians from town and city schools, who are living isolated from their villages and have learned the white man's songs in an institutional environment, and have never been advised to stop and think what a tremendous part this chanting took in the building of their church during its first century. As for myself, I get much enjoyment from well-rendered chanting after the traditional Fijian method, and in the back parts of the group, in the mountains and in the islands, where one hears much of it still, he learns to appreciate quickly enough when it is well done; and it was no good turn to the Fijian worship when a much later edition of the Fijian hymnbook dropped the chants and left the musical people without a written record of this art so truly theirs. Yet despite this, and despite Western progress, these chants survive, handed down in the truly ancient manner by the old women.

V

The First Bau-Rewa War was a thoroughly well-planned campaign by means of which Cakobau simply devastated the Rewa delta, reducing it to a state of famine and, closing in by pincer movement on the chiefly centre at Rewa, Bau had mobility (as Ratu Edward Cakobau expressed it to me); she dominated the coastline and shut up the mouth of the river. Her warrior states threw a line across the delta from Bau to the river and slowly worked towards Rewa itself. In front of this advancing line, ambushes were daily events. Gardens no longer existed. Kadavu and Beqa, Rewan subject states, were at war with each other. A rebel Rewan chief was in possession of Nukui, a town at the mouth of the river. Famine reigned. Continual vigilance wore down the Rewan villages. The end was in sight.

Of all the earthly possessions the missionaries had in their keeping, none was more valuable or more indispensable than the printing press and its accessories, and these were housed at Nasali, Rewa. For months the missionaries at Viwa had been cut off from Jaggar at Rewa, and the story of the rescue of Jaggar and the printing press by the captain of the *John Wesley* is an epic, suitable for a story or an article in itself; but for the present purpose its importance lies not in the rescue, but rather in the fact that at this particular juncture the press and the printer to work it were suddenly removed from Rewa to Viwa. Though Jaggar was removed largely against his will, yet there can be no doubt whatever that it all turned out very much to the advantage of the Fijian church, for his arrival in Viwa coincided with what was one of the greatest literary drives of the history of the church in Fiji. One does not have to argue the advantages of having writer, printer, and machinery together in one place. Undoubtedly it speeded up production and accomplished much that would have been absolutely impossible while Viwa and Rewa were so shut off from each other through the war.

So that though their fortunes may have seemed mysterious at the time, there was not a man among the missionaries who would have doubted, had he been able to look back from a distance as we can, that even through the calamities of war, men and things were being brought together in a remarkable way for a supreme effort at an extremely critical juncture. It all turned out very much for the furtherance of the gospel.

Even supposing that nothing else had been accomplished at Viwa during those eventful years, the printing programme itself was a momentous accomplishment. Every necessary aid for worship was provided in abundance—at first scripture portions and paraphrases, many of them suitable for chanting, hymnbooks, catechisms, ritual for morning and evening prayer, short sermons for native preachers, membership tickets, and so on.

But greatest of all these projects was the appearance of the complete New Testament in the Bauan language, all Hunt's own work, with the exception of the Fourth Gospel, in which case he had accepted the translation of John Watsford.

The production of the Viwa Testament is a story of triùmph under difficulty, of patient research and a continual, critical testing of his own work. Hunt worked from the original Greek, and worked to a system, with assistance from the English version and what commentaries he had available, and when he had to choose between literal words and clarity of idiom, he chose the latter.

After some years of experimentation the Language and Translation Committee had determined that the Bauan was the most suitable and the most likely to become the *lingua franca* of all Fiji, and in this dialect the Viwa Testament was produced. Nettleton, who was stationed at Viwa not very many years later, considered that Hunt's translations were superb. He commented thus:

Hunt's hymns are mellow and sweet in the Fijian Churches. He lives in the vernacular Scriptures, the vernacular ministry, the theological text-books, the hymn-book and the transfigured lives of the people (1906).[11]

VI

The written Word needed the preacher to expound it, so Hunt planted at Viwa the seeds of what was shortly to become Fijian theological training.

Here selected men were trained as teachers and preachers of the Word. It was for them that Hunt prepared his lectures and sermon outlines that became the basis of preaching for decades to come, and indeed some of it was still in use when the writer came to Fiji.

But Viwa was not purely a place for theological education, for Hunt had a carefully graded system of schools there. This was part of what was known as the Viwa Plan, a forerunner to the Glasgow System introduced by trained lay educationalists a few years after Hunt's death, but still before the conversion of Cakobau. Similar schools, following the Viwa pattern (i.e., graded) were to be run on all the mission stations, and the educational aids prepared for Viwa were also made available in other places. Viwa was the experimental school, and thus became the model. It also carried education to a higher stage than the institutions at the other stations, which sent their best students in to Viwa for this higher group. From this group the teachers and preachers came. That, in a nutshell, was Hunt's Viwa Plan.

Cakobau was tremendously impressed by the schools at Viwa. There has been a tendency to think of these schools as rather primitive in type, but really nothing could be further from the truth. The educational standards of the centres at Viwa and Lakeba and later at Levuka were quite high, even judged by English standards. Watsford, who was with Hunt at Viwa, was himself a trained teacher from the King's School, Parramatta, before he entered the ministry, and the infant school at Viwa was his. He made profit from some of Hunt's methods, and composed many jingles for helping the Fijians to learn their lessons—history, geography, hygiene, and religion—yes, and even tables were set to rhythm. He prepared sets of cards for teaching common words and used them as our modern educationalists do.

The women's school concentrated more on sewing, handcrafts, hygiene, domestic duties, and so on, but reading and Scripture were also taught. Mrs. Hunt was a competent speaker and writer of Fijian, and had most of the responsibility of this institution. It is not generally known of Mrs. Hunt that, after the death of her husband, when she returned to England she was used by the Bible Society for assisting the full Fijian Bible

---

11   The centenary of the translation of the Viwa Testament was commemorated in Suva by the presentation of a pageant on the writing and translating of Scripture, terminating with the Viwa Testament. It was written and produced in Fijian by the writer, and presented by the students of the Bible School, Davuilevu. *The Missionary Review* published a special number for the occasion (September 1947). It contains articles on the subject by ten different writers.

through the press. A capable woman was Mrs. Hunt, and a most suitable wife for her husband in every way.

The educational system of Viwa, I have already mentioned, was graded and well organised, and special classes were arranged for special groups. Hunt's greatest project was his special organisation for training preachers of the Word, whom he sent forth armed with scripture portions at first, New Testaments later, and also preaching points, sermon outlines, and catechisms. He saw to it that the wives of these men were well versed in the catechism and in sewing. In fact, the wholeness of the homes of these early teachers was one of the great points of Christian witness in the heathen villages where they were received.

Sometimes a chief would visit Viwa and ask for a teacher, and sometimes Hunt would visit a village and offer a teacher; but in true Fijian style Hunt always threw the responsibility back on the chief. Would he promise to find the man a house and gardening land and to give him protection? This threw the chief back on his honour and an affirmative reply would secure him his Christian teacher, and give him the right to speak about Christianity in the village. That is not to say that all these promises were honoured—indeed they were not, but the teachers knew the risks they took. They were an intrepid lot.

And many a timid Christian youth had fled to Viwa in a panic for protection, to be sent out later as a soldier of the King, to stand firm, and many of them to endure unspeakable persecution and perhaps to die for Christ.

These Christian agents spoke worlds for the personality of Hunt who had fired them with zeal, but not for this only, for they were also the fruit of his educational system.

VII

More widely still, as far as the heathen Fijians were concerned, was the dispensary Hunt established at Viwa. Its fame spread to the extremities of the group, and folk came for treatment, even from places a hundred miles away.

As we have already seen, Hunt learned much in simple medicine during those days he lived with Lyth at Somosomo, yet he did not always feel disposed to use such opportunities of contact for direct evangelism, for mainly he sought to win converts rather than proselytes. He has actually left a written record of his mind on this subject. Yet on the other hand, some would be saved after these contacts, and the Great Physician Himself did use such occasions for speaking of sin and salvation. Hunt judged his cases on their individual merits, and usually found it better to do his medical work for its own sake, and often one who had found healing or comfort would shortly open up the subject of salvation of his own accord. Sometimes much later one would return to make enquiries. The missionaries were by no means in perfect agreement as to the use of medicine in evangelism, and Hunt for one, though he seldom missed an opening for evangelism in the normal course of events, always thought twice before pressing too hard with a man physically and mentally weakened by sickness.

This remarkable efficient dispensary worked according to timetable, and the bell rang daily at the correct hour and treatment was administered. In the dispensary Hunt gave himself entirely to this task. No man could possibly have accomplished what Hunt did without working to a system. And of course hundreds came for his treatment and elected to remain to hear his sermons.

VIII

It is easy for a missionary to be so taken up with the virtues of a native agent that he becomes more or less blind to his shortcomings. And on the other hand, the converse is equally true.

Although Hunt was never fully satisfied with his native agents, he was not unappreciative of them. A good agent was "wealth above rubies" to him, a weak one had to be nursed and watched. In the pioneering days it was inevitable that the best men got the toughest assignments. We read of the tasks assigned to Josua Mateinaniu, Paula Vea, Joeli Bulu, and Malakai Butuki, and we realise at once that we are in the company of heroes—men who should stand in glory beside those who performed similar tasks in the days of Nero and Domitian. I make that claim without reserve or qualification—neither in courage nor in faith were they any less.

And Hunt, whose whole ministry was based on the biblical model, knew how to use his men. Where possible, and especially in dangerous assignments, he sent them in pairs. He demanded regular reports and encouraged correspondence.

Every now and again he brought his men back to Viwa for a change of air and a rest before going out again. This had many points of advantage. These tried warriors made good impact on the young men in training and proved a real inspiration to them. On the other hand, it was a rejuvenator to them to come again into Viwa, not only physically, but also from the spiritual point of view also; they had benefit in procuring new publications, preaching material, hymn tunes, and so on.

Quite apart from all this, Hunt tried to keep in touch with his men by visiting them in person. Each year he did a long round trip which took him away for a number of weeks. He circumnavigated Great Fiji and the Great Land, and was known as far away as Rotuma. Many of the villages are names only today in the memory of old men, for they were burnt or evacuated in the persecutions which followed Hunt's day. Hunt was known by all these people—the distances he travelled and the places he visited simply stagger those of us who know these parts today.

So here we see the father of his people and of his students—keeping in touch with them, sharing their dangers, inspiring them, never idle, never letting them feel he has forgotten them.

And before long all Fiji was hearing the preaching of Hunt and seeing his ever-restless passion for souls as it was reflected in the lives and ministries of his native agents.

It was out of this system of keeping contact that the organisation of the Fijian church ultimately grew. It was neither an English nor an Australian church. It was Fijian through and through, for it grew from the relationship of a loving chairman and his team, from their intense fellowship, from their joint suffering and burden bearing, from their corporate passion to win Fiji for Christ.

Hunt had inspired his team with this vision, and though it is true that Lau was the first part of Fiji to become Christian, it was from Viwa and not Lakeba that the Fijian church really took root. There were, of course, many Lauans and Tongans in that fellowship—able men and deeply religious—but metaphorically speaking, Viwa and not Lakeba was their spiritual home. Lakeba and Bau may have been the Jerusalem and Rome of Fiji, but Viwa was its Antioch.

This may have been partly due to the centrality of Viwa in the group, its proximity to Bau, and the crossroads of Fijian intercourse, but more especially it was due to the intense emotional experiences which swept the place from 1844 onwards; I am speaking now of spiritual conversion, from sin to life, not the formal conversion from a pagan to a Christian system. This distinction in Christian experience was clearly stated by Hunt on several occasions in his journal and correspondence, and also by his colleagues. Both of these seemed to be genuine religious experiences, the first leading the person to reject the ancient religious system and place himself under Christian instruction, and the second some time later was more a counterpart of what we would call conversion at home. These conversions came in waves, and the missionaries called them "revivals" for the want of a more suitable term. Literally, they could not be revivals, but were Pentecostal movements.

The dynamic figure of Paul tends to overshadow his lieutenants—Luke, Silas, Aristarchus, Timothy, Tychicus, and the others—but Paul himself would have been the first to admit his real dependence upon them for those difficult assignments to which he appointed them all in turn, and which actually represented the building of the church in the Roman Empire.

A similar situation existed in Fiji. Fundamentally it was John Hunt who was the "chosen vessel" to mould the soul of the young church; but he, like Paul, gave responsibility to his assistants during his lifetime, and eventually passed on leaving his inspiration in the hearts of his native lieutenants.

We have seen that the Viwa Fellowship, by means of these native agents, spread to the extremities of the Great Land and Great Fiji, and multiplied by division and growth, like organisms or cells. The dynamic radiance and enthusiasm of these agents took possession of the places to which they were sent in much the same way as a banyan seed takes root in the cleft of a great tree, ultimately to envelop the whole tree within its very self.

These men were of a great variety in character. Some were assigned to special tasks of limited duration, and some were just left to do the best they could to lead a clan to Christ; some had the task of holding the fort until a more qualified agent was available, and some had to spy out the land or break entirely new ground. Usually they were given some rank or status—maybe a teacher or perhaps an exhorter. And when the flood tide came and chiefs from every part were crying out for instruction, many ordinary folk whose qualifications were nothing save that they could read were often sent to visit villages to read the Bible and Hunt's sermons.

This was a desperate measure, and alas the home congregations were much impoverished by such an exodus of its members. Both Viwa and Lakeba passed through periods of serious depression on this account, but in Viwa in particular they were short lived, for the Holy Spirit was mightily at work there. The same may be said of Ono-i-Lau and later on of Kadavu.

Hunt did not ask every converted man to become a full-time agent of the Mission. He realised the importance of having a Christian chief at the head of civil affairs, and we must remember to his credit that he encouraged men like Varani (who passed through a remarkable experience of conversion in 1845) to retain their posts in tribal administration. Varani would have made a great native minister, but he made an even greater "leading Christian layman."

So we note that the Viwa Fellowship gave birth to those two excellent bodies of God's workmen—the native ministry and the Christian lay officers—who meet side by side in synod today. Although the lay group had no synod voice for half a century, we should not fail to note their place in the Viwa Fellowship, and in every local congregation in the Fijian church.

IX

The Viwa Fellowship was the fruit of a genuine Pentecostal experience. In form it compared with what is generally described as the Evangelical Revival. It took place among the people who had for some time professed the "form" of Christianity, but had not yet experienced its "power." It was deeply emotional, with tension, fainting, and the many other forms of enthusiasm that accompanied the Evangelical Revival. It began in 1844 in Viwa and recurred from time to time in the following years.   .

Each outburst was followed by intensive pastoral attention, and its results were thus consolidated by effective follow-up—the point where much good evangelistic work in the church is often lost. Decision was followed up by direct challenge to activity or service and often dangerous assignments. Hunt saw that the machinery of the Viwa church provided opportunity and place for folk to work at all stages of religious development. In this respect the Fiji movement showed where others often failed—viz., in effective follow-up and opportunity for service.

For decades the subjects of this spiritual movement carried its potency to all corners of Fiji. Nor was it limited to the inhabitants of Viwa.

Three times a week as the sun rose yonder over cannibal Gau, native agents of the coastal villages near Viwa came in all kinds of primitive craft to Viwa for Hunt's special dawn class in Christian theology. Now although these were basically compiled from Hannah's lectures at Hoxton, Hunt called no man his master, and was himself a scripture expositor of the first order. Again, he was a good observer of native custom and natural history and a master of illustration. His illustrations were local. England he loved, but he never tried to project it into the congregations of Viwa—he drew his pictures from the forests of Fiji, the sailing of canoes, the habits of fish and fishermen, and the handcrafts of the women. His sermon and lecture outlines were solid theology, but his illustrations were so apt and his local idiom so pure that his people saw the Christian theology in every common object about them, and the voice of God in warning or in comfort spoke forth from daily events, and the familiar characters of Fiji could be classified mentally by his congregation according to their biblical prototypes.

Yet the preaching and teaching of John Hunt was certainly not what we call allegorical preaching—it was thoroughly sound biblical exposition; for Hunt knew his Bible well, not merely to quote texts, but he knew its background, he knew the human situations out of which its choicest passages sprang, and he saw those same human situations about him in Viwa, and a listener who did not see the points he made must indeed have been dull.

We do not wonder then that prayers became fervent, that hearts cried out and people wept, and all sorts of extraordinary things happened. Then from those who sat or knelt on the tear-stained floor of the chapel would come forth an enthusiastic chant of primitive music, once used for a song of pagan hero-worship—but now with the words of the *Te Deum*. "Thou art the King of Glory, O Christ!" they chanted, and some would shout for joy and others burst into tears; and Hunt, so far removed from the fields of Lincolnshire, would be so possessed by the essential Fijianness of it all to say, "This beautiful piece never seemed so beautiful as now," and to shed his own tears with those of the penitents.

Whatever we may think of these forms of emotionalism, there is an element about it which we must not overlook—that it was this movement which created the Viwa Fellowship, from which came Fiji's own native ministry (as distinct from the agents brought from Tonga) and the evangelistic drive which took the gospel and the singing church into every corner of the Great Land and Great Fiji. The New Testament and the hymns they spread were the result of Hunt's literary industry, and he was their father in this mass movement which translated this gospel and these hymns into their own personal experiences. When Hunt said, "There is a Church in Fiji," he knew there was a living fellowship—that cells were developing, dividing, spreading, multiplying—and this was some years before the conversion of any real paramount chief, or any great victory in battle. And even later on, when Cakobau set the Fijian church in the heart of the social system, he was happy to see its control left in the hands of the Fellowship, and in time he found himself truly one of them. Cakobau died a member of the evangelicals, and it was a worthy death as he sighed softly and uttered his last words—"Hold me Jesus. My faith in Thee is strong."

Hunt had not died in vain.

X

Hunt's Viwa ministry might well have claimed a whole book in itself. It was the task for which he was clearly born. The fame he no doubt could have won in Oxford or Australia he turned aside, for "the Voice" led him on. He might have satisfied his heart's desire and ministered in Africa, but the winds of God carried his ship to the Pacific. He might well have grown discouraged in Somosomo, and thinking himself a failure as a missionary, returned to the colonies or to England—for work still awaited him there. Others have done this and lived to serve worthily elsewhere.

But when God sent Hunt to Fiji, he gave himself wholly to this place. Even upon his arrival in Fiji he was still in the preparation stage. That is something every missionary has to learn—that when he reaches the field he is still unready for his task. So often a new worker comes into a primitive or semiprimitive environment, full of the latest ideas of Western scholarship—all very useful and important, but as yet, unrelated in his mind to the strange new world in which he has arrived, and of which, as yet, he knows practically nothing. Without first settling down to master the language, the customs, and the outlook of the people, he blusters into violent reforms (by Western standards quite justifiable), finds he is more or less ineffective, and retires within a few years with an entirely erroneous picture of the native people, to settle down in an environment he knows and perhaps to be a most useful man there. But he leaves a scar on some mission station or institution that suffered from his misdirected enthusiasm. Had he been willing to be led for a while, and to regard his first years as a getting to know the people and trying to think their thoughts—then, in God's time, a task would certainly have opened up to him. Then, and not before then, would the real value of his scholarship be apparent. This is the missionary task as men like Hunt saw it. But such a conception is hardly possible to people who think it would be an interesting experience to take a job on the mission field for four or five years. To use the mission field as a personal end is a tragedy of the first magnitude.

There is only one justifiable reason for going to the mission field—a conviction that it is God's will. It has to be a clear call, and an unconditional venture into the unknown with God. Be the missionary a doctor, a minister, a teacher, a nurse, or a social worker, he must realise that it is God's work, and God takes his time in preparing his servants, and that preparation may continue for some time on the field of labour before the psychological moment arrives. This kind of submission, or guidance, invariably has a cost. It could hardly be otherwise—one has to be absolutely willing to be guided, to wait, to go on patiently, till the sacred moment arrives, and then to give the utmost, regardless of cost.

It has already been suggested that all the elements of Hunt's preparation period were concentrated in the brief Viwa ministry, that everything that had gone before seemed to be leading up to this hour. Then let us take stock.

Here he drew more than ever before from the theological work he had from Hannah in Hoxton, and likewise the pastoral guidance of Entwistle and his study on the classical languages as he had from Jones. For a few years he had cultivated these things until they were no longer Hannah and Entwistle and Jones, but Hunt himself. They bore fruit in his finest literary work, the Viwa Testament, and in his aids for its interpretation and his theological work in English on the doctrine of entire sanctification—as choice a piece of biblical theology as one could want to meet.

The four-month voyage and the two months in Australia had widened his knowledge of men and the world, and of Pacific missions. From Cargill he had received his introduction to the Fijian language and it had stood by him well; and Cross had introduced him to the people and missionary method, and in particular the value of pictorial paraphrases in presenting the gospel. In this, Hunt was a true son of William Cross and went on to perfect the pioneer's method. The fullest fruit of this was seen at Viwa. In Somosomo he drew deeply from Lyth's medical resources, and together they ploughed a new furrow in the field of native worship, producing the first hymnbook and other aids to worship. It was in Viwa that the Fijian really saw the quality and beauty of these, and thence they spread.

Somosomo had taken him into the valley of the shadow—death, sickness, suffering, and failure. But through it all his faith stood the test, as did the faith of Hannah his companion of the way. This learning of the discipline of absolute submission enabled them to say to many a persecuted refugee at Viwa—"Events are God's. Duty is ours." And so they were able to encourage the timid to go out as the strong.

Thirty long years of preparation for a ministry of six years and death by utter exhaustion—but how every element of that thirty had been concentrated in the six. And what did that six years mean to Fiji?

The gospel in the vernacular was sent out to every corner of the group, and teachers to interpret it. From that gospel Fiji got her *lingua franca*, the first and greatest step towards the unification of the Fijian race. In that six years the hymns of John Wesley and their essential theology possessed the souls of the native agents and ultimately through them became indigenous. Here was established a city of refuge, a centre of evangelism, and a place of healing, both physical and spiritual—in the pagan heart of Fiji. Here at the crossroads of the heathen kingdom was a model settlement, with better gardens, graded schools, tremendous activity, and cheerful radiance—a living witness to every weary mariner or native traveller who chanced to come that way. Here came the never-to-be-forgotten Pentecostal experiences which transformed this great potential into a realised activity—and power simply streamed forth from Viwa as teachers and preachers went forth charged with the Spirit to see repetitions of this outpouring in the more remote parts of Fiji. From all of this there grew a remarkable form of Christian witness which has become a priceless tradition of the Fijian church and, of which I myself can truly say, has in my own days still called forth thousands of her younger sons and daughters to repentance.

As Jesus spoke of "their hour" and "his hour"—Viwa 1842–48 was surely Hunt's "hour."

XI

"Tread softly on this earth," said the Fijian who welcomed Dr. Sangster the other day at Viwa, where he turned the sod where the first post is to be inserted for the new Hunt Memorial Chapel. The speaker was a direct descendant of Ilaija Varani, one of the grandest of Hunt's converts. To me it was a sacred moment as I handed the spade to Dr. Sangster after a few words about Hunt's work for Fiji. It seemed right that this sod should be turned by the modern preacher who has done most to revive the doctrine of entire sanctification, which was so greatly Hunt's.

Not only was this particular doctrine the subject of his special study throughout the whole of his Fijian ministry, but it was itself the subject of his life, and of the truth of this several who knew him personally have left written testimony. He thought it. He taught it. He lived it. This was the secret of his tremendous power.

Hunt himself used to state his life's desire was threefold:

(1) The conversion of Fiji

(2) The translation of the Scriptures into Fijian

(3) The revival of the doctrine of Scriptural Holiness

On this subject he engaged in a personal correspondence with Calvert, and these letters were published posthumously and ran to many editions, being accepted by the Australian Wesleyan Church as their standard textbook on the subject for fifty years—i.e., until Methodist Union.[12]

Even this secular historian, who has not hesitated to criticise the Mission at any point he could, spoke of "the saintly John Hunt." His devotional life in private was intense—and surely here was the source of his power.

Hunt lived for a time in a house that had been made from the salvaged timbers of two wrecks, and when the winds blew hard from the sea, the timbers of the old house would

---

12   An excellent summary of Hunt's doctrine of entire sanctification is given by his most recent biographer (Birtwhistle 1954, ch. 14), who shows that Hunt developed some aspects of the doctrine, not found at all in the writings of his contemporaries; for instance, the social aspect, the view of daily work as a divine vocation.

strain and creak like the ship at sea. Was it the salt in the air, or the swell of the sea itself calling, or the wind drawing forth its answer from the old ship-timbers of the house? Whatever it may have been, it *was* there in the very timbers, we may say as the soul of the house, as it were. In the same way the doctrine of holiness was whispering in every timber of Hunt's life, in the fabric of his thought, his teaching, and his living. And that is the John Hunt which Fiji remembers today, and as you approach his grave the Viwan says quietly—"Tread softly!"

ROAD TO BAU

I

Among the scores of unusual tasks Hunt set for himself was one of seemingly little importance which, strangely enough, the Fijians remember to this day. This was the construction of a path across the island of Viwa from the settlement, which faced the sea, to the small bay which faced the chiefly island of Bau, still grimly cannibal at the time.

"John Hunt cut this path," they will tell you as you begin to climb; "first of its kind in Fiji." No doubt the first part of that pronouncement is true, the second does not matter. The Fijians tend to take things as symbolical whenever they can, and the thought of Hunt the road maker has not been missed.

That path was the most direct route from the Viwa settlement to the heart of the king of the Cannibal Isles.

It would be quite wrong for me to leave the reader with the impression that the battle between heathenism and Christianity in Fiji was over, or was won in Hunt's lifetime. What I have really tried to do is to show side by side the two armies, the forces arrayed against the missionaries, and the forces on which they had to draw. The final battle is beyond the scope of this book. Hunt did not see it. But he had prepared the organisation which carried the day eventually; the vision, the inspiration, the preparation was his. Without Hunt's Viwa—its literary activity and publications, its evangelical mass movements, its training of native evangelists, and the Viwa Testament, there could have been no victory for many a long day.

That Hunt was to openly construct a road in the most direct route to Bau, the fearful fortress and stronghold of all that was "too disgusting to mention" (to retain our own phrase), was literally to apply against Cakobau his own strategy.

Hunt knew there could be no security until Bau was won, and Bau could not be won without Cakobau. The church could never become part and parcel of the social system until Bau made it so. Until Bau was won, there could be no end of persecution or war. Hunt desired Cakobau as he had previously desired and won Varani. So he built the road to Bau.

Cakobau had persecuted the Christians. Every wave of conversions had been followed by a trough of persecution, especially when useful warriors had been among the converts, and throughout all the days of the Hunts' residence in Viwa the sword of Cakobau hung by a thread over their heads. Yet he had never engaged in a policy of annihilation against them, which he could well have done. Through his women folk, he had in a way pegged out a distant claim in the new religion. He drew much from Viwa resources, and Hunt was a popular interpreter with him when the white strangers visited Bau. In fact Cakobau had so taken Hunt into his heart that time after time, when his whole mind was set on massacre, Hunt had fearlessly calmed him and saved much bloodshed. Christians and heathens alike never ceased to wonder at the quiet power Hunt held over the man all Fiji feared.

Yet Hunt never lived to see his conversion. Hunt lay down life's burden with a dying prayer for Cakobau. Observe it was Cakobau who was in his heart to the end—and Cakobau marvelled at the triumph and loveliness of his passing.

II

Historians, biographers, and preachers have devoted much space to their accounts of the death of John Hunt—far too much space to his death, triumphant though it certainly was, and not enough to his message. I shall not repeat what has become so familiar, but substitute rather the dirge composed by his Fijian friends for the occasion. It is a good example of a typical dirge and was composed for heroes on their passing, and I apologise for the shortcomings of my translation, which seems to have lost some of the stately solemnity of the original.

> Beside the *koka* tree
> Sleeps Mr. Hunt.
> The devoted Joseph
> And Josua go to
> The house of Kuva, and enter
> To make a long coffin.
> Completed, it is carried
> To the mission house.
> Black cloth is cut
> As a covering for the coffin.
> Mr. Hunt is lifted within,
> The coffin closed,
> Fastened and borne away.
>
> So Mr. Hunt is buried
> And his widow cannot be silent
> Mr. Calvert comforts her
> They hold each other's hands
> And move off to Navakavua
> And ascend to Mataidigo
> To the far end (of the chapel).
> The tide has gone out.

The widow will not eat.
Her heart breaks with grief.
She merely sips a hot drink.
Black material she has prepared
As a veil from her hat
And to shade her face.

Beside the *kura* tree
Stand the Viwans who loved him.
The zealous one is dead.
He crosses from one house to another
Between the stone and wooden houses
Products of his zeal during life,
Whence the landscape could be surveyed.

Beside the vasa tree (where Hunt's house was)
The lady calls
Joseph, let us go
And waken the missionary.
They enter and shake his hand.
There is much weeping
The woman enquires
"Why are you dying?"
"Is the sickness so heavy on you?"
The missionary replies
"The sickness pains within."
And then again he adds
"My Dear, let your mind rest
You must not sorrow."

Beside the *kura* tree
The Viwans move off together
The chief of the land announces
"Let us go and pay our last respects
At the mission house
And carry forth the Zealous One
Let us march in twos
Thence to Mataidigo and lay him to rest."

Everyone grieves for the departed friends
The Europeans also are overcome.

I have retained as much as possible of the dirge, even though its sequence of events is obviously wrong, for the stanza printed in italics is clearly the earliest in the true sequence of events. This is common in these compositions, and probably represents a particular movement of the *meke* that accompanied the dirge, that was more suitably inserted at this place than at the beginning. The dirge would have to begin by announcing that Mr. Hunt sleeps. A dirge like this would be the highest honour the Fijians could pay to the departed missionary.

III

As one stands on the hilltop of the chiefly island of Bau today, the place being sufficiently high to see in all directions, the long mainland coastline is dotted with fish fences, and there is no longer the fear of savage warriors lurking among the mangroves, to fall without warning on defenceless fishing parties. I live on this hilltop, and a few yards from the house is the Christian cemetery of the Cakobau family, and away beyond it over the water is the headland where the Battle of Kaba was fought. In the opposite direction the coastline is also peaceful enough now. There was a time when it was continually at war with Bau, for Bau was in the act of crippling the kingdom of Verata when the gospel first came to Fiji. In the same direction but much nearer is the place where once stood the sacred ironwood groves of Cakobau's people and their religion. Cakobau destroyed these groves of his own volition to prove his change of heart, and to let there be no doubt about it. On a clear, still morning after rain, nothing in the world could be more peaceful than this coastline, which was but so short a time ago so continually bathed in blood.

My hill stands in the midst of Bau, the village surrounding me below. The Fijian drum beats out its message day by day, but like a giant endemic banyan nearby, once the shrine in which a fearful god appeared to its devotees, the fear has gone, and little children play marbles under the shade of nearby trees. Before me stands the great Council House. Once it was a temple, majestically sinister. Every post in the building was planted in human arms, these supporters of the temple being buried alive as a just sacrifice to so great a god. Before this great temple there once stood a killing stone, where the skulls of unhappy victims were dashed before being put into the ovens. That same stone is a baptismal font in the Bau church today, and its temple is the chiefly Council House, the symbol of law and order.

More immediately beneath me is a place called the Pig's Head, beside which the old cannibal ovens stood. On this piece of land there stood, in ancient times, the largest building on the island—the strangers' house. No place entertained more visitors than Bau. If only places could speak, what tales the Pig's Head could tell of the way old Bau entertained its visitors.

But it was in this strangers' house six years after the death of Hunt that the mighty Cakobau "bent the knee to Jehovah," as the phrase was. As might be expected, his form of Christianity was rudimentary, but he grew—he grew mightily.

Before he died he built a great church in Bau, and he built it to stand the test of time. He built it in the midst of the town as a memorial to what God had wrought. From the foundations of the ancient temples of Bau—or at least of seventeen of them—he assembled enough stone to make the walls of his church up to three feet thick, and its front door faces the site of the old strangers' house and the disused cannibal ovens, and before the congregation there stands to this day the baptismal font, which was once a killing stone, as a continual reminder to all his people of the greatness of their salvation. The instrument of death has become the instrument of reception into the flock of Christ.

Further out along the skyline at sea we read the same story. The distant shadow of Gau, which had a fearful record of cannibalism in pre-Christian times, lies on the horizon to the right. In the same direction but nearer is a small island where prisoners were kept until required for the ovens. Directly in front of me lies Moturiki, where Calvert narrowly escaped the ovens, and beyond it a cloudbank hides the mountain tops of Ovalau, where Ilaija Varani was murdered on a peace mission. On my left and much nearer lies Viwa. It is the dominant object of the beautiful seascape. Everything else is setting or background. To stand on the hilltop at Bau and look out is to see Viwa. And that is metaphorically true also in matters of religion and culture.

From my study window, at the moment of writing this closing passage, two small Fijian craft are moving slowly off over the still water towards that little bay where lies the roadway which John Hunt made to bring cannibal Bau nearer his heart of love.

Along that pretty pathway after the death of Hunt, his students planted crotons and other brightly coloured shrubs. It was to them a sacred path. But better than this, they used it—as he had intended when he made it—as a road to Bau. Preachers—scores of them—passed along that road. They carried with them Viwa Testaments, catechisms, and hymn-books—Hunt's books. They took them to Bau, the Rome of old Fiji.

REFERENCES

Birtwhistle, Allen. 1954. *In his armour: The life of John Hunt of Fiji.* London: Cargate.

Eason, W. J. E. 1951. *A short history of Rotuma.* Suva, Fiji: Government Printing Dept.

Henderson, G. C. 1931. *Fiji and the Fijians 1835–1856.* Sydney: Angus & Robertson.

Hunt, John. 1849. *Entire sanctification.* London: Wesleyan Conference Office.

Nettleton, Joseph. 1906. *John Hunt: Missionary pioneer and saint.* London: Charles H. Kelly.

Rowe, George Stringer. 1860. *The life of John Hunt, missionary to the cannibals.* London: Hamilton, Adams & Co.

Thurn, Everard Im, ed. 1925. *The journal of William Lockerby.* London: Hakluyt Society.

Tippett, Alan R. 1954. *The Christian: Fiji 1835–67.* Auckland: Institute Printing and Publishing.

Waterhouse, Joseph. 1866. *The king and people of Fiji.* London: Wesleyan Conference Office. Reprint, 1997, Honolulu: University of Hawaii Press.

Williams, Thomas. 1858. *The islands and their inhabitants. Vol. 1 of Fiji and the Fijians.* London: Alexander Heylin.

the AUTOBIOGRAPHY OF JOELI BULU

THE MISSIOLOGY OF ALAN R. TIPPETT SERIES
DOUG PRIEST, SERIES EDITOR
ALAN R. TIPPETT AND TOMASI KANAILAGI, TRANSLATORS

WILLIAM CAREY
LIBRARY

CONTENTS

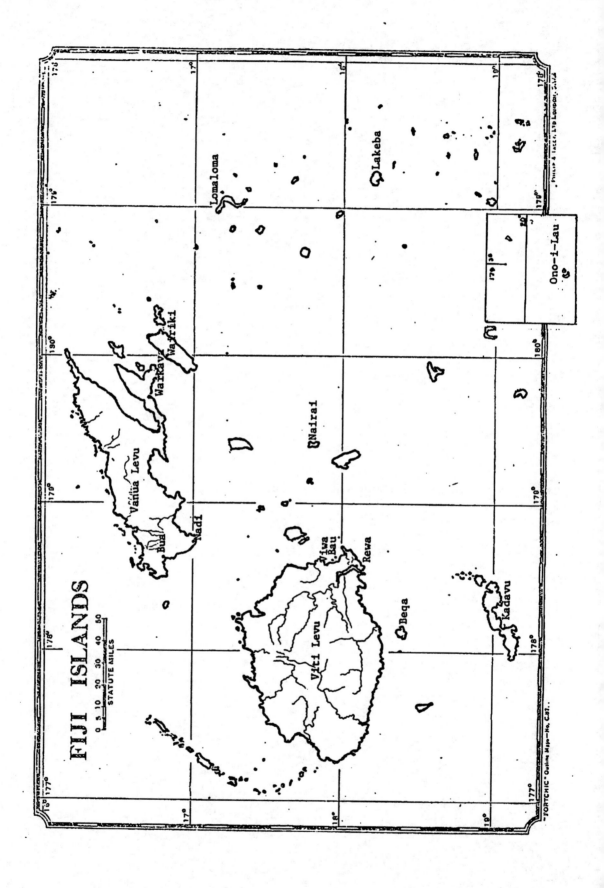

FIJI ISLANDS

STATUTE MILES
0 5 10 20 30 40 50

Vanua Levu

Buä

Nadi

Waikava

Wairiki

Nairai

Viwa
Bau

Rewa

Viti Levu

Beqa

Kadavu

Lomaloma

Lakeba

Ono-i-Lau

Philip & Tacey, LTD London, China

"FORTCHIC" Outline Maps—No. Cal.

INTRODUCTION

This is a professor/associate research project in ethnohistory, an attempt to make available a valuable autobiography with historical and cultural footnotes that should make it meaningful to present-day readers.

We took the original script and worked through it together line by line, checking sequences, trying to ascertain the dates and occasions of the specific events narrated, and working out the chronology of the life and missionary appointments of the man telling the story. In addition to our independent research, we worked together on the script for two or three hours weekly for six months before we were satisfied with our annotations. We used not only published volumes on the Fiji mission, but drew also from notes made at numerous archives in the Pacific, where we had done work prior to the commencement of this project.

The autobiography tells the story of Joeli Bulu, a Tongan converted in Vava'u, Tonga, during the Great Tongan Awakening of the early 1830s. Bulu was caught up in the enthusiasm of the overflow of the Awakening which finished in the mission to Fiji, when he was merely a few years old in the Christian faith. It is a lively story, full of faith and action. Joeli lived long enough to see the Fijian people won for Christ and break forth themselves in Christian mission to islands beyond their own reefs. He died a few years after the establishment of the mission to German New Guinea. Thus his life in Fiji spanned the whole dramatic period of Christian pioneering.

Joeli Bulu wrote his autobiography from memory, in a black notebook somewhere about 1869. He was a sick man at the time, and was thought to be dying. Lorimer Fison persuaded him to write it and translated it for publication. The manuscript is written in the Fijian language, which both of us understand and use. Fison's translation appeared in 1873, but was soon out of print and is a collector's piece today.

The story needs to be told for another day and generation, and this we have tried to do. We have restructured the narrative in historical form and modified some of Fison's terms to update the translation. Some of his informative footnotes have been retained, and some we have expanded. We have added many footnotes at points which need explanation for readers today—especially at points of custom. We have tried to relate to the standard histories of Fiji, and to provide some biographical data for characters long deceased but who were well-known to Fison's audience. Fison finished off his edition with some material of his own. This we have retained in its proper chronological position. Our hope is that by these passages and our own footnotes the reader will capture something of the personal relations of Bulu and Fison in the 1860s and 1870s.

At least until Fison was awarded his Master of Arts degree by the University of Rochester in New York—Lewis Henry Morgan's university—he hid much of his writing behind anonymity. On the title page of his redaction of the *Autobiography of Joeli Bulu*, he called himself merely "a missionary." Thus, we hope we have exposed something of the deep and personal relations between the two men, which is one of the really choice interpretive factors of the whole work. Fison persuaded Joeli to write the record. Fison translated it. It seems only right that the personal correspondence of the two men should be preserved with the manuscript. We think that the letters we have cited in this volume make our own redaction worthwhile.

Joeli did not die as expected in 1869, but lived on for some years. The last part of his life has never been recorded. Although Fison outlived him by thirty years, he never set down the events of his closing years. This we have recaptured as best we could. Information about Joeli for this period is scattered and scrappy, although the sociopolitical and religious background is well documented. It may well be that, as Fijian mission archival work becomes more established, this chapter can be rewritten with more detail. Meantime, we do at least indicate the issues which claimed the interests and prayers of Joeli in his last years.

His last decade was spent in historic Bau where he served as Ratu Cakobau's pastor. Cakobau [1804–83], a most notorious warrior and cannibal to the time of his conversion in 1854, had become a remarkable Christian thereafter and formed a strong attachment to Joeli; as did all his family. But those were eventful years of increasing acculturation and political experiment leading up to the cession of Fiji to Britain (1874) and the establishment of colonial government. Joeli played a major role as spiritual advisor in high places. Unfortunately his journal stops with the hurricane of 1869, but no account of the life and work of Joeli Bulu would be complete without an editorial chapter to cover those last years. We have tried to focus on the events and trends which are known to have been Joeli's concern at the time, and terminate our reconstruction with an eyewitness' account of his death. His life, conversion, ministry, itineration, and death were in so many ways like that of John Wesley that we can almost hear the praise of his last words as "Best of all, God is with us!"

Alan R. Tippett
Tomasi Kanailagi

[Editor's Note: Tomasi Kanailagi was born in the Fiji Islands on 25 January 1939 and was educated at the Davuilevu Educational Centre, passing through the Bible School and subsequently the Theological Institution. He wasan ordained minister of the Methodist Church in Fiji, and served with the Bible Society in the South Pacific. He held the Diploma of Theology from the Melbourne College of Divinity, and a Bachelor's degree in Divinity from the Pacific Theological College. He was deceased some years after completing this manuscript.]

TABLE OF DATES

Significant Dates for the Reconstruction of the Autobiography

ca. 1810	Joeli born at Vava'u, Tonga
ca. 1833	Converted at Vava'u [Cargill and P. Turner, missionaries]
1834	Friendly Islands district meeting decided on the mission to Fiji
1835	Mission to Fiji. Embarkation, 8 October. Arrived Lekaba, 12 October.
1838	Joeli's canoe voyage to Fiji. Arrived Lakeba 26 June.
1838–39	At Lakeba with Calvert. Left November 1839.
1839–45	At Rewa with Calvert and Jaggar
1839	Conversion of Namosimalua at Viwa
1842	Rescue of Aisake at Kadavu
1843–45	Bau/Rewa War
1845	Joeli left Rewa, end of November. Sack of Rewa, 1 December.
Nov. 1845–56	At Viwa with Hunt
1846–48	At Nadi, Vanua Levu, under supervision from Viwa
1846	Hunt's visit to Vanua Levu
1847	Hunt's return visit to Vanua Levu
1847	Bua and Nadi stations opened, November
1848	Hurricane year, Bua and Nadi, January and April
1848	Joeli left Nadi via Bua (in canoe), thence to Ono (in *John Wesley*)
1848–ca. 1856	At Ono-i-Lau
1850	Ordained by Hazlewood at Ono
1854	Conversion of Cakobau at Bau
ca. 1856–58	At Nadi, Vanua Levu
1857	Destruction of Nadi by Tui Levuka and Mara
1858–ca. 1863	At Cakaudrove (at Wairiki)
1861 or 1862	Joeli's wife died
1862	Wainiqolo killed
1862	Decision to transfer Wairiki station to Waikava. Move effected, 1863.

ca. 1863–66	At Cakaudrove, resident at Waikava (Fawn Harbour)
1865	Calvert's visit to Waikava. Joeli in charge.
1866	Joeli Bulu and Akesa Muala married by Fison at Lomaloma, 11 August
1866	Joeli and Fison voyage through Lau. Joeli's second visit to Ono.
1867	Massacre of Baker and his party in the interior of Viti Levu
ca. 1866–77	At Bau. Cakobau's chaplain.
1869	Nairai hurricane (March)
1873	Fison's redaction of *Autobiography* published
1874	Cession of Fiji to Britain
1875	Measles epidemic
1875	Mission to German New Guinea (New Britain, New Ireland)
1877	Died 7 May at Bau

1

THE GREAT AWAKENING IN TONGA

I was born at Vava'u[1] in the heathen days, nor was it till I was a big lad that the *lotu*[2] came to our land. When I heard the report of it, I was full of anger, and my soul burnt with hatred against it. "And shall our gods be forsaken?" I cried in great wrath. "As for me, I will never forsake them."

There were many others also of my mind; and we were one together in our hatred against the *lotu*, until one day when we heard a man talking of it who said that it promised a land of the dead different from the *Bulotu*,[3] of which our fathers spoke—even a home in the sky for the good, while evil men were cast into a dreadful place, wherein there burnt a fire which none could quench. On that very night I went forth with the lads of our town.

---

1   Vava'u is one of the groups of islands in the Friendly Islands, or the Kingdom of Tonga. It is also the name of the largest island in that group. It lies in the northern part of Tonga, 18–19° S., 174° W. of Greenwich (see map).

2   *Lotu* is the term for "Christianity" in the missionary literature. The word is of Tongan origin, as far as Fiji is concerned, but was used in Fiji before Christianity arrived; *lotutaka* = to pray for, *vakalotuya* = to Christianise, or cause to embrace the new religion from Tonga. Worshippers bowing low to the floor (even before Christian times) were *cuva vakalotu*.

3   *Bulotu* (cf. *Pulotu* [Samoa] and *Burotu Kula* [Fiji]) is the Tongan abode of the dead. According to Lorimer Fison:

A strange and beautiful legend tells of a speaking tree being there, and a fountain of life. Maui, the king of the gods, fished up Tonga from the bottom of the sea, and thither a number of the younger gods fled, leaving Bulotu. As a punishment for this rebellion, they were made *Maha Mahaki* (subject to decay and death); and they were not permitted to return to Bulotu. These runaway gods thus became the fathers of the Tongan race.

Fijians say that Burotu is sometimes seen by those who are sailing from the windward islands towards Kadavu, always with the sunlight strong upon it; but when they steer for it, it always fades at their approach, growing fainter and fainter as they draw nearer and nearer, until it utterly disappears, and they sail in speechless wonderment over the spot where they saw it standing, green and beautiful, in the midst of the waters. The people of Matuku say that burnt out torches of a strange make, with handles of shell, sometimes drift to their land; and, when they find them, they say, "See the torches from Burotu." Moreover, an old legend has it that Burotu was formerly to be seen from the hill-tops of Ono; but that two goddesses, who perfidiously drowned in the Ono passage many boys and girls belonging to the Levuka tribe, hid it thenceforward from mortal eye. Even now, on moonlight nights, the drowned children are heard singing in the Ono passage; "and this," says the legend, "is ever the song they sing:

Tuvana e colo, Tuvana e ra,
Ko Nasali sa cere baba;
Ko Burotu erau sa vunia tu ga."

(*Tuvana of the mountain, Tuvana of the plain,*
Nasali is plainly in sight;
as for Burotu, they two are hiding it.)

It was a fine night, and looking up to the heavens where the stars were shining, this thought suddenly smote me: "Oh the beautiful land! If the words be true which were told us today, then are these *lotu* people happy indeed," for I saw that the earth was dark and gloomy, while the heavens were clear and bright with many stars; and my soul longed with a great longing to reach that beautiful land. "I will *lotu*," said I, "that I may live among the stars."

But I feared my father and our kinsfolk, for they were all heathen, and great was their hatred against the *lotu*, so that it was many days before I could make up my mind. But I could not rest because of the great longing within my soul, and at length I went away to another town, where dwelt 'Ulukalala,[4] a Christian chief, and made my request to one of his people who took me to him saying, "Here is the son of Mafitangata; he is come because he wishes to *lotu*."

"Good is your coming," cried the chief, for great was his joy. "But why do you want to *lotu*?"

"I have heard," was my reply, "of the good land whither you go after death; wherefore do I wish to *lotu*, that I also may be a dweller in the sky."

So they prayed over me. And thus it was that I turned to Christianity, but of its meaning I knew nothing. One thing only I knew, that I wanted to live among the stars.

When my father heard what was done, he was very angry; and calling together all our kinsfolk, he sent for the heathen priest and told him that I had cast away the old gods and why. Then the priest became inspired after their lying fashion and uttered a lamentable cry: "Why has he forsaken me? What have I done to him that he should hate me? Have I not always watched over and kept him ever since he was but a little child? And now that he is a big lad, he turns his back upon me."

Then were my friends very mad against me when they heard these words, which they believed to be the words of the god (for when a priest was inspired, we used to think that it was not he who spoke but the god), and they sprang to their feet in hot wrath, saying, "Let him be clubbed! He shall die today!"

And I was afraid when I heard these words and saw the deadly anger in their faces, so I said to myself, "It were well for me to lie to them, that I may live." And I cried out, "Take pity upon me. I will cast away the *lotu*." With these words their wrath was appeased but no sooner had I spoken than a great grief sprang up in my breast. "I have thrown away the good land," said my soul within me, and stealing away into the forest I knelt down and prayed to God: "O Lord, I have cast away the *lotu* because I feared the anger of my friends, but I lied to them, I lied to them, for I wish to hold it still." And thus day after day I used to

---

4   Also known as Finau. 'Ulukalala II was the Tongan warrior chief who had become notorious for his destruction of the English whaler *Port-au-Prince* in 1806. In this event twenty-five of the crew were killed, and the remainder spared only to service the salvaged guns. One of these was William Mariner, the major primary source for pre-Christian Tonga (see Wood 1975, 14–15).

hide myself in the forest and pray to God, though indeed I knew not what to ask him for. All I knew of the *lotu* was the good land among the stars.

When 'Ulukalala heard that my father had made me turn heathen again, he was very angry, and our friends were afraid of his wrath, so they made a great feast, to which the priest was called, where they bade farewell for me to the heathen gods and gave me over to the *lotu*. So I went away to Hakoka,[5] the town of 'Ulukalala, where I lived until war arose between the *lotu* folk and the heathen, wherein we were victorious; and when we had beaten them, they said that our God was stronger than theirs, wherefore they all *lotued*, and I went back to my father.[6]

All this time I knew but little of religion—my soul was dark—but I tried to be good, because of the great longing I had after the beautiful land in the sky; and so ignorant was I that I thought I could get there by my own strength alone. Then came Mr. Thomas[7] to Vava'u, and standing under a tree in the public square he preached to us from the parable of the tares among the wheat. It was this sermon that pierced my soul, for I had thought that I was one of the wheat, and now I found that I was among the tares. As I heard, I wept and trembled, for I thought, "I shall never see the good land"; and it seemed to me that the devils were waiting for me behind the trees which grew in the square, to drag me down to that awful pit of which I had heard, where burns the fire that none can quench.

When the sermon was over, and the people rose to go, I sat in my place, quaking for fear and weeping in great anguish, for all the strength had gone out of my body; and I could not rise till some friends raised me up and led me away, staggering like a drunken man. When we reached the house, I fell down within the doorway, weeping bitterly; and our people, looking upon me and seeing that my face was like that of a man in great pain (for the anguish of my soul was written upon my face), thought that some evil disease had taken hold upon me. "What is the matter with you?" they asked; and I said, "Pray for me. Pray for me, I beseech you." So they knelt down and prayed for me, first one and then another till they were tired; and then they sat looking at me, not knowing what it was that made me weep. But I found no comfort in their prayers for my body, whereas it was my soul that was sick; so I rose, and going to an empty outhouse I knelt down there by myself, weeping and praying before the Lord, for now I felt that I was a sinner: the wrath of God lay heavy upon my soul, and I hated myself because of my evil ways. "Oh, what is that repentance whereof the preacher told us?" I cried. "Lord, let me find it that I may live"; for so dark was my soul that I did not know that this sorrow and fear of mine were marks of repentance. Thus I

---

5   In Vava'u.
6   Not a good motive for conversion, but a common one nevertheless. It shows that the converts at this point still held the power orientation of pre-Christian animism and called for Christian instruction in the true nature of the Christian faith.
7   Rev. John Thomas, missionary to Tonga from 1825. He was established at Hihifo by 1826 and had their first baptisms (seven) in 1829. He stayed in Tonga until 1850, and returned again later—1855–59.

continued for a long while, no longer thinking that I was fit for the good land among the stars, but seeking the Lord in prayer with many tears; and often did I hide myself in the forest and pray to God[8] that he would give me this repentance, while so great was my fear that if but a bird flew suddenly past me, I started and trembled, thinking that the devils were come to drag me away.

When the Christian people saw my earnestness, they had compassion upon me and came near to me, teaching me all they knew of the Way of Life. The missionary also took pity upon me and comforted me with many good words, so that I began to understand somewhat more of the Way; but still my sorrow did not leave me, and I could find no rest for my soul. Thus I went on for many days, seeking the Lord with tears but finding him not; and at length I was appointed to help in the work. So I went forth to teach others—I who wanted teaching myself; but indeed I did what I could, exhorting all men to flee from the wrath to come, from which I also was fleeing with all my might, though whither to go for safety I knew not.

At last there came a day [1834] whereon the missionaries (of whom Mr. Turner[9] was one) assembled us together to hold a love feast[10]—us who were employed in the work; and when we had sung a hymn and prayed, then Mr. Turner stood up to declare the work of God in his soul. My heart burnt within me as I listened to his words, for in speaking of himself he told all I had felt, and I said to myself, "We are like two canoes sailing bow to bow, neither being swifter nor slower than the other." Thus it was with me while he told of his repentance, but when he went on to speak of his faith in Christ, the forgiveness of his sins, and the peace and joy which he found in believing, then said I, "My mast is broken; my sail is blown away; he is gone clean out of my sight, and I am left here drifting helplessly over the waves." But while I listened eagerly to his words, telling of the love of Christ to him, my eyes were opened. I saw the way, and I, even I also, believed and loved. I was like a man fleeing for his life from an enemy behind him and groping along the wall of a house in the dark to find the door that he may enter in and escape, when lo! a door is suddenly opened before his face, and straightway with one bound he leaps within. Thus it was with me as I listened to the words of Mr. Turner: my heart was full of joy and love, and the tears

---

8   Retiring to pray in the forest was a common pattern in the islands for people struggling with the significance of re-jecting their old religion (Tippett 1970, 17). This was reported by William Ellis, John Hunt, Lorimer Fison, and others. Even planters observed it.

9   Rev. Peter Turner arrived in Tonga 7 August 1830. In February 1835 he went to Niuatobutabu and Niuafo'ou islands towards Samoa, whence the awakening was spreading. All references to Peter Turner in Joeli Bulu's writing must fall between these dates. Peter Turner should not be confused with his namesake, Nathaniel, who was also in Tonga 1827–31.

10   The love feast was a Wesleyan institution, an attempt to restore the New Testament communal fellowship. The prac-tise was used in the Wesleyan churches of the Pacific and was quite appropriate for its spiritual purpose of building the *koinonia*. This it achieved without disturbing the indigeneity of the churches. However, it never had the same "staying power" as the class meeting which continues to this day and serves much the same purpose. The initial impression of this institution on Fijian converts is described by Cargill (1841, 190).

streamed down my cheeks. Often I had wept before, but not like my former weeping were the tears which I now shed. Then I wept out of sorrow and fear, but now for very joy and gladness, and because my heart was full of love to him who had loved me and given himself for me; and Mr. Turner, seeing the tears raining heavily down from my eyes, called upon me to speak. "Stand up, Joeli," said he. "Stand up, and tell us how it is with you."

So I stood up, but it seemed to me as if my soul were parted from my body, and I remember nothing more until I found myself lying on the mats, Mrs. Cargill[11] supporting my head upon her lap while the missionaries held me by the hand, weeping as they looked down upon me. "What is this?" they cried. "What ails you, Joeli?"

"I live!" said I. "I live! Let me rise, that I may declare the mercies of God." And even while I spoke, there arose a great cry in our midst and a burst of weeping, for the hearts of all were strangely moved; and Mr. Turner stood up with tears streaming down his cheeks and cried aloud, "Let us spend the rest of our time in prayer and praising God."

Oh, what a day that was! Never can I forget it. The prayers, the praises, and the tears of joy! There were many like myself who had long been seeking the Lord, and how many of us there were who found him on that day I do not remember rightly, but we were very many. Nor did we break up our meeting until the night had come over the land, and even then we were loath to part. Before we went away Mr. Turner said to us, "Blessed be God for the great thing which he has wrought among us today! But this is only the beginning of a greater work. Let us now go, each man to his own house, and pray that the heavenly rain, which has watered our souls, may fall on all the land, for the land is athirst."

And this word of his came to pass, for when a teacher named Aisea,[12] who was with us in our meeting, went to preach at another town, the same great work broke out there also. And so it went from place to place until it reached the town of the king, whither we all went to help it on and to rejoice over the great things which our God was bringing to pass. This was the time when King George[13] repented of his sins, and lay weeping on the chapel floor until he could bear no more, but fled away to his own house, where he ceased not to seek the Lord with strong crying tears until he found him, to the joy of his soul; and then we were all gathered at his house that he might tell us what God had done for him. And still the work went on from house to house and from town to town; strangers also, who had come sailing over to us from the other islands, carrying it with them when they went back to their homes—a work great and glorious, such as I have never seen since those days.

---

11   Margaret Cargill, wife of Rev. David Cargill, subsequently a pioneer missionary to Fiji in 1835. The best source for her life is her husband's *Memoirs of Mrs. Margaret Cargill* (1841). She was born in Aberdeen, Scotland, 28 September 1809 (nee Smith); married 6 September 1832; arrived at Nukualofa, Tonga, 24 January 1834; sailed for Fiji, 8 October 1835. This reference dates the incident Joeli is narrating as in either 1834 or 1835.

12   Aisea Vovoli of Neiafu.

13   George Tūpou I, also known as Taufa'ahau. This conversion took place 31 July 1834, and is reported by Cargill (ibid., 76).

As for myself, I lived in great peace and joy, for everything was going on well, and I used to think that, if we had all died in those days, we should have gone straight to heaven in one great and mighty band. Oh that I could see such a work as that here in Fiji. I have worked for it, I have prayed for it, I have waited for it; and if I could but see it coming, if I could live through but one day of it, then would I say with joy and gladness like Simeon of old, "Lord, now lettest thou thy servant depart in peace, for mine eyes have seen thy salvation."

After a while Mr. Turner went away from Vava'u, and Mr. Thomas came in his stead. In those days there was a great friend of mine, one Jacob Fekeila by name, the teacher at Leimatua (which was about as far from the town where I was stationed as Bau is from Kaba),[14] and with him I used to meet every Friday that we might pray together and help one another on the way to heaven.[15]

One day, as I was going to see him, there met me in the path a man who told me that the word of the missionaries in Fiji had come to Tonga, begging for teachers to help them in the work of God; and while he was yet speaking, my soul burnt within me, and a great longing sprang up in my heart to go away to that land and declare the glad tidings of salvation to the people that knew not God. I spoke no word, for indeed I could not speak, but turning my back upon the man, I went on my way towards Leimatua, weeping as I went because of the fullness of my heart.

There I found my friend waiting for me in the little house which he had built as a house of prayer. "What is the matter with you?" he asked, for he saw the tears in my eyes; and I told him of my meeting the man in the path, and of the great longing which had sprung up within my soul.

"Good," said he. "Perhaps it is the will of God concerning you. Let us pray about it"; and kneeling down, we prayed for each other and for Fiji also—asking, moreover, of the Lord to put it into the hearts of the missionaries to send me to Fiji if it were his will that I should go; and after our prayer was ended, I went back to my own town.

That night I could not sleep, but lay thinking of Fiji and weeping as I thought of how there were many thousands there who were living in darkness, not knowing the true God. At last I could refrain no longer and, rising to my feet, I said to my wife, "I cannot sleep. I must go to Neiafu."[16]

---

14 The references to Bau and Kaba in Fiji (not Tonga) were inserted by Joeli Bulu for Fison's benefit and any reader familiar with Fiji. Kaba is a headland three or four miles from the island of Bau. Bau was the chiefly location of Ratu Cakobau in Joeli's time.

15 This was typical of early Tongan Christians. They maintained their faith in God by meeting like this for regular prayer at specific times.

16 The largest town (i.e., capital) of Vava'u.

Now this Neiafu was the town where the missionary lived, and there also dwelt a Christian chief, Sailasa Faone by name,[17] with whom I often met for prayer. So I went to him and told him all that was in mind. "Lie down now and sleep," said he when he had heard my words. "In the morning we will ask the missionary about it."

In the early morning, before the sun had well risen, there came a man called Aisea Vovoli to the house where I had slept.

"Are you here, Joeli?" he cried. "Good is your coming, for I was just going to seek you. Mr. Thomas has sent me for you."

So I went to the mission house, and Mr. Thomas said to me, "Joeli, a letter has come from Fiji begging for help, and ever since I read that letter I have been thinking of you."[18]

Then I told him why I had come to Neiafu, how Fiji was ever before my eyes, and how the desire to go thither lay like a burning coal at my heart. "Good is the will of the Lord," said he. "It is plain that you must go. Come, Joeli, let us kneel down and ask God's blessing upon you." And thus the matter was settled.

Great was the weeping of my friends on the day of our departure. My wife and I, we also wept at parting from them, but though my eyes were wet, yet was there joy in my heart, for the Lord comforted me. We sailed to Fiji in a canoe, hoisting sail when the day was far spent, so that the land was still in sight when darkness came down upon the waters. We went sailing through the night before a pleasant breeze, through all the next day also, and the following night; but on the second morning Moce[19] rose out of the waters in our course, and landing there we offered up our thanksgivings to the Lord, because he had brought us thither safely.

---

17   A Tongan preacher who subsequently went to Fiji as a missionary, arriving there 26 June 1838 in company with Joeli. He was a hereditary chief, born in one of the islands of the Haofuluhao group. He began his missionary work in Fiji under William Cross at Rewa after preaching at the dedicatory planting of the first post of the chapel at Bucainabua, Lakeba, 23 July 1838.

18   The Friendly Islands district meeting of December 1834 determined on expanding their work into Fiji and selected Cross and Cargill to go. The decision had been carried out, and there had been a mission in Lakeba, Fiji, from the end of 1835. This episode must have been in 1838. Over those years regular contact had been maintained between Fiji and Tonga by large deep-sea canoes—the first mail services between Fiji and Tonga. Cargill was stationed at Lakeba in 1838, and the letter mentioned here must have been written by him.

19   As Fison points out, they had come through dangerous waters with many reefs during the night. Moce is about twenty miles from Lakeba, their intended destination. Moce is a coral island with a large and beautiful lagoon. After their arrival at Lakeba, one of their number, Jeremaia Latu, was appointed to this island.

2
MISSION TO FIJI

Lakeba, 1838

Thence we went on to Lakeba, where Mr. Cargill[20] rejoiced greatly at our coming; and I set myself to learn the language and to help in the work.

After I had been here some little time, Mr. Hunt and Mr. Calvert came out from England, bringing with them a printing press.[21]

Mr. Hunt went to Rewa,[22] and I was appointed to help Mr. Calvert in the printing, which I did until it was the mind of the missionaries to send me to Rewa,[23] whither I went with Mr. Lyth, who had also come down from Tonga to preach the gospel in Fiji.[24]

---

20   David Cargill [born 20 June 1809, arrived Tonga 24 January 1834] had removed from Tonga 8 October 1835 and arrived in Lakeba on the 12th. By expertise he was a linguist, holding an M.A. degree from Aberdeen in that field. His major contribution to the Fiji Mission was linguistic. Joeli's party arrived on 26 June 1838 and were immediately "at home" because of the large number of Tongans resident at Lakeba. Even so, like a good missionary, he began immediately learning the language of the people.

21   John Hunt was born at Hykeham Moor, Lincoln, 13 June 1812. He had a theological training at the Hoxton institution and was an effective evangelist both in Britain and in Australia. He departed from England for Fiji 29 April 1838. James Calvert was born at Pickering, Yorkshire, and served as a postmaster and printer. He trained "also at Hoxton" before entering the Wesleyan ministry. Hunt and Calvert arrived in Lakeba on 22 December 1838 in the *Letitia*. Thomas Jaggar was also with them. With the arrival of Hunt and Calvert the Fiji enterprise was constituted an autonomous mission district, independent of Tonga. Calvert brought a printing press with him. It was set up at Lakeba, and Joeli was employed there as Calvert's offsider. In February 1839 they printed the first *Catechism*.

22   Rewa was one of the great kingdoms of Fiji. Cross had removed there from Lakeba arriving 8 January 1838—an important decision by which the missionaries determined to concentrate their missioning on two localities, one in the windward islands and the other in central Fiji. Calvert and Jaggar were to remain at Lekaba and Hunt to join Cross. After twelve days in Lakeba the voyage continued via Moala, where the captain desired to trade, until on 7 January 1839 Hunt arrived at Rewa.

23   Joeli had worked with Calvert from June 1838 to July 1839. Now he removed to Rewa with Cargill and Jaggar, Calvert remaining alone in Lakeba. The printing press was taken to Rewa, which probably accounts for Joeli's removal at this juncture. This reflects the most significant feeling of the missionaries with respect to their policy of diffusion. Cross removed to Viwa in August 1839. Cross, Cargill, Hunt, and Calvert had met at Rewa in 1839 and determined this deployment immediately upon Lyth's arrival from Tonga. Lyth and Hunt were to open new work at Somosomo.

24   Richard Bursdall Lyth, born 1810, was both a trained surgeon and an ordained Wesleyan minister. He served in Tonga from 7 October 1836 and spoke the language fluently, using it a great deal in Fiji after his arrival in July 1839. In Tonga he had witnessed the effects of the Great Awakening, and was probably better prepared for mission in Fiji than any other missionary. Lyth's travels during July 1839 permit us to date Joeli's arrival in Rewa.

Rewa, 1839

There were but few Christians at Rewa in those days, and many were the sufferings which we had to endure. We were often abused and threatened, our goods were stolen, and the heathen stoned us when we met together to worship God. But none of these things moved us, for we believed that our God was stronger than the devil, and that he would prevail.[25]

We lived at Nasali,[26] the river being between us and the town; and awful were the sights which we saw from day to day, for Rewa was then a great kingdom, strong and full of people. All the open spaces in the midst of the town, which are now empty and grass-grown, were then covered with houses, and the hearts of both chiefs and people were hardened and lifted up, so that they defied the living God; wherefore has he smitten them down and destroyed them, and the mounds whereon stood the houses of the living are now full of the bones of the dead.[27]

Day after day we saw the bodies of the slain brought to the town and the refuse floating past us as we stood upon our bank of the river, for the Noco[28] people were then fighting among themselves; and when anyone was killed, the body was brought to Rewa and presented to the king. These were not eaten, for Noco belongs to Rewa, and they were killing one another in their own quarrel; but their bodies used to be thrown down on the flat opposite our houses, and there the children used to drag them up and down, sometimes on land, sometimes in the water, singing the Song of Death.[29]

Moreover, the Tokatoka and the Nakelo tribes were always at war in those days.[30] They lay in wait for one another in the paths: they hid themselves in the long reeds on the river

25　Joeli had moved from the windward islands, where the Tongan residents had heard the gospel readily because of the reports of the Great Awakening at home in Tonga. When they went to Rewa they were penetrating into Fiji proper, and the land was at war. Those who became Christian were subjected to all kinds of petty persecution, which they endured because they trusted in God, whom they regarded as actively in control of the end results.

26　Nasali is on the opposite side of the Rewa River from Lomanikoro, the location of Rewan chiefly residence. The original site has been eroded because of the changing course of the river. A few years ago the graves of Mrs. Cargill and her infant child were removed across the river to the compound of the superintendent minister (see *Fiji Times and Herald*, 17 April 1953, for a full description).

27　This is an interesting historical description of the place in the early 1870s, but the judgement described here refers to the fall of Rewa before the Bauan forces in December 1845. Joeli had lived in Rewa for a little over five years. The gospel had been preached, but the resistance had been extremely strong, and Joeli interpreted the fall of Rewa as divine judgement on the rejection of Christianity by the Rewa chiefs—Qaraniqio in particular.

28　A district of Rewa in the river delta with a fortified town that Cakobau destroyed in 1847, killing many and taking about two hundred prisoners.

29　This neglect of burial rites was a symbolic way of expressing contempt for the dead, as also was the notion of allowing the children to use the bodies of the dead as playthings, and the throwing of the entrails into the river. The children chanting a dirge was their "playing cannibal war" (cf. the children of the marketplace "playing funeral" in Luke 7:32).

30　Tokatoka and Nakelo were caught in no man's land between Bau and Rewa, quite apart from their own rivalry. Tokatoka was one of the best defended towns in the delta, with a network of war trenches, well described in the primary sources. In the Bau/Rewa War they grew tired of the continual battering by Bau and her allies, who shut off resources by land and sea. In the face of famine the town "went over to the Bauan side," like many smaller villages of the delta. So loyalties shifted. The kingdom of Rewa was itself hopelessly divided, not only by Bauan intrigue but also by discord among its own chiefs. Many villages which appeared to be on the Bauan side were rather loyal to Cokonauto banks, whence they fired their guns and threw their spears at the women as they came down with their waterpots or their fish baskets, at the canoes as they passed by, and at the children at their play. Seldom could you pass their towns without hearing the death drum booming forth from one bank or the other; and the bodies of these slain also were brought to Rewa, either to the king or to Qaraniqio,[31] his brother, who took opposite sides in the quarrel, though not themselves coming to blows about it. These bodies also were not eaten. Having been presented to the chiefs, they were sent back for burial; but we saw that the Tokatoka men always cut out the tongue, the heart, etc., before they brought a dead body to Rewa. Men from Suva and other places were always eaten; and Rewa being then on friendly terms with Bau,[32] whole canoe loads were often brought thence as goodwill offerings, at which times we looked on sights that made our hearts sick with a deadly sickness.[33]

Well do I remember one day when Bau and Viwa had smitten Telau[34]—the little island opposite Viwa, which stands empty at this day—how a large war canoe came in heavily laden with the dead, who were taken ashore and piled up in a great heap on the low flat opposite to our houses; and when the Bau messenger had finished his report, the king said, "Do what

---

and against Qaraniqio—an internal matter of which Bau took advantage. [For a detailed account of these wars, see Tippett (1973, 33ff.), based on the journals and letters of Hunt and Jagger, who lived in the thick of the war, one in the territory of each of the contestants.] Joeli Bulu at this time was with Jagger at Rewa.

31   Qaraniqio was the war lord of the kingdom of Rewa and the brother of the Tui Dreketi (whom he subsequently succeeded). Even before taking this office he held great power and authority and often acted in opposition to the decisions of the king, who was more disposed to be friendly with Christianity. Qaraniqio was hostile. At the time Joeli was writing, his body lay, ironically, in a lofty burial mound close to the mission house at Rewa. He was also known as Dakuwaqa. Both names had religious significance. Despite his cruelty the Rewans held him in high respect. Fison left the following record of him:

A woman, one of his household, brought him food which was badly cooked.

"What is your hand given you for?" he asked in a quiet tone. "It is given you to cook my food. And now what is the use of it? Cut it off, Koroi Qavoka; cut it off."

The cruel deed was done, but the king's anger was not yet appeased. "Let her eat it," he cried; and the bleeding arm was thrust into her mouth.

This Koroi Qavoka is still living—a Rewa chief of high rank. I know him well, and he is always very kind and obliging, ready to help with anything within his power. I asked him once whether this horrid tale were true. "It is true," said he with a placid nod. "I cut her arm off. It was taken away and cooked for eating."

Qaraniqio died of dysentery. Missionary Moore had given him medicine shortly after a peace mission to Bau. Qaraniqio's death was interpreted as due to the medicine, and his supporters destroyed the mission house by fire, Moore and his family barely escaping.

32   The First Bau/Rewa War lasted from 1843 to 1845, so this reference to friendly relations must be dated early in 1843. The Suva affair was actually one of the main causes of the war; Jagger describes the event in a letter to Britain (25 May 1843).

33   Joeli had entered a part of Fiji where cannibalism was "the order of the day." Originally ceremonial in its function it had been secularised because of the introduction of Western firearms and ammunition some twenty-five years before the arrival of the missionaries. He had never seen anything quite like this before in spite of the Tongan reputation in war.

34   Telau, a small island a mile and a half north of Viwa. The chief responsible for sacking this island on Bau's behalf was Namosimalua, and the principal actor was Varani. They came from Viwa, which has remained the territorial overlord of Telau ever since. It was a terrible slaughter, and the island is empty of population to this day.

you like with them," whereupon there rose a sudden yell.[35] A great rush was made down to the waterside, and the bodies were dragged hither and thither as the people struggled with one another over them, many clutching at the same body, cutting them up limb from limb, tearing them asunder, and snatching the pieces out of each other's hands. And the yells rose louder and louder as the people grew ever fiercer in their eagerness; women and children also mingling with them in the struggle, their shrill cries rising high amid the uproar.[36] Many years have passed since that fearful day, but sometimes, even now, I see that struggling crowd and hear that awful yelling in my dreams, and when I wake I thank God for the *lotu*, which has wrought so wondrous a change in that proud and savage tribe.

Where the missionary's study is now built, on the raised mound called Cakauyawa,[37] there stood a house in which the hands of the slain were hung up and smoked. I have seen the roof full of hands, hanging there in the smoke, the fingers drawn up like the claws of a roosting bird; and the chiefs would sit around the fire and point up at them with a laugh and savage jest, making their mock at their dead owners.[38]

I was at Rewa when the chiefs of America [captains] came in their warships and took Ratu Veidovi away, because he had killed some of their people who were fishing for *beche de mer* in the old times.[39] The king of Rewa, with the queen and others also, went to see the

---

35   The politics of this decision are interesting. No doubt the Tui Dreketi did not want to offend Bau by returning the offering. Neither did he want to involve himself in the sack of Telau. So he accepted it and secularised it, leaving it to the rank and file.

36   They could not have done this fifty years earlier when *bokola* (flesh for the oven) was taboo to women and children. It illustrates how the old religious values were already decaying when the missionaries arrived.

37   This must have been the second position of the mission house, which was originally at Nasali. Today it is again on level land, but in Lomani-koro, not at Nasali. Joeli used to designate the location of the mission at Nasali by the biblical name Zoar. He told the missionary Jaggar:

This is a Zoar, for in heathen settlements the bodies of the people are diseased, and they cannot cure them; and their souls are sinful, and they cannot save them. But when they come to these premises they obtain a cure for body and soul; for their bodies are generally healed; and, receiving instruction, they believe in God, and their souls live thereby. Therefore this place is a true Zoar. (Gen 19:22)

Cargill said, the analogy having been put forward by one who had himself passed through the experience, it was accepted, and the station at Nasali was called Zoar in those days before the fall of Rewa.

38   This custom was an institutionalised form of revenge in pre-Christian Fiji, to remind the household that their enemy, so-and-so, had died an ignominious death. Death could be honourable (burial alive or strangling normally) or dishonourable (various ways of cooking, eating, leaving to rot, giving to the children as a plaything or for target practise, or preserving an organ for display on the wall or rafters of the house).

39   In September 1834 Veidovi had been employed to pilot the American brig, *Charles Doggett*, to Kadavu for the collection of *beche de mer*. The vessel anchored at Ono-i-Kadavu, and the crew was engaged in a project on shore as part of their trade contract with the people. Veidovi and the local chief determined to seize the ship and cargo by attacking the crew, ten of whom were clubbed, among them eight American citizens. It appears that this was all done in the interests of Qaraniqio. The members of the crew remaining on board turned the ship's cannon on the attacking party which took refuge in a cave, thus permitting the vessel to escape capture. This was one of the matters investigated by the U.S. Expedition of Commodore Wilkes [actually by Captain Hudson of the *Peacock*, second ship of the squadron]. Veidovi was taken by a trick, but was tried and convicted on the evidence of a beachcomber, Paddy Connel, who having been on board the *Charles Doggett* had witnessed the event. In any case Veidovi had boasted of his achievements. The date of this capture of Veidovi which Joeli witnessed was 22 May 1840, so Joeli

ship, and the American chief kept them on board, saying that he would not let them go unless Veidovi were given to him.[40] When this news was brought to the town, there was a great uproar, and the warriors ran together, vowing to kill us all, because they thought the missionaries had a hand in this deed. Then were we in great fear, but a Rewan chief [a Christian sympathiser] came over to us; and when the warriors appeared in sight, he went up to them and presented an offering of atonement for us, begging that we might not be killed.[41] So we escaped, but indeed we thought that our time had come.

The chiefs hardened their hearts and set their faces against the *lotu*, but in spite of them the work went on, though slowly,[42] and doors were opened here and there. Thus we found an opening to the island of Kadavu,[43] whither two teachers were sent—even Aisake,[44] a Fijian, and Eparaama,[45] a countryman of my own (who was afterwards with me at Nadi, and who was lost at sea in a great hurricane—he and many others).[46] They lived at a town called Suesue,[47] and the *lotu* was making good way when Eparaama, having come from Kadavu to make his report to the missionaries, was forbidden by Qaraniqio to return[48];

---

had his Rewa narrative somewhat out of historical sequence. This is not to be wondered at, since he was writing of his experiences about thirty years later.

40   This tactic was effective. Veidovi was handed over to the Americans and went willingly. He was taken away in irons with his Hawaiian barber for a companion. If he actually served his sentence he was, even so, never heard of again in Fiji except in the storytelling.

41   The presentation of a whale's tooth might be an atonement for a sin admitted, or a request for freedom from blame in a matter not admitted. The Fijians soon differentiated between the kinds of whites in their midst, but were still ready to exact vengeance on any white man who came along. Retribution was a strong law—"an eye for an eye, and a tooth for a tooth." Any white eye or tooth was equal to any other. Many an innocent missionary paid the price for the offences of white whalers, sandalwooders, and convicts. The story of Erromanga demonstrates this. The action of the Rewan chief here shows the Fijians were not without a sense of justice. Nor was this the only time Joeli's life was spared by the offering of a whale's tooth on his behalf.

42   The leader of this opposition was Qaraniqio, the strong man who frequently defied even the Tui Dreketi, and who had the support of the younger chiefs.

43   Kadavu was under the authority of Rewa, and Qaraniqio had no intention of allowing the church to grow there, it being too far from his sight. Actually several attempts were made to plant the church in Kadavu, both on the north and south coasts, but the small Christian communities were wiped out by the heathen. It was almost a decade before an effort at church planting was effective, and then the thrust did not come from Rewa. Sometime after Bau had defeated Rewa, Paula Vea, another Tongan, was dispatched to Yale by Varani of Viwa. Joeli had been long removed from Rewa by this time. The case he describes on this page refers to a small congregation commenced in September 1841, which the Tui Dreketi had approved.

44   Aisake Ravuata.

45   This Tongan always appears in the records as Eparaama. We do not recall seeing his full name.

46   In 1848 Eparaama was with Thomas Williams at Bua. He had been appointed to Lekutu, but under heathen pressure fled in fear. He was in Tiliva in September and appointed to the Yasawas in February 1849, when his wife was brought from Viwa to accompany him. Apparently she was timid, and I believe he never went to the appointment and was ashamed because of his wife's obstructions. Soon after this he lost his life in a hurricane.

47   On the north coast of Kadavu at the mouth of a strongly flowing stream. The location still bears this name, but the village has been removed to the top of the nearby cliffs. It is now marked on the map as Naikorokoro. The evangelism of Eparaama and Aisake won some response, and a nearby village had enquired about the procedure for becoming *lotu* (Christian) as a group. Tui Dreketi had granted them permission to convert, and this stirred up Qaraniqio.

48   Eparaama was detained by Qaraniqio, and thus Aisake was left alone in Kadavu. He kept in contact with Jaggar (at Rewa), reporting to him in 1842 that there had been five attempts by the heathen to drive the Christians away, all stimulated by Qaraniqio.

and we heard that a canoe belonging to the Vusanamu tribe[49] was being made ready for sea, the chief having sent orders that they were to go to Kadavu and kill Aisake. When we heard this report, we were in great perplexity, for we could not leave our comrade to die without making on effort to save him, but what to do we knew not. At length we begged a double canoe[50] from one of the chiefs, and I was sent to look after Aisake and to bring him away if I could. A miserable sailing was that, for the wind was strong, the sea ran high, and the rain came pouring down all the day, so that we could not see whither we were steering. We were wet, and cold, and wretched, being, moreover, in great fear that the sea would swallow us up, but the Lord watched over us and brought us safe to land. It was late at night when we reached Kadavu, and very dark, the rain still falling heavily, and we anchored the canoe in deep water so that we might hoist sail at once and flee, if need were, for we durst not run her on the beach for fear lest we should be attacked; in which case, if she were aground, we should all have been killed while trying to get her afloat.[51]

"Who will go with me to the town?" I asked, and two of our people volunteered. So we three went together, creeping stealthily along the beach towards the town, for we knew not whether Aisake were living or dead, the Vusanamu canoe having got the start of us.

Presently we were aware of a smell—the smell of an oven[52] wherein a man is being baked—and a great fear came upon us. "It is all over!" said I. "We are too late," and groping along the sand in the darkness, we found the oven with a club hanging over it—the

---

49   According to Lorimer Fison who had personal dealings with the Vusanamu:

These are also called Tonga-Viti, or Tongan Fijians, being the descendents of a number of Tongans who fled from their own land to Fiji, bringing with them, as their god, a large turtle-shell, which was said to have come down from Lagi [the sky], and concerning which there is a curious legend.

50   *Drua*, the largest of all the Fijian canoes, used for war and transporting tribute. Some of these were over one hundred feet long. They were used to sail between Tonga and Fiji.

51   Joeli must have been a fine navigator. He brought his craft in to the bay of deep water on the Naikorokoro side of the headland. There is no reef here; the deep water comes right to the beach. It is treacherous enough in daylight, but to achieve his purpose in a rainstorm at night was no mean accomplishment. One has to beach the canoe on the crest of the wave, and the craft has to be pulled up high on the beach before the next wave. It takes great effort to launch her again. The story of the planting of the church in Fiji is dotted with daring exploits at sea. Many of these adventures were told of the Tongan evangelists like Joeli Bulu and Jemesa Havea, both of whom left written accounts of their experiences in hurricanes. But the Fijians like Josua Mateinaniu were no less in number or in their exploits. The account of Jemesa Havea is still extant, is written in Fijian, and badly needs translation and annotation like this present volume.

52   Lorimer Fison, who had been ten years in Fiji when Joeli wrote his autobiography, left us the following footnote to this reference:

Fijians, to bake a pig, a turtle, or a man, dig a hole in the ground sufficiently large for their purpose. They fill it with wood, which they set on fire. Into this fire they throw a great number of small stones. When the wood is burned down, and the stones well heated, they clear out the oven, lifting the stones quickly and nimbly. They line the oven with green leaves on which they lay the pig, or whatever else the baking may be, having cleaned and made it ready while the fire was burning. Hot stones, wrapped in leaves, are thrust within the pig's body. Green leaves are now strewn over it, the hot stones thrown in atop, and the whole carefully covered with the ashes and with earth. Presently a light vapour arises, diffusing a fragrant smell. A pig thus cooked is wholesome and juicy eating.

This is a description of a *lovo*. One knows the food is cooked by the smell which rises from the hot earth.

club, I suppose, wherewith the deed was done. "It is Aisake who lies baking here," we said and, weeping, we returned to the canoe. After telling our comrades what we had found, we went ashore again, being fully resolved to make sure as to his fate, though we doubted not that the man in the oven was he. Through the rain and the darkness we groped our way to the town and, creeping into Aisake's house, we crouched down within the doorway, scarce daring to breathe, lest his murderers should be sleeping there, and at our wits' end to know how to find out who were in the house. "Let us put something on the fire," said I in a low whisper. "If they are here, we can escape before they are fully awake," and gathering together the leaves and bits of reeds which lay in the fireplace, a bright flame soon shot up from the hearth, by the light whereof we saw a mosquito curtain hastily lifted up from within, and we heard a startled voice crying, "Who's that? Who is there?"

"From Rewa we. Who are you?" said I, hand and foot ready for a spring, that we might rush to the door and escape.

"Metuisela," answered the man. "Is that you, Joeli? Who is with you? Why are you come?"

"It is I. Our people are with me. But where is Aisake?"

"He is sleeping here behind me," answered Metuisela, pointing to the end of the house. "Wake up, Aisake. Joeli Bulu is here."

"Hush!" said I. "Speak low. Who, then, is the man in that oven on the beach?"

Great was our rejoicing when we saw Aisake alive and well, and he told us that he whom we had found in the oven was a Kadavuan man whom the Vusanamu had killed at the command of Ratu Qaraniqio. He told us, moreover, that the murderers had said nothing to him, save that the chief was resolved that there should be no more *lotu* at Kadavu; so we got Aisake and his family on board the canoe as soon as possible and took them back with us to Rewa.[53]

It was while I was living on this station that I fought with a great shark.[54] Here are the marks of his teeth on my arm, where you see this big scar. Truly that was a wonderful deliverance.

---

53   So ended the first attempt to evangelise Kadavu. The rescue included also Aisake's family and the small Christian group. The second attempt came with a number of Christians who escaped from Rewa when the town fell before the Bauans in 1845. In 1846 they appealed to Hunt at Viwa for a teacher, but we hear no more of this until October 1848, when Lyth found a teacher there with eleven church members. Lyth baptised eleven more at Matanivanua near Ravitaki on the south coast. This congregation was scattered by war, but they requested another teacher in 1849, and again one was sent; but this third attempt also failed, and by 1852 there was no church at all on Kadavu, all the Christians having been massacred. The firm records of the Kadavu circuit did not begin until 1857 when Varani of Viwa had sent Paula Vea to give the Kadavuans the church.

54   This is probably the most repeated story in Pacific mission history, probably because the wound left such a scar which Joeli carried to the end of his life, and every missionary writer who met Joeli in the flesh had seen it. Professor Henderson (1931b, 58) threw doubt on the story by generalising about native testimonies. However, the narrative is well attested, quite apart from the presence of the scar. We are disposed to accept it as reliable. Lorimer Fison was quite satisfied that "Joeli's word is a good and sufficient voucher for the truth, and those who know him best, know that no further testimony is needed." In any case, Fison said that there were still eyewitnesses of the event alive to validate the account.

One night I dreamt that a shark bit my arm—this arm here, where you see the deep scar—
and I woke in great fear; but finding it was only a dream, my heart was glad.

For many days afterwards, when I went to bathe, I feared to go down into the deep
water, but stayed close to the shore, lest my dream should come true. But one day a young
chief, who was *vasu*[55] to Bau, called me, saying, "Come out for a swim, Joeli," and I refused,
for I feared the shark. Again he called me, and again I refused; but when for the third time
he shouted for me to come, I saw that he was bent upon it, and I did not like to say "no" lest
his heart should be evil against me. So I went with him.

In the river there were many boys swimming their toy canoes, and laying hold of one,
he said, "Take a canoe, Joeli, and let us see which will win—yours or mine." So I took one,
and presently seeing that his was shooting ahead, I gave mine a push to make it go faster;
whereupon he also pushed his, and soon we were swimming in the deep water, following
our canoes. "Let us go to the other bank," said he, and we swam across the river, a great
crowd of Bauans and Rewans following us. They all climbed up the bank, but I stayed in the
river, for it was in my mind to swim back and return to my house. As I was wading towards
the deep water, I saw two little waves coming towards me on the surface. "It is a shark,"
I thought. "My dream is true." I was afraid to turn back, for I was too far from the shore.
So I stood still, hoping that the shark might not see me, and the little waves came slowly
on. Holding my breath, I stood, and by and by the waves disappeared. Then I said, "It was
nothing," and I struck out to swim for Nasali.

Suddenly something struck sharply against my thigh. It was the shark biting me, but
I did not feel much pain, thinking it was only one of the young men who had dived and
caught hold of me. I put my hand down to seize him, and lo, it was a shark! Then was it with

---

55   Kinship studies were a specialty of Lorimer Fison who had been started on this aspect of research by Lewis Henry
      Morgan, the American anthropologist. Fison's description of a new Fijian *vasu* at the time, runs as follows:

      A man's nephew is called his *vasu*; but *vasu* is a title of office rather than of kinship; for the nephew has strange rights
      with regard to his uncle, and can take his property unquestioned. It is even said that, a chief being at war with his
      nephew, the latter actually went to his uncle's house and took thence gunpowder, etc., none daring to say him nay. It
      should here be noted that the sons of a man's brothers are not called his nephews in Fiji, but his sons, he being their
      great-father, or little-father, according as he is older or younger than their fathers. It is the sons of his sisters only
      who are his nephews. This is only one of the peculiarities of the most remarkable system of kinship which prevails
      among these Polynesian races, and which is found among the North American Indian tribes as well as among the
      Tamil and Telugu tribes of Southern India; affording conclusive proof of a common origin for all these widely scat-
      tered races [showing how Fison had accepted Morgan's theory]. When a great lady is given by one tribe or kingdom in
      marriage to another, her son is *vasu* to the tribe or kingdom from which his mother came; and has many privileges,
      giving him great power and influence among them.

      Hazlewood, in 1850, also allowed for the use of the term *vasu* for niece, but the power lay mainly with the male *vasu*,
      and the bigger and wealthier the town of his uncle the greater the value to his own locality. When the emphasis
      is on the person, the term is *nona* or *kena vasu*. When it refers to the institution—the relationship—the pronoun is
      postfixed: *na vasuna*. Thus we may distinguish between the personal status and the functional role. When both the
      mother and father are of high rank, the power of the *vasu* is very great, and he is known as the "big *vasu*," a *vasu levu*.
      The person is ceremoniously established in the status. In the period of history we are discussing, the ceremonies of
      the *vasu* were elaborate and significant.

me as if my soul were clean gone out of my body. A great darkness fell upon my eyes, and I could no longer see the shore or the people or the houses; all was dark.

One thing only I remembered—the *lotu*—and I said, "Today my life is at an end. Let me now pray once more to my God." I prayed, and in one moment the darkness was gone, though still I could not see the shore or any earthly being; but as I looked upwards, it seemed to me that the heavens opened, and I saw the throne of God, and a great multitude clothed in white raiment and shining with a blaze of light. Oh the glory of it, the wondrous glory! It was gone in a moment, like a flash of lightning on a dark night, but I saw it, I saw it! As plain as noonday I saw it, and my soul was glad and strong within me. I wished not to live. "Let me die today," said my heart, rejoicing. I no longer feared the shark. It was as nothing to me, though my flesh was torn and my blood was flowing.

But now he let go my thigh and came at me again to bite me. Then I seemed to awake, as it were, out of a dream, and my soul grew hot against him as against an enemy who wished to kill me. When he drew near and opened his mouth to bite, I thrust my hand down his throat—down, down as far as I could thrust it, for I thought I would tear out his heart and so kill him. His teeth closed on my arm and tore the flesh,[56] but still I worked my hand downwards with all my might; and at length he could no longer bite me, but opened his mouth as if he were sick. Then I snatched forth my hand and, clasping him round the body with both arms, I lifted him up as high as I could, holding my head down so that he could not bite me.

Thus I staggered with him towards the shore, and I could hear his jaws clashing together over my head as he tried to bite, but I held him fast, and I believe that I should have got him to land, only that, when I reached the shallow water, my right arm, which he had bitten, fell powerless to my side, whereupon he slipped out of my grasp and began to swim away, though very slowly and feebly.

So hot was my wrath against him that I turned and caught him again by the tail with my left hand, but now the shore and the trees and the people seemed as if they were going round and round. A deadly sickness crept upon my heart; a mist came over my eyes; there was a sound in my ears like the roaring of the surf; I fell down and knew no more. And this is how the Lord delivered me out of that fearful strife.[57]

We had not much to cheer us in those days. But few turned to serve the living God, for the people were eaten up of savage pride, and the land was full of all manner of heathen

---

56   Thirty years later Fison described the wound:

The scar of this wound is frightful to look upon even now. It extends all round the arm, and goes down to the very bone, which seems in one place to have only a covering of skin over it.

57   A fine description of the thoughts of life and death that passed through a man's mind in a few short seconds. It reveals a number of true, old Fijian idioms—"as if my soul were gone out of my body" [a pre-Christian explanation of sickness unto death (from the Lau-Tonga part of Fiji) was to have the soul stolen from the body; this might be done by sorcery (*yalovaki*)] and "my soul grew hot against him" (the intense anger of a man against an opponent).

abominations, some of which I have already told, but there were others concerning which I dare not even speak. It was when war broke out between Bau and Rewa that we had to look upon the worst sights, for then the people grew mad with rage, and there was no end to the killing of men and the strangling of widows.[58] Truly these were awful times, for there was no peace, nor any sense of safety either day or night. The chiefs were divided among themselves, every man's hand being against his neighbour,[59] while the enemy were pressing upon them from without, so that things grew worse and ever worse as the Bauans gained ground, until the missionaries had to leave,[60] and after a little while I also went away in the *Triton* to Viwa, where Mr. Hunt was living[61]; nor was it many days afterwards before Rewa was sacked and burnt to the ground, its people being slain with a fearful slaughter.[62]

---

58 All forms of war, and the killing and the cannibalism which accompanied them, demanded the strangling of widows. This was considered an honourable way to die and was demanded for theological (eschatological) reasons, that the dead might arrive in the afterlife with a consort and appropriate retinue. The strangled people might include slaves also, and perhaps a few warriors and a herald, in the case of a great chief who would supposedly be deified.

59 See chapter 4.

60 In August 1844 the *Triton* took the missionaries to the district meeting at Viwa. The chiefs were set against the *lotu*. The mission house needed rethatching, but no labour could be obtained. Food was extremely scarce. The possibilities of survival in Rewa were slim. The district meeting decided to withdraw temporarily, and the *Triton* returned to Rewa to effect the removal of mission equipment. The missionaries ceremonially requested the chief's permission to withdraw. Joeli Bulu remained at Rewa with a colleague. The most important equipment was the printing press (which had been in Rewa since July 1839) and a supply of paper. These were removed to Viwa.

61 Joeli stayed at his post until the end of November 1845 with the small Christian group who escaped to Kaba a few days before the fall of Rewa.

62 1 December 1845.

3

VIWA INTERLUDE

[Editorial Note:

Joeli Bulu says very little about this "Viwa interlude." He mentions it only because he was sent from Viwa to Vanua Levu to "spy out the land" as a suitable place for evangelistic thrust. But he did live at Viwa from the end of November 1845 for a period of time, and even while he was penetrating the Nadi area before the establishment of a proper mission station there in November 1847, he was under instructions from Viwa. This period of two years was a formative one in the ministry of Joeli Bulu, and this brief reference is important with respect to the light it throws on the Wesleyan missionary methods in Fiji.

It was significant for Joeli in that it brought him under the direction of John Hunt, the most dynamic personality of the Wesleyan mission to Fiji, and it is significant for an understanding of the journal because it shows how the Wesleyans used an islander to open up a new area. Josua Mateinaniu was engaged in the same role at Bua, a few miles along the coast from Nadi, at the same time.]

When I stayed some time at Viwa, Mr. Hunt sent me over to Vanua Levu in a canoe that I might go throughout the land as far as I could and see whether there were any place where we could gain a footing.[63] The white men were then living at Solevu[64] on that land, and thither I went first in a little canoe, narrowly escaping being wrecked on the way, for the wind being strong with a heavy sea, we ran bows under into a great wave that rose up suddenly before us, and in a moment the canoe was full of water.[65] Springing to my feet, I threw all our boxes overboard with everything we were carrying, and then, leaping into

---

63   Here is a specific statement of the purpose of this policy.

64   This was a large settlement of white traders and adventurers who had married Fijian women and from whom much of the present Euronesian population of Fiji has descended. The company had originally lived at Levuka but had so incurred the displeasure of Cakobau because of assistance they gave Qaraniqio in the Bau/Rewa War that they had to remove to a place further from Bau, and to do so at short notice. They first tried Makogai, but determined that Solevu in Vanua Levu offered better facilities for defence. They settled in Solevu Bay at a location known as Nawaido, but they found the place unhealthy and too seldom frequented by Pacific shipping. Without chiefly protection they found themselves repeatedly under pressure from hostile Fijians. Just prior to this episode one of their cutters had been plundered and five of the crew had been killed. Things went from worse to worse and after an epidemic of dysentry they appealed for permission to move to Levuka and left Vanua Levu shortly after Joeli.

65   This is one of the several ways a Fijian canoe may come to grief—*aoko na mua*—usually caused by too much weight up forward.

the sea, we held the canoe up until it could be bailed out.[66] So we escaped with our lives, though with the loss of nearly all we had in the world.

When I reached Solevu, I found that there was an old priest of a heathen god at an inland town called Muanaicake, who had been to Bau, where he had heard of the *lotu*, and returning to his own town he called his kinsfolk together and told them that he was resolved to turn his back upon the old gods and worship him alone of whom he had now been told.[67]

So I went to his town, and great was his rejoicing when he heard who I was and why I had come. "Good is your coming," said he. "I thank God that he has sent you to teach us dark-minded men the way of life."

He gave me a house to live in and cared for all my wants; and I went about from town to town, talking with the chiefs and the people and telling them of the one true God, and of Jesus Christ the Saviour of sinful men. When I went to a town, I used to ask for the chief's house and, entering therein, made my report after the Fijian fashion, to which answer would be made according to their custom[68]; then I used to talk about ordinary matters, telling any news that might be stirring; and when we had thus got into friendly talk, I would speak of the *lotu*, and of the good things which are written in the word of God.

Many of the people listened eagerly to my words, declaring that the things whereof I spoke were good things indeed, and better than those which they had heard from their fathers, but the heathen priests hated me and spoke evil of me continually.[69]

After staying at Muanaicake for many days and going throughout much of the land, I sailed back to Viwa that I might make my report to the missionaries. And when Mr. Hunt heard my story, then was his soul hot within him, and with tears of joy he gave thanks to God for his mercies to me.[70]

But when I was appointed to go back and dwell in that land, my heart sank within me, and I feared to go; for though I had been well received, yet I knew that the priests would stir up evil against me, and I said, "I am going to my death." Nevertheless, though I was sore afraid, yet it never entered my mind to refuse to go, for I knew it was the will of God concerning me, so I bade farewell to the missionaries and sailed away in great heaviness of soul.[71]

---

66   This is the recognised safety precaution—every man overboard except those bailing until the canoe is safe again. [The reader is referred to Tippett (1968, 106–10) for a situational description of the laws of sailing.]

67   The priest's name was Rai. We have this from a letter of John Hunt who had visited him before Joeli went to Vanua Levu. The probability is that Hunt had told Joeli to follow up this contact. We note the pattern: Rai was convinced of the truth of the *lotu* and called his kin together before registering his conversion.

68   With the support of Rai and his family, the door was open for an itinerant ministry. He was approved, provided for, and protected. He followed chiefly custom, reporting first to the chief wherever he went and speaking to the group through him. He established himself in the normal way and used opportunity for witness whenever appropriate.

69   He was getting a hearing from the rank and file, but as he gained a hearing the priests felt threatened—a regular pattern.

70   Hunt receives the report with enthusiasm. It is adequate for seriously considering a firmer appointment to Vanua Levu.

71   How long a space of time lies between Joeli's report and his firm appointment we do not know. We only know he faced it with some trepidation. He knew the people would receive him. He knew also the threatened priests would obstruct his work. However, he resigns himself to the sovereignty of God.

4

MISSION TO BUA AND NADI

At first things went well enough. Almost every day there came to me those who wished to *lotu*, sometimes one by one, sometimes twos and threes, and sometimes in little bands, until the work grew too great for me, and I sent to Mr. Hunt begging for help.[72] He sent me my countryman Eparaama, of whom I have spoken before.[73]

But when, after a little while, the work still growing on our hands, we asked for further help, then he sent us word that he could give us nothing but his prayers, that we could have no more men, but must do the best we could by ourselves; and indeed there were no men to be had in those days. So I said, "We must find our helpers here"; and we gathered the best of the young men together every night at my house, reading and praying with them, and teaching them all we knew, so that they might be able to teach others. And truly these young men were of great use to us, for some of them did good service in the work, not fearing even to die, that they might help the cause of Christ.[74]

But when the devil saw that we began to be many, and that his people were escaping alive out of his hands, then he bestirred himself to bring mischief upon us and to hinder the work of God.[75] The priests were his great helpers in this evil work. When any misfor-

---

72   This was the common pattern for the beginning of a movement to Christ—people coming in many small groups. The *Journal of Thomas Williams* (Henderson 1931b) reflects the same thing at Tiliva a few years later. Sending to Viwa for help was the normal procedure. He was in the Viwa circuit. Hunt was his superintendent.

73   Eparaama the Tongan reappears. This was the man Joeli rescued from Kadavu, and we shall meet him again. He figures prominently during the 1840s, but we do not know his other name. Joeli and Eparaama put together a congregation of about eighty persons. They built a chapel at Nabukaivete. Shortly afterwards, Hunt visited them. He was welcomed at Muanaicake by Rai and stayed five days, very pleased with the way Joeli had organised the congregation. This was in 1846. Hunt paid another visit in 1847, before the establishment of the Nadi mission station.

74   The shortage of trained pastor/teachers was due to the rapid expansion of the church. For years the Lakeba and Viwa circuits were deprived of their best leadership by the missionary demands of other parts of Fiji. Many of the circuit records reflect this, and it explains the educational slowdown in the central stations. Local congregations were frequently deprived of male leadership, because everyone was out on a missionary purpose in a pagan locality. Joeli soon recognised this, and this valuable statement shows how he realised the importance of the missionary principle of selfhood. He did the best he could with the best he had available and trained his own leaders. This is what John Hunt meant when he said, "There is indeed a Church in Fiji." Even though the mission organisation lasted for a century, the institutions planted in the villages were indigenous churches.

75   The regular pattern—a little growth and then persecution—begins, often stimulated by those who feel most threatened, the heathen chiefs.

tune happened, they would become inspired and cry out, as they lay convulsed and foaming at the mouth, that the gods had wrath against the land because of us; so that the hearts of the heathen people were turned against us, and we began to suffer persecution.[76] They dug up our plantations, defiled our bread-pits,[77] killed our livestock, and vexed us in every way, until our people could bear no more and wanted to fight; but I held them back, saying, "Let us endure in patience, according to the word of our Lord: it may be that the evil days will soon be past." But they grew worse, and even worse.[78]

I had a fine pig in those days—a pig large and fat—which never wandered away from my house, but stayed always about the door eating the leavings of our food; and one day, when I came back from the weekday preaching, I found it was gone, and there was a trail in the dust where it had been dragged along the ground. All our people came running together to my house. "Joeli," they cried, "we can endure these things no longer. It is our pigs today; it will be ourselves tomorrow. Let us go and have it out with them."[79]

"Stay you here," said I. "If we all go, there will be fighting; therefore I will go alone, and beseech them to take pity upon us, and cease these masterful doings."

"Nay, but we will die with you," they cried.

"Not so," said I. "Stay here, I beseech you, and wait for my return. The Lord will bring me back alive. Stay here, therefore, you, and pray for me." So they let me go alone.[80]

76　The common attack was for priests to blame the Christians for any misfortune and to stir up the heathen against them. Christian mission has had to deal with this problem since the days of Nero.

77　This was a serious persecution because it destroyed stored food which was an insurance against emergency. We have Fison's description of the process, which is as follows:

Fijian *madrai*, bread, which is made by the women, is of various kinds, whereof that made from bananas is the most highly esteemed. Here is the recipe: To make Banana Madrai—First choose a dry spot, well above flood-mark, and dig a hole of a size proportioned to your stock of fruit. Line the pit carefully with long leaves, the ends of which must be somewhat higher than the surface of the ground at the pit's mouth. Peel the bananas, and pile them neatly one layer over another until the hole be filled. Fold down the projecting ends of the long leaves so as to cover the mouth of your bread-pit, and lay flat stones on the top, or cover with earth if stones are not to be had. Fermentation will ensure; and you must change your leaves once or twice during the process. Open the pit, say, at two months' end, and you will find the contents reduced to a sort of pulp, and giving forth a stench which, though an utter abomination to you, is yet a sweet-smelling perfume to Fijian nostrils. Take out enough for two or three days' food, and close the pit again. If you wish to make your *madrai* especially nice, sprinkle grated cocoa-nut and sugarcane juice over the pulp. Take green banana leaves, and broil them on the embers of your fire (having first drawn out their fibres) until they are thoroughly soft and pliable. Tear them into shreds of sufficient size. Make up small packages of the evil-smelling pulp in these shreds, tying them with the fibres. Boil for an hour, and your bread is ready for eating.

[We believe that only the plantain, *vudi*, was used in this manner. Neither of us have tasted this, but have heard from older informants who always spoke of it as *madrai vudi*. Sometimes *yabia* and *dalo* are reported to have been used.]

78　A demonstration of Joeli's pacifism. No one could ever accuse him of any lack of courage in danger, but he did not believe in aggravating a dangerous situation.

79　The early Christian party were not afraid to face the heathen and felt the tension could only be relieved by their fighting for their rights and justice.

80　Joeli felt that belligerence on the part of the Christians would at best only bring a temporary solution. He knew, as the local Christians did not, what widespread resources of the heathen would be arrayed against them. He believed that there could be no peace in any way but by trust in the Lord only.

Now the heathen town was separate from ours, though close to it; and when I went up thither, I found all the townsfolk gathered round an oven wherein fire was burning, and by the side of it lay my pig, all cleaned and made ready for baking.

"Good is the baking!"—thus I saluted them. "*Kobo!* The bigness of the pig! Why, it's very like a pig of mine."[81]

"Why do you come here asking about pigs?" they cried. "Are you angry? Are you angry? What are you going to do?"

"Nay," said I, "I am not going to talk with you, for I see that you have evil in your hearts against me. I go to the chief."

With these words I turned from them and went up to the house of the great chief, whose name was Masiwawa.[82]

"I have come, sir," said I to him, "that you may tell me wherein we have offended. Your people have ruined our crops, killed our livestock—even now are they baking a pig of mine—and we hear that, when you have taken all our goods, you intend to eat us also. What, then, is the root of it? Tell me now why you are angry with us; and if we have done any wrong, we will not refuse to make amends, or to be punished. It is true that we have turned our backs upon our gods, but we have not forsaken you. No, sir, our faces are towards you still. You are the chief of this people, whether heathen or *lotu*, and we are no whit behind the heathen in our willingness to serve you. Tell me now, have you ever shared out to us any work which we have not done, any house which we have not built, any feast which we have not made? Why, then, should your soul be evil against us?[83] Your priests say that the gods are angry. Let them show their anger by punishing us, if they can prevail against the God who is our defence. We do not fear them.[84] It is you whom we fear."

Then said the chief, "True are your words, Joeli. True indeed are your words. There shall be no more of it. Be of a good mind. Overlook that which is past, and I will see that you shall be troubled no more."[85]

Thus spake Masiwawa, and I verily believe that all would have been right between us. But even while we were yet talking together, we heard a sudden tumult without, and shouts of defiance; and rushing forth, I saw that our lads had come up to look after me, and

---

81   *Kobo* is a local word expressing admiration, amazement, or disapproval, depending on the tone of the speaker.

82   This was the correct approach in Fiji. One does not go to the offenders, but to their chief. The former leads to discord and the latter to justice.

83   This is a good typical speech for such an occasion. It is humble but direct. It demands an explanation and offers to make an atonement in a way which would appeal to any chief's sense of justice. It points out that the Christians are loyal to the chief and carry their responsibilities—that rejection of the old gods did not mean rejection of the social system. [There is a similar record in which Cakobau himself admitted that his Christian subjects were more loyal to him and responsible than the heathen.] It shows how careful Joeli was about correct cultural procedure.

84   A good argument, and one that was used by Christians in the first century. The Fijian once had a phrase for an impotent god—*kalou lasu*, but in old Fiji it meant "one who could not carry out his boast or duty or live up to the expectations of his worshipper." Today the word means "lying."

85   The chief responds in justice. His chiefly image is at stake, and he knows it.

there they were bandying angry words with the people round the oven. So I ran between them, crying, "Why have you come? Did I not tell you to wait for my return?"

"We waited," said they, "till we could wait no longer. We are here to die with you. You shall not die alone." And hardly could I persuade them to go back with me, for they were thoroughly roused.[86]

The heathen now resolved to kill us, and their messengers went to all the neighbouring towns, calling on the warriors to gather together for the attack on the following morning. We heard all that was going on, for we were not without a friend or two among them; and we were told that they had resolved, after making an end of us, to attack the white men also at Solevu, that the *lotu* might be utterly trampled out in the land.[87]

So I sent a messenger to Mr. Whippy,[88] who was headman among the whites, warning him of our danger and theirs.

"Good is the word of warning," said he. "See, here are guns, and powder, and lead and flints. Go back to Joeli, and tell him to send some of the young men to fetch them."

When the messenger returned, there was great joy among our people because of the weapons of war. But I said, "We will not take them, lest our enemies say that we are defying them. Go one of you down to Solevu, and tell Mr. Whippy that we thank him for his care of us, but that we will not take the weapons, lest the heathen should say we want to fight, and lest they should be angry with him also, and thereby evil befall him." And when Mr. Whippy had heard these words, he said, "It is good. Let the guns stay here. If evil comes upon you now, it is your own fault. But tell Joeli that we shall not forsake you. We shall go up, and see how you fare."[89]

---

86   This often happened in Fiji. The rank and file of the Christian party were not sufficiently removed from heathenism to understand Joeli's theology of confidence in God. They saw his pacifism as a threat to their solidarity rather than as theological. It was a Fijian communal value to stand together as a group—survival depended on it. They were so aroused that their behaviour threatened everything Joeli had achieved by chiefly confrontation.

87   Joeli is describing the early stage of a normal Fijian war situation. Not only is this little Christian settlement threatened, but the church at large throughout all the land and also the white community at Solevu, some of whom were interested in the missionary work because it offered educational facilities for their education. Before their departure for Solevu John Hunt had held a class for them in English. Many of the wives were full members in good standing.

88   The leader of the Solevu settlement, David Whippy, who figures prominently in the Fiji records of the period, was an American born in New Hampshire who came to Fiji in 1822. He was still alive in Fison's day, a great worker in the interests of the Fijian Euronesian community. Fison spoke of him as one whom these Euronesians look up to, with much respect, and he has striven hard to train them to habits of industry and sobriety; but I fear that his success has not been such as he had deserved. Nevertheless, whether successful or not, he is a man worthy of honour, for he has set his face manfully against all kinds of evil; and [according to Fison also] Joeli does no more than express the common opinion when he speaks of him as "a kind man, just and upright in all his dealings."

Someday the biography of David Whippy will have to be written (hopefully by one of his descendants). He played such a formative role in the opening up of Fiji to trade and commerce, the pioneer cultivation of cotton, and supported the mission and its educational system.

89   We see here the two possibilities before every isolated Christian community in a pagan world—to arm and defend themselves, or to refuse to do so, and thus put the enemy in the wrong if an attack should eventuate. Joeli's attitude was to take the pacifist course and to "trust in the Lord" and not to resist unless actually attacked. In this event they

This was during the night. In the early morning we heard the war trumpets sounding from three different points, and our people gathered together in the open space in front of my house, waiting for the battle. I went out to them and cried with a loud voice, "Sit down. Let every man sit down. Let them see that we do not want to fight. Sit down and wait for the will of God. Then, if they fire upon us, let us spring to our feet and fight for the lives which He has given us."[90]

So they all sat down in silence, each man with his weapon lying across his knees, and the blast of the war trumpets sounded nearer and nearer, louder and ever louder, until the enemy appeared in sight on the edge of the forest—a great multitude of heathen warriors, all painted and armed for war. When they saw us, they set up a shrill cry, and as with a confused noise they came forward towards us, I spoke to our people, encouraging them.[91] "Sit still," said I, "the Lord will fight for us."

But when Eparaama saw a number of the heathen leaving the main body and making a circuit as if to get round to the back of our house, he ran to prevent them, and certain of the young men also ran with him; but I called them back and made them sit down again with the others.

"Eparaama," said I, "do you not know that we die today—you and I, and the rest of us here? Why, then, should you go forth to meet your death, and to bring it upon yourself? Let the Lord bring it upon us, and it will be well. Perhaps even now He will save us alive."[92]

And the heathen came up to where we were sitting. Those who had guns pointed them at us; those who were armed with clubs raised them to strike; the spearmen poised their spears, making them quiver before our eyes; and the bowmen bent their bows[93]: but not a shot was fired, no blow was struck, no spear was thrown, and no arrow flew in our midst. What held them back I cannot say; this only I knew, that for a long while they stood there threatening us with their weapons of war, while we sat in silence, speaking never a word; but our hearts were crying to the Lord for help, and He heard our cry.

At length, after the enemy had been for a long time thus threatening us, and we expecting every moment death at their hands, I saw a chief coming towards us through the town with a whale's tooth in his hand. Walking forward between us and the heathen, he sat down and presented the tooth to them, begging that we might live, and that there

---

would defend themselves with clubs, not with guns. This was probably the better way, because he knew his party of young Christians would be hard to hold were they armed.

90 This was the regular pattern of Fijian war—war trumpets on three sides. There was only one for escape, and they probably had a trap of some kind on the fourth side. Joeli's instructions were explicit. He would not allow his party to put themselves in the wrong. They were to sit and wait until attacked. For a description of the military tactics of Fijian war just before this period, as reported by missionary observers in their journals, see Tippett (1973, 38–80), which covers a number of episodes from these northern islands.

91 This again is typical. The war party bursts in and shouts its war cry (na oibi ni valu) and rushes forward.

92 Obviously they were hopelessly outnumbered, but as with the narratives of the Old Testament, the Lord could deal with statistics if He was disposed to do so.

93 This reference to weapons—mixed Fijian and European—is typical of the culture contact period.

might be no fighting.[94] And when the chiefs had heard his words, they drew off their men to a distance, and sat down holding a council; whereupon we also withdrew.[95]

Presently Mr. Whippy came in, leading the white men and the half-castes, all with their guns, and the bayonets fixed. "Here we are, Joeli," he said, "we have come to look after you." A kind man was this Mr. Whippy, just and upright in all his dealings, and always ready to help forward the good work. [Once, when a letter came from Lakeba saying that Mr. Calvert was ill of dysentery and lying at the point of death, and directing me to forward the news to Viwa that Mr. Lyth might know (for he was well skilled in medicine), then I being in a great strait because there was no canoe in which I could sail, Mr. Whippy sent me to Viwa in his schooner with his own men and brought me back again, never asking so much as a yam for payment.][96]

But, to go on with my tale, after a while two old chiefs from the heathen war party came to me, bringing with them a whale's tooth as a token of peace; and sitting down before me in my house, they kissed my hands, sniffing at them, after our fashion in Fiji and Tonga, one taking one hand, and one the other.[97]

"Joeli," said they, "we know this day that you are a true man, and that your God is a great God. Wonderful are the things which we have seen today, for there was rage in our hearts, and it was in our minds to kill you all; but when we came to where you were sitting in silence on the ground, all the strength departed from our hands, and we could do nothing against you. It is you, Joeli, who have saved us alive. If we had killed you, it would have been shedding our own blood, for are not all your people our kinsfolk?[98] Therefore are we sent to ask pardon for our anger, to thank you for your longsuffering, and to tell you that we shall never forget your love to us.[99] Let this tooth of a fish[100] be the burying of an ill will

---

94   This is the symbol of a respectful request of appeasement. In many cases it would be an atonement or request for forgiveness, but here the Christians are not in the wrong. Here is a chief who recognises that the Christians are not the aggressors and offers an appeasement (*ai vakamudu ni valu*) on their behalf, and a request for the fighting to terminate. This was a social mechanism to permit withdrawal without losing face, and reflects a basic sense of justice even among the heathen.

95   Both parties drew aside to discuss the new situation. This was the normal procedure in peacemaking. The chief presenting the whale's tooth was spoken of as the mediator (*dau tataro*), from the verb "to intercede" or "to stop a quarrel"; a complex of words which has obtained deeper theological meaning since the preaching of the Christian gospel.

96   A typical reference to the regular pattern of how everyone depended on Lyth's medical services and how folk helped each other with the use of canoes and cutters.

97   The whale's tooth is the return offering (*na kenai ulivaki*), an agreement to make peace (and indirectly an admission of wrong on the part of the party making war). The "sniffing" is symbolic of the restoration of peace. It is followed by a typical speech of reconciliation on behalf of the offenders.

98   There is more in this than is apparent. The laws of kinship and retaliation would have been set in operation. The heathen would also have demanded the strangling of the widows of the dead because they were of the same kin and they feared the recently dead who were unmourned in this ceremony. The killing would certainly have had a chain effect.

99   Here the words of the speech show it is an atonement.

100 A whale's tooth—not strictly a fish at all. Ceremonial designation varies in different parts of Fiji—treasure (*kamunaga*), ancient stone (*vatu makawa*), stone of the land (*vatu ni vanua*), or tooth of a sea creature (*bati ni ika*).

between us. Know this, moreover, that if any man hereafter does you any harm, he shall be clubbed, whosoever he be, and an oven shall be his grave."[101]

Thus did the Lord deliver us on that fearful day. I said that I could not tell what it was that held the heathen back, but I know that it was the mighty power of God. Not once, nor twice, but many times, when there was none to help, had He delivered me, as He will ever deliver all them that put their trust in Him, until the time come for them to enter into the joy of their Lord; and then, whatsoever it be that takes them away, whether disease or shipwreck or the club, all will be well.

After this affair we had no more trouble, but went in and out among the people, preaching to them and explaining the *lotu* from town to town and from house to house, none daring to make us afraid. Many cast away heathenism and joined with us in the worship of the one true and living God, while even among those who still held to the old gods there was so friendly a spirit toward us that we were like Job after the Lord had turned again his captivity, for all that we had lost was restored to us more than fourfold.[102] And when Mr. Hunt (he who lies buried at Viwa)[103] came to look into the state of the work, he rejoiced with us and praised our God for His wondrous mercies.[104]

Moreover, there was another thing which turned the hearts of the people towards me. When the news of the attack upon us reached Viwa, Namosimalua and Varani[105] were very angry and came sailing from Viwa with many warriors to avenge us; and at a council which they held with the Great Lady and the chiefs who ruled in those parts, it was resolved that Masiwawa should be put to death and his town burnt with fire; but Varani persuaded them to wait till I returned (for I was away from home at the time), and he sent a swift-footed young man to bring me back.[106] As soon as I heard from the messenger what

---

101 This is a ceremonial boast, a "certification" or "oath" cementing the pact. It dates back to cannibal times. The penalty—to be put in a cannibal oven—is a dishonourable death. This is a strong oath.

102 Joeli's theology was accepted at its face value, and there followed a period of responsiveness and the little church began to grow.

103 The grave of John Hunt is near the little church at Viwa today, beside that of Joeli Bulu. The church is a memorial to Hunt, and the grave a place of frequent pilgrimage. A synod deputation of missionaries and Fijian ministers visited the place for a memorial service on the occasion of the centenary of Hunt's death in 1948.

104 Hunt visited Nadi (Muanaicake) in 1846, and again in 1847, staying a number of days. The place was still in the Viwa circuit.

105 Namosimalua and Varani of Viwa. Their names are frequently met together. They left a trail of destruction behind them in their pre-Christian days. Their exploits included the wasting of whole villages and islands, and plundering of foreign ships. But both had now become Christian, and the missionaries (including Joeli) were under their protection. The significance of their having become Christian was not yet understood in Bua, so there was a general fear of their presence. Namosimalua had become Christian in 1839 because of his loss of faith in his old gods and the desperate hope that the Christian God had more power to protect him. Varani's conversion was more spiritual, and resulted from the personal work of John Hunt who taught him to read—the only Fijian we know to have learned to read before his conversion on Good Friday 1845. This happened while Joeli was at Bau.

106 The Great Lady (*Marama Levu*) carried a lot of power as either the firstborn or only child of the *Tui*. The resolution to kill the local chief, Masiwawa, and to burn his town to demonstrate their concern and sense of justice over the matter, was probably for no reason but their fear of Namosimalua and Varani; but Varani the warrior had become Varani the arbitrator, and he will permit no action until he has heard Joeli on the matter.

was going on, I hastened back with all speed, being in great fear lest I should be too late to prevent the attack on Masiwawa's town; which, if it had been made, would have undone all the good which had been done, and would have turned the hearts of the people against us once more.[107] When Varani heard of my return, he came to me at once, and having told me the news, he asked me what my mind was upon the matter.

"Ratu Varani," said I, "if you love me, if you love the God whom we both serve, let this thing go no further." And with that I told him all that had happened, how no harm had come to us, and how all the heathen were now very friendly, so that the work of God was greatly prospering. "And now, if you make war upon this people," I continued, "you will make them our enemies once more, and you will, moreover, bring an evil report upon the *lotu*. Wherefore, I beseech you, let there be no fighting."

"Good," said he, "good are your words. I will persuade Namosimalua. Fear not, Joeli; there shall be no war."[108]

And he did according to his promise, taking the Viwans back to their own land in peace, whereat the Great Lady and the Nadi chiefs were very wroth, but I cared little for their anger, because I knew that what we had done was right in the sight of God, and because all the heathen folk were now tenfold friendlier than before. "Now we know of a truth that Joeli is our friend," they said; and more of them than ever came over to us, turning their backs upon the old gods, till the work grew to such a greatness that missionaries were appointed to the place[109]—even Mr. Watsford[110] and Mr. Ford[111]—who built their houses at Nadi, whither I also went to live with them.

It was in their time that the dreadful hurricane smote us, and the great flood also, which left scarce a house standing on all that coast.[112] Eparaama, the teacher who was

---

107   This is sound thinking. Joeli would not yet fully know the strength of Varani's Christianity—it being so recent. He knew that any punitive action like this would create a feud which would only mean the extinction of Christianity, at least in this locality—a fact in which some historians, like Henderson, have failed to allow for in their judgement of missionary pacifism.

108   Varani responds to Joeli's plea for peace. We note that Varani assumes the responsibility of convincing Namosimalua.

109   The establishment of a mission station on the assumption that there was a responsive population and enough converts to plant a church. The pattern was normal—two Western and one or more island missionaries. The others came from Viwa in the *John Wesley*. The same procedure was followed in Bua, where the missionaries were transferred from Somosomo. The two stations were opened in November 1847. Varani was on board the *John Wesley* as pilot. Until this point Nadi had been a section of the Viwa circuit. The Nadi station opened with a Christian community of about 350 persons (including about thirty whites at Solevu). Joeli and Eparaama appear to have been there for less than two years—five years as suggested by Henderson is too long and does not fit the facts.

110   John Watsford arrived in Fiji in 1844 from Australia, where he had been a school teacher. He served in Viwa, Ono, and Vanua Levu. He left Fiji in October 1849 and returned to Australia. His family suffered sickness and death, but he had mastered the language very well in a very short time.

111   James Ford landed in Fiji in November 1846, after a long voyage, during which he was sick for the duration. He was removed to Australia in 1848, but died soon after.

112   13 January 1848—the hurricane hit both Bua and Nadi. At Nadi the mission house was deroofed, and the inmates had been immersed in six feet of water and suffered extremely from exposure. Mrs. Ford had labour pains. Groceries, paper, medicines, and books were ruined. [See *The Journal of Thomas Williams*, 13 and 19 January (Henderson 1931b); also Watsford's description in Henderson 1931a, 305–7.] Watsford's child died of exposure, and Mrs. Watsford never

with me when the heathen came down to kill us, was lost in that storm—he and nearly all of them that were with him in the canoe, some two or three (I forget how many) escaping alive to the shore.[113]

It was in vain that we propped and strengthened the mission house, for it could not withstand the fury of the storm, but fell on its side, giving us barely time to escape. We fled from house to house, one falling after another, until at length the flood came down from the hills, a great and awful wave, sweeping everything before it and destroying what the storm had left. I carried Mr. Watsford's little child, who was very ill, holding her close to my breast and walking backwards against the wind to shield her from the rain, which was driven with such force before the furious blast that it struck and stung like little stones.

When the flood came down, I saw a great lot of bamboos drifting past; and leaping into the water, I swam to them and brought them to the shore. With these bamboos we made a raft on which we carried the missionaries, with their wives and children, across the flood to a little house on the hillside which the water did not enter, though it came up to the very doorway before it began to abate. We were all thoroughly drenched and very cold; and not being able to endure to see the ladies shivering, and to hear the moans of the little children, I swam back to the mission house, thinking that I might perhaps find dry clothes for them. But it was full of water, and I could find nothing dry until, on a shelf on that side of the fallen house which was highest from the ground, I saw a large bundle of Fijian cloth which the rain had not wetted, for it was sheltered beneath the roof. This I took back with me, and in it the missionaries wrapped themselves, their wives, and their children, putting off their wet clothes.

After the flood went down we returned to the house, and a pitiable sight it was, for it was full of black mud, which the waters had left, and nearly everything was utterly spoilt. Moreover, after a few days the poor little child died, to our great sorrow, for we all loved her.[114]

[Editorial Note:

1848 was a calamitous year in Vanua Levu. It began with two hurricanes, resultant sickness and death, loss of leaders, etc. Being now a circuit in its own right, the first annual report dates from 1848. It was signed by Watsford, but the handwriting is Hazlewood's. He had replaced Ford. The report contains another account of the hurricane and its effects. One event which came out of the hurricane was the wreck of a canoe at Nasavusavu, one Christian teacher escaping to witness on shore. He found twelve persons there who had become Christians and five more ready to join them. The Chief Lady of the area accepted the gospel and asked for the appointment of a Christian teacher to the town—a typical narrative.]

---

did recover from the effects of the hurricane on her health and had to be sent to Viwa for the attention of Dr. Lyth. Mrs. Ford gave birth and became dangerously ill of dysentery.

113   Eparaama, three other Tongans, and five Fijians, all members of the young church, perished.

114   She died of aftereffects 31 January 1848.

5
APPOINTMENT TO ONO

At length I was removed from Nadi to Ono.[115] The *lotu* had become firmly established there long before,[116] but trouble had arisen because of the teachers, who had grown proud and wanted to live as chiefs among the people, taking upon themselves to interfere in the affairs of the land, whence much ill blood had arisen; and the work was thereby sadly hindered. Wherefore, it being thought good that a missionary should live there for a time until the wrong things could be set right, Mr. Watsford was appointed to Ono,[117] and after him Mr. Hazlewood.[118] But when the growing evil had been checked and uprooted, then the missionaries decided that Mr. Hazlewood should remove to Nadi. "For," said they, "Ono is but a little island, while on the great land there are many ten thousands who know not God."

---

115 This is Ono-i-Lau, 21 degrees south, the southernmost outlier of Fiji. The first European to discover the Ono group was the Russian navigator Bellinghausen (1820).

116 This is itself a great story of events (or a whole series of events) which happened before Joeli came to Fiji. The people of Ono had heard of Christianity before they ever saw a missionary and had actually turned from their old religion. In May 1836 a canoe of Tongan converts returning from Lakeba to Tonga was blown off course in a storm and sheltered at Vatoa (fifty miles from Ono), where the Christians heard of the events at Ono. One of the Christians separated himself from the company and went to Ono to give Christian instruction to the "blind" seekers of truth there. He taught them to pray, to worship on the Sabbath, and built a chapel. They already had a congregation of forty persons. An Ono youth, Aisake Ravuata, was converted in Tonga, learned to read, became a preacher, and returned to Ono to help the church there early in 1838. When he arrived he found a church of 120 adults. No white missionary had yet visited Ono. Another similar story of those early days is that of Lasarusa Drala, an Ono convert who became a missionary to other parts of Fiji. As a result of these happenings a Tongan teacher, Joni Havea, who arrived in Fiji with Joeli, was appointed to Ono. Jeremaia Latu, another member of Joeli's party, also visited Ono (May 1839). Missionary James Calvert visited Ono early in 1840 and baptised 233 persons and united sixty-six couples in Christian marriage. When Thomas Williams visited Ono in 1842, only three people remained heathen, and they became Christians during Williams' visit. The same kind of thing happened at Doi, another island of the Ono group, when Pentecostal experiences resulted from the preaching of Necani Cataki on Whitsunday 1845. Over two hundred converts responded in a two-week period. The pattern was similar to the Tonga Awakening of a decade earlier. [This Necani Cataki became one of the early Fijian ministers (d. 1864).]

117 Watsford removed from Viwa to Ono in September 1846 because the Tongan teacher, Silasa Faone, who had chiefly rank was somewhat authoritarian and, as Joeli puts it, "interfered in the affairs of the land." But this was not the only reason. The Roman Catholics had heard of the Awakening and were trying to effect an entrance. The missionaries were touchy about Roman Catholic activities since the Tahiti Affair when Depetit-Thouars had appropriated a Protestant mission field in Oceania for a Catholic nation in 1843, just three years before.

118 David Hazlewood (1819–55) arrived in Fiji in 1844; served in Ono, Taveuni, and Vanua Levu; and was a great linguist. He prepared the Fiji grammar and dictionary and translated the Old Testament.

So they appointed me to take charge of Ono.[119] And when I heard thereof my heart sank within me, for I thought of the evil which had arisen under the former teacher, and I was afraid that the chiefs would be suspicious of me also—all the more especially because he (the teacher) was a countryman of mine. Wherefore did I go to Ono,[120] even as I had formerly gone to Nadi, in great fear and heaviness of soul.

But my fears were vain, and my soul heaviness was turned into gladsome lightness, for the Lord helped me, the people loved me, and the work of God grew and prospered exceedingly. Thus indeed have I ever found it. Often have I gone to my work in great fear, expecting evil, and wishing that my way lay to any place other than that to which I was going; but instead of trouble I have found peace, laughter instead of tears, deliverance out of every danger, and great success in the work of the Lord; while on the other hand, sometimes when I have gone expecting good things, being perhaps somewhat puffed up and trusting in my own strength, everything has gone against me, so that I have been ashamed and confounded.

It was during my stay on this island that I was thought worthy of being solemnly set apart for the work of an assistant missionary, whereat great was my rejoicing; though I durst not take the glory thereof to myself, but gave it all to God who, I well know, had done this great thing for me.[121]

All the while I was at Ono I saw no lessening in the love of the people towards me, and we lived happily together, helping one another in all things, both worldly and spiritual. They would come to my house, one after another, and put down within the doorway a fowl or fish, or a basket of yams or *dalo*, or whatever else they had, so that my house was always full of food beyond our needs.[122] In vain did I tell them not to bring so much. The more I spoke to them the more they loved me and the more they brought, so that we could not eat all that was given; and even our pigs had more than they could devour.

Wonderful were the things which I saw and heard on this little island—tales of the olden times and of the first coming of the *lotu*; the people of God rejoicing and giving

---

119 This was a major policy change in the missionary strategy. Joeli was soon to be appointed as a native assistant missionary. His was the first such appointment, and he is amazingly humble about it.

120 Joeli and Watsford removed from Nadi, 25 September 1848, in the canoe *Kurabui* to Bua, and thence in the *John Wesley*, Watsford to go to Lakeba and Joeli Bulu to Ono. Other stationing moves at the same time were Calvert from Lakeba to Viwa, and Hazlewood from Ono to Nadi. John Hunt, the chairman, was dying, and Ford also was removed, to die soon afterwards. Jaggar had fallen from grace and had to leave the district. In these painful circumstances, after two bad hurricanes, and with the country torn by several wars, the strained missionaries selected Joeli Bulu as the most promising of their indigenous workers for trial in this new status. As we look back over history, it was a momentous decision because the Fijian indigenous ministry sprang from this.

121 "Solemnly set apart," i.e., ordained. Nearly two years have elapsed between these two events. He had been in Ono since October 1848. This event took place in August 1850. Joeli had proved himself as a "missionary probationer," and Hazlewood went from Nadi to Ono in the *John Wesley* to inspect the work and to ordain Joeli as a Wesleyan minister— the first South Pacific Islander to be ordained in Fiji. Thereby was commenced a great tradition.

122 Yams (*uvi, kawai, kaile, tivoli*, etc.). *Dioscoreae*, species (Linn.). *Dalo* (cf. Polynesian *taro*). The Fijians distinguish over eighty varieties. *Colocasia esculenta* (Linn.), etc.

thanks, as sinners wept under our sermons and cried for mercy, so that many a time I had to come down from the pulpit and pray with them—while the words which I often heard from dying lips made my heart glow and burn within me; and I know that there are many graves at Ono whence they who lie sleeping there shall rise with joy at the resurrection of the just. As for tales of the old days, there is no place like Ono for them.

And as for the first coming of the *lotu*, this was the way of it: An Ono canoe went sailing to Lakeba with sinnet and mats for the king; and when it returned, the crew brought back a wonderful report about a new worship which certain white men had established at Lakeba—even the *lotu*.[123] They knew but little about it, but there were many who, when they had heard the account of the one true and living God, found their hearts strangely moved and, taking a present to a heathen priest, they asked him about this God and besought him to tell them how they might worship him. He said:

> I know all about Him. If you want to worship Him, I can tell you the way. Kneel down, and bow your faces to the ground. So. Now hold your breath. Let no man draw breath again till I give the word.

And the poor men held their breath till they were well-nigh choked. Three times did the priest make them do this, and then he said:

> Keep silence. I will now report you to your God. O Lord Jehovah, these are Thy people who wish to serve Thee! As for me, I turn my back upon Thee yet for a while. Looking away from Thee, I worship another god. But do Thou take knowledge of these people. Shelter them, and do them good.

Thus it was that the *lotu* first came to Ono, and this priest was the first teacher the people had. But I think that they did not get much good out of his teaching, because he taught them little else than that they should bring many presents to Him. "For," said he, "this God of yours is very fond of wealth."[124]

As for their weeping under our sermons, this is the way with the people of Ono. They were a warmhearted folk, easily moved to either good or evil; wherefore some have said that they are the best tribe in Fiji, while others have declared that they are the very worst, according to what they have seen in the days when they dwelt among them. I lived with them in the good times, and I used to think that Ono was a little heaven. Never shall I

---

123 There had been an epidemic in Ono in 1835. Their offerings to their gods were ineffective, and they were disillusioned about their religion. This visit with tribute must have come late in the same year after Cross and Cargill had established themselves at Lakeba, but it is by no means the only Christian origin story in Ono. The gospel was penetrating the group in various ways through various people.

124 There are numerous accounts of this particular episode which must have taken place at the end of 1835. Each account adds something to the whole story. This is obviously not borrowed from any of the others. Thomas Williams said the priest was a Namuka man. He discussed the incident in much the same way in his journal (4 January 1842), when he heard it from the Christians who had come to Bua from Ono by canoe. There had been a war between heathen and Christians in 1841 which left the latter victorious, and he had apparently asked them about the Christian origins. It is interesting that in turning from their own gods they employed a priest from another island than their own.

forget the warmth of love which the people showed me; and whatever evil may have arisen in the after days, I know that hundreds of them are now singing the new song of Moses and the Lamb, and I expect they will come to meet me when my name is called, and lead me to the good land of which I used to tell them. I was not speaking idly when I said that their dying words used to make my heart glow and burn within me, and if I could tell of them all, the account thereof would never be finished. Therefore will I tell you of but one or two deathbed scenes, that it may be known how some of these people die.

Taniela Kepa,[125] as he lay dying, said to me:

> Every day have I an assurance of the pardon of my sins. I know that, if my life
> here were to end today, I should enter upon life eternal in heaven.

On another day I asked him whether the love of God were still with him, and he said:

> In the night was my soul full of peace, for I found the love of God; and He helped
> me, so that I had many happy thoughts in the midst of my sickness.

Then I read to him the twenty-first chapter of the Revelation, and the dying man rejoiced as he listened to the words of the book. He said:

> I am going to heaven. I am ready. There is no doubt on my mind, for I know that,
> if I die today, today shall I begin to live in heaven.

Then said I, "Let us pray." While I was at prayer he burst into tears and, when the prayer was over, he was still weeping, so I asked him why he wept.

> I weep for love to my Lord. He also loves me, and His love is greater than mine.
> Plain as noonday is it to me that my soul is saved, therefore I fear not to die; for
> I know that, when my soul is parted from my body, I shall live forever with my
> God, through Jesus Christ my Lord.

With many other good and precious words did he speak of the love of God to him. But his sickness grew ever worse, and when on the following Sunday I went to see him, the signs of death were on his face.

"How now, Taniela?" said I, and he answered, "I am ready to be gone today. My departure from this world to the world above is now near. What day is this?" I told him it was the holy day, whereupon he said, "This Sabbath I shall spend in heaven." So I asked him how he knew this, and he said, "It is the Lord's will that I go to Him today."

"Has He then appeared to you?" I asked.

"Yes," said he, "I see Him now, though you cannot. Let your words be few. My Lord is here, and He calls me away. Look! Behold the Lord!"

His eyes were fixed, nor did the eyelids quiver; and his face lost its look of sickness as, gazing upwards, he stretched forth his hands and died. Thus went this man of God to heaven, and useful to us was his dying; more useful than all his sermons, and all his words

---

125 An Ono class leader and preacher.

as a class leader,[126] was the manner of his death to us who remained alive, for therein we saw how good a thing is true religion. And this is the account of Taniela Kepa, the true servant of God.

There was another man of Ono, Rupeni by name, whom I visited when he lay dying; and when I asked him how it was with his soul, he said, "My soul is at rest, for I know the love of God, but my disease is heavy indeed upon me. Nevertheless, my trust is in the Lord my Saviour."

Then said I, "Let us pray," and while we were praying he could not rest because of his great agony, but cried aloud, "Lord Jesus, have pity upon me!"

When our prayer was over we sat watching him and talking with him about his soul. It was plain indeed that he was ready to die, so I went away again to my own house.

When daybreak came over the land I went again to see him, and when he saw me, he said, "I am very ill. I know that the time of my departure is at hand, when I must go to the land whereunto I have made myself ready." And when I asked him whether he was sure that he would enter heaven, he said, "Yes. Long ago was I sure that my soul lived through faith in Jesus"; and looking on his face as he spoke, I saw that it was like the face of a man who has found a great treasure.

Then he commended his children to my care. "Joeli," said he, "if you love me, take pity on my children. Teach them the Christian religion, that they may thereby know Jesus their Saviour."

"I will take care of them," said I. "Trouble not yourself about them, but attend to your own soul."

Then he said, "Of a truth the love of God is with me. Great indeed is my pain, but this pain of mine is not worthy to be compared with the good things which our God will soon give me on the right hand of His lordly throne."

Presently, as we were talking together, he said, "Now is the time of my going near at hand." And seeing that he had but a little while to live, we thought we had better take him to the great house,[127] because he was of the blood of the chiefs, and many people were coming to see him, so that the house wherein he lay was crowded. Nor was it long after we had carried him away before he died (as we thought), while his friends were gathered together that they might kiss him and perform upon him the "custom of the dead."[128] Great then was the wailing because of their grief that their friend was dead—a man so useful in the land.

---

126   Taniela had been a class leader (*qase ni siga*), an office also held by men in the early Wesleyan Church.

127   *Vale levu* (the chiefly house), built up higher than the others, in a most prominent place, and used for ceremonial occasions—welcome, farewells, councils, funerary ceremonies, etc.

128   *Somate*—the funerary rites over the body before going to the grave, when mourners wail because of the death, a ceremony of respect from the ingroup; and visitors present mourning gifts of bark cloth (*masi*) and a whale's tooth (*reguregu*), i.e., respect from the outgroups.

But in a little while we saw that he was breathing gently. Then he opened his eyes, and lifting up his hand he beckoned us to be silent, saying, "Weep not, weep not."

Then there was a great silence in our midst, and we were afraid, for we thought he had been dead. But the dying man spoke again: "Why are you weeping?" he asked.

"We are weeping," answered one of his friends—"we are weeping because of your death."

"Weep not for me," he said; "weep for yourselves. As for me, I live. The Lord and His angels are hastening to take me with them. But yet once more will I speak a little to you. Be earnest in the Christian religion. If you love me, hold fast the *lotu.* While I was in health, I believed that which is told us in the Holy Book, and thence came to me pardon for all my sins. I read of heaven in the Bible, and believed it; and now this very day shall I look with mine eyes upon the things which I believed, though I saw them not—those things that Paul spoke of, whose words I have so often read, where he tells of heaven and of my Saviour. Now am I going to possess them all."

"Rupeni," I cried, for my soul was hot within me, "tell me once again—for my own sake, and for the sake of these others—tell us whether you now find the truth of the *lotu.* Tell us whether you now trust in our Saviour, and whether He comforts you."

Then he smiled, and his face shone. "Do you see that post, Joeli?" he asked. "Yes," said I, "I see it."

"Do you see it plainly?" "I see it quite plainly," I answered, surprised that he should ask me such questions, and fearing that his mind was wandering. But he looked earnestly in my face and said, "Joeli, as plainly as you see that post, so plainly do I see the Lord. Do you not see Him? Look! The house is full of angels. My Saviour is hastening me away. Farewell. Great is my love to you." And laying his hand upon his breast, he raised it gently two or three times, and so fell asleep. Thus ended his mortal life in this world, but angels took the hand of his soul and led him up to heaven.

We, with his father, his wife, and his friends, even we, heard and saw these things. Our souls were filled with joy. It was not to us like a day of death, but like the day of a feast, as we saw the love of God to him that was dead. Our faith in God was made even as a burning fire, and we said, "There is nothing in the world like true religion."

6

RETURN TO NADI

Very different from the comforts and encouragements wherewith the Lord blessed me at Ono were the hardships and disheartenings which I met with at Nadi, when I was appointed there again.[129] Grievous indeed was the state of things which I found there, for war had broken out, and the heathen were raging furiously, being fully resolved to drive the *lotu* out of all the land.[130] We could not stir out of the town without danger, for the enemy were lurking in the forest round about, where they killed two of our men who had gone to cut grass for thatching our chapel. They smote one of our outlying towns with a great slaughter, the remnant of death fleeing to us with the dismal tale; and to crown all, our missionary died,[131] so that we were left as sheep without a shepherd. The enemy grew bolder and ever bolder as our people grew weaker and more discouraged, until at length they came in great force and began to build a war fence against our town, surrounding us so that none might escape. We expected nothing less than utter destruction. But the Lord delivered us once more, for a great storm arose with heavy rains, lasting for many days, from which we were well sheltered within the town; but they, having no shelter, stayed till they were half dead with the cold and wet, and then fled away, every man to his own town; whereupon we sallied forth and destroyed the war fences which they had built.[132]

---

129 He had been away from Nadi for about eight years. He appears to have transferred back in late 1856 or in 1857.

130 In point of fact 1856 had been a year of great church growth in Nadi as also in Bua (following the conversion of Ra Masima, the new Tui Bua). In Nadi, clan after clan renounced heathenism, but no teachers were available to teach them. Those available were located in the geographically central towns. By June 1856 every male full member of one year's standing was serving as an evangelist or scripture reader. Yet it was because of this very growth that the heathen felt threatened and war sprang up. Gardens, houses, chapels, and communities were plundered. The Christians had to defend themselves. At one stage they possessed a fort in the mountains and were never dislodged in many heathen attacks. Missionary efforts secured a temporary respite, but it was an unhealthy peace. All through 1857 the church continued to grow, but the heathen determined to stamp it out. After the conversion of Ra Masima, who now legitimatised conversion, the heathen aggression became a rebel movement.

131 The unnamed missionary was John Crawford, a new appointee who died of dysentery very soon after his arrival. A great many missionaries and members of their families died of this disease—not a few of them in Vanua Levu. Crawford arrived 20 June 1857, was in Nadi by October, was sick of dysentery by December, was then taken to Levuka, but died after five weeks of illness, 20 January 1858.

132 We cannot identify this episode.

But though we were thus saved from destruction, yet we were still in great straits, for when the fine weather returned, the enemy lay in wait for us in the forest as before, killing those who went out to search for food, so that we durst not go far beyond our war fence, and sharp hunger made itself felt in our midst; wherefore I resolved to take my wife and children to Bua that they might live. "If we fall in with the enemy by the way," said I, "if we meet them in the path and they kill us, we can but die; and if you stay here, you will die of hunger."

So we rose up and went to Bua, making a circuit for fear of the enemy; and here the Lord wrought out a great deliverance for us, for as we were passing across an open place, bare of trees and every kind of shelter, a great company of heathen warriors went marching by. We were full in their view and they in ours, but they saw us not, though we saw them so plainly that we could have counted every man of them; and I believe that the Lord blinded their eyes, even as He blinded the eyes of the Syrian army who were sent to kill the prophet in the olden days.

Leaving my wife and children at Bua, I went back to Nadi and stayed with the people, comforting them as well as I could and exhorting them to put their trust in God; but our faith was very weak, for indeed, what with hunger and fear, we were in a bad way.[133]

After some time I went again to Bua to see my family, intending to stay three days; but while I was there a young man came running after me to tell me that the king of Levuka[134] had come over from Ovalau with a large war party to help the heathen, and that he wanted to see me. I spoke about it to Mr. Wilson,[135] the missionary at Bua, and he told me not to go; for, said he, "a letter has come from Mr. Binner,[136] saying that the king of Levuka has promised to see that no harm come to the teachers, and to spare the lives of the people also. It is useless for you to go. Why should you go when you can do no good, for the town is surely taken before now?"

---

133 He had left his wife and family at Tiliva, the Christian centre at Bua beside Nawaiwai, where the missionary lived, opposite Bua town, the locality of Ra Masima, the now Christian chief, and under his protection.

134 This Tui Levuka had died before Joeli wrote his manuscript about fifteen years later. He drank himself to death. Fison, who remembered him well, said in 1863:

  There happened to be a ring around the sun at mid-day just before his death, and many of the Ovalau natives looked upon it with awe, as a sign that the powers above were taking note of the coming of so great a chief. He used to be a remarkably fine-looking man, with a natural grace of bearing and courtesy of manner which many an English gentleman might envy; but of late years he had become a confirmed drunkard, and his excesses told miserably upon him, both body and soul. Our country is surely laying up wrath against a day of wrath by the infernal liquor traffic, which fully deserves the strong term which I apply to it, for it is a trade in "the bodies and souls of men." It is working fearful evil in Fiji—fearful evil, fearfully on the increase.

135 William Wilson arrived in Fiji in 1854, immediately after the conversion of Ratu Cakobau, and spent his two eventful years at Viwa. A son was born there in February 1855. He went to Bua in August 1856 exchanging appointments with John Malvern. He left in February 1860. All Joeli's references to Wilson in Bua therefore fell between those dates. Wilson died in 1881.

136 John Binner, trained in the Glasgow Normal Seminary as a teacher. He arrived in Fiji May 1852 and was appointed to Levuka where he reorganised the school system. He died at Levuka, 2 April 1863, and was buried there.

And so it was, for upon the king's promise to spare their lives, the townsfolk opened their gates to him; whereupon all the heathen warriors rushed in and burnt the town. They wanted to slaughter the people also, but the king would not have it so. "Let there be no killing," said he, and they were afraid to go against his word. However, he allowed the townsfolk to be taken away captive among their enemies.[137] Thus ended the war, and therewith my stay at Nadi also.[138]

I lived now with Mr. Wilson at Bua, helping him in the work; and once, when I went with him in the mission schooner to the back of the land,[139] we came near being killed at a town called Mouta—he and I. This was the way of it: We went to see a powerful chief called Ramere, but when we landed at his town we found that he was gone to a great trade feast at Mouta—whither Mr. Wilson decided to follow him. We pulled far inland in the schooner's little boat, up a winding river; and when we reached the town we found it crowded with heathen who had come down from the hills to trade.

As we went along the path, there came swaggering up to us a big man who, without more ado, seized Mr. Wilson by the nose and shook him to and fro after a most unmerciful fashion, putting him thereby to great pain of both body and mind; and when, having got rid of this tormentor, we came to where the chiefs were sitting in the public square, they did not care to listen to our report, for they were busy with their market.

Meanwhile the people crowded around us, pushing and jostling one another, pinching us (especially Mr. Wilson), and feeling our arms and legs, so that we had no peace. Wherefore we left them as soon as we could and, slipping away out of the crowd, we looked for a place wherein we could hide ourselves till morning, for the night was coming on.[140]

---

137 This pattern of enslavement was common in Fijian war, usually with tragic results for the women. This destruction of Nadi and the mission station may be dated in April 1857, and was the work of Tui Levuka and Ratu Mara. Although there was no massacre, the persecution and enslavement were brutal. As always, anything Mara could do to hurt the Christians after 1854 was thought to hurt Cakobau.

138 Nadi, as a circuit, disappeared from the station sheet, and the work in this area was superintended from Bua until after the departure of Wilson (February 1860), who lost his wife nine months before. [William Whittley was ordained in Australia in December and designated to take Wilson's place. Actually he never reached Vanua Levu, but served round Levuka and Bau. His wife died and he returned home after eighteen months.] For a very brief time the circuit was "Bua and Nadi," until 1860 when new stations were opened in Vanua Levu.

139 *Daku ni vanua*, a Fijian idiom for the eastern side of an island, the leeward. The town of Mouta was a place of refuge used by Tui Macuata in Northern Macuata when Macuata was under attack by the Bauans under Varani and Rivota some seventeen or eighteen years earlier. It was a long way from Bua and a market centre, strongly fortified. A village of only fifty people survives there today in what is now called Labasa Tikina.

140 During 1858, while the church expansion was operated from Bua, it was unsafe for Christians to go about except in large parties. In April, over one hundred Christians were murdered thus by roving bands, and many Christian villages were destroyed. Yet in spite of these factors church attendance increased by hundreds. Offerings of yams and oil for the self-support of the church increased enormously. In 1859 nearly three thousand conversions were reported, and in all Vanua Levu (and Taveuni) some fourteen thousand people were attending Christian worship—a good example of how a church can grow in spite of persecution and war. But this advance was made in the face of great danger as this incident reveals.

At length we found a little hut at a distance from the town, which might perhaps have been a storehouse for yams; and here we lay down in one corner on the grass, with which it was strewn, hoping they would not be able to find us. But after dark we heard shouts in all directions, and looking forth we saw a great number of men with torches in their hands coming towards us, shouting and yelling and calling one to the other. So we commended our souls to God and prepared for death.

"Here they are!" cried a tall fellow as he stood in the doorway with a torch in one hand, and a battle-axe held over his shoulder by the other; and raising his torch, he set fire to the thatch, but some of those who came running up behind him put it out in a moment—why I know not, unless it were that they were unwilling to lose the house.

Then he sprang in and flourished his axe over our heads, the others also threatening us with their weapons of war. Whether they really intended to kill us or not, I cannot say—perhaps they were only trying to frighten us; but they continued acting thus far into the night, crowding upon us with threatening words and weapons, one houseful going out only to make room for another, who acted in like manner, making a terrible noise, while we sat in one corner of the hut with our backs against the wall, looking them in the face and praying silently to our God. At length they left us in peace, and we passed the remainder of the night as best we could, in doubt as to whether they would come back again and make a full end of us or not.

In spite of all this, Mr. Wilson took me with him into the town in the morning and asked leave to preach,[141] which was granted, somewhat to our astonishment; and standing up in the midst of a great crowd of heathen, he told them of the one true God, and of Jesus Christ our Saviour; after which we went down to our boat, in no small wonder that we were allowed to leave the town alive.

---

141 This is a typical story of the period. It reflects the courage of these Christian missionaries. Having once made contact, they would not retreat without witness. It also reflects the nature of their penetration into the heathen area.

7
APPOINTMENT TO CAKAUDROVE

[Editorial Note:

   After the destruction of Nadi and the short period of the supervision of all the work from Bua where Joeli Bulu had worked with Wilson, and upon the death of Mrs. Wilson and her burial at Bua in 1859, and upon Wilson's departure with his three small children for England in February 1860, the Wesleyan circuits of Vanua Levu were reorganised. A new station was established at Wairiki, Taveuni, for superintending the new Cakaudrove circuit. The pioneering party comprised two missionary families (Carey and Waterhouse) and two Tongans (Bulu and Fotofili). The Bua circuit was to be carried on by Thomas Baker and the new appointee from Australia, William Whittley. These names appeared on the 1860 station sheet, but Whittley never worked in Bua.]

My next appointment was to the Cakaudrove kingdom,[142] Eroni Fotofili[143] being sent with me. We lived at Wairiki,[144] where we saw much fruit of our labours, for many turned from heathenism. The women and the children were especially zealous in the schools, learning to read with great quickness; while not a few of the young men gave themselves to us as our sons in the gospel, and these we were careful to teach, and train as helpers in the work. Nor, in spite of all the evil that befell us afterwards, was this labour of ours altogether in

---

142   There had been a previous mission to this part of Fiji from May 1839 to September 1847. They had been invited there by Tui Cakau and Tui Kilakila; but this had been for reasons of prestige and trade supplies. The missionaries had been forced to live by the cannibal ovens and no proper station was established. Tui Kilakila had forbidden any of his people to convert to Christianity on the penalty of death in the oven. Openings in Bua and Nadi had led to the missionary evacuation of Somosomo. Now, twelve years later, we take up the narrative again. In the interim Tui Kilakila had died a tragic death of leprosy, and his people blamed his rejection of the gospel. The Christian gospel spread by means of converts from Bua and Nadi, where the persecution had led to the diffusion of the faith rather than its extermination. This called for a new station somewhere closer to the centre of growth.

143   Another Tongan. Subsequently he went to New Britain but died in Sydney on his way home in 1876, one year before Joeli himself died.

144   A coastal town a few miles from Somosomo, close enough for direct liaison with the chief but safely out of reach of his cannibal ovens. The Annual Report of the Nadi Circuit (June 1856) describes the calamities that afflicted the Somosomo chiefly family and the decimation of the population, which all led to a movement of national repentance. Four village teachers, trained at Lakeba, had been sent there from Nadi to explore the evangelistic potential. Interest was also expressed in the Natewa Bay area on the mainland (also part of the kingdom of Cakaudrove). This is an interesting picture of a field, green but not ready for harvest during the 1840s, which had suddenly ripened unto harvest.

vain; for some of these youths are workers together with us at this very day, among whom is Ratu Wiliame Vutikalulu, the native missionary who is now stationed at Tokatoka.[145]

Ratu Golea (who is now Tui Cakau[146]) was a heathen, but nevertheless he was very friendly towards us, helping us in many ways, so that we were cheered in our work and went joyfully on from day to day, hoping for still better things. Then two missionaries were appointed to the station, even Mr. Waterhouse[147] and Mr. Carey.[148]

After living for some time at Wairiki in great discomfort and feeble health (for it is a place of much rain and of burning heat), it was thought good to remove the station to Waikava (Fawn Harbour)[149]; and thither I also went, having the training institution given into my hands.[150] I went, but my wife went not with me, for she died at Wairiki, and there I buried her.[151]

Some time afterwards the chief Ritova[152] sent whales' teeth to Golea—whales' teeth of war—praying him to go down to help him in his fighting at Macuata. Five times came the messenger, and five times he went back with a refusal[153]; but at length Golea consented, and two of his men were sent for me that I might go with the war party. I was away from home at the time holding missionary meetings, but when I came back the matter was talked over, and it was deemed prudent that we should keep ourselves altogether apart from such affairs, cleaving to our right and proper work of preaching the gospel and teaching

---

145 Wiliame Vutikalulu, a Cakaudrove man who became a native missionary like Joeli himself; one of Joeli's first trainees who was at Tokatoka in the early 1870s when Joeli was a few miles away at Bau.

146 That is in 1873; a heathen but not opposed to the *lotu*, probably because of popular opinion about Tui Kilakila's opposition and death.

147 Joseph Waterhouse, one of an illustrious missionary family, several of whom served in Fiji and other parts of the Pacific, and whose father was the first Wesleyan General Missionary Superintendent in Oceania. Joseph arrived in Fiji in 1850 and left in 1864 or 1865. He returned for the second time in 1874 to take over the Theological Institution at Navuloa until 1878 when Fison took his place. He had about nine years experience in Fiji at the time of this appointment.

148 Jesse Carey arrived in Fiji 1859, and this was his first appointment in Fiji. He stayed until 1874, when significantly enough he was relinquishing the theological training programme to Joseph Waterhouse, who had first introduced him to Fiji fifteen years earlier.

149 The kingdom of Cakaudrove included both Taveuni (on which Wairiki was situated) and the opposite coast of Vanua Levu. This transfer was a major shift, moving away from the chiefly centre. It provided a better harbour and a better climate. The early missionary deaths due to unhealthy locations make a tragic story. The move to Waikava (Fawn Harbour) was probably made in 1862 after the district meeting in May.

150 This is evidence of the organic growth of the church. Joeli is put aside for a special task of training leaders. Many of the men he trained eventually became Fijian ministers. His ministry in this way over the years was no less than his pioneering evangelism.

151 Some years later, feeling he could not perform his ministry effectively without a partner, he remarried. The ceremony was performed by Fison. His new wife was Akesa, who long outlived him.

152 Ritova was a chief of Macuata and was involved in many wars over two or three decades. Waikava is a long way from Macuata and in the region under Somosomo. The great kingdoms of Vanua Levu were involved in this war in the early 1860s. The possibilities of widespread ramifications were serious, as Joeli well knew.

153 Here are the ceremonial customs of request and refusal with the symbolic whale's tooth; the *kerei valu* (request), and *na kenai diwiki* (its rejection).

from house to house.[154] So it was decided that I should not go. The *lotu* people also refused to join in this war. "Why should we kill those who have done us no harm?" they asked. "Let the chief go, since it is his mind to go. As for us we will stay at home and attend to our plantations." "It is well," said Golea. "Stay and look after your gardens. I shall go and attack that folk; and when I have done with them, I will make a raid upon you."[155]

These words sank down into the hearts of our people, and they of Laucala sent to Wainiqolo, the Tongan chief who was then at Vanua Balavu, praying for help. Now it has been said that it was I who brought this chief down to fight against Golea; but indeed it was not so, for I had no hand in it, nor did I even know of the message sent by the Laucala folk.[156]

The warriors went away in many canoes, and it was not long before we heard of burnings and slaughters, as town after town was taken, none being able to stand against them. Then the missionaries, being assembled at Levuka for their yearly meeting,[157] spoke to the British consul, beseeching him to use his influence to stop the war, which had already caused such awful woe; and he sent a messenger to Golea with a request that I should go with him.

"Let us first go to Tui Cakau," said I. "It were well for us to tell him of our errand, and to ask for one of his messengers to go with us in the path." So we went to the king and laid our request before him.

"Sleep tonight," said he, "and in the morning we will hold council." But when the council was over, we found that no help was to be given us. "Go you two," said the king. "Go to Golea, and tell him the consul's words. As for us, we will sit waiting here until you return."[158]

So we went on our way, and when our canoe drew near to the shore where the army was, we saw a great cloud of smoke rolling up from a burning town, which the chief had taken on that very day. Going ashore, we found that he had climbed up into the mountains

---

154 This reference reminds us that the early church in Fiji followed up the preaching with family instruction in the homes. This was a well-organised practise established by Hunt in Viwa in the 1840s.

155 Golea interpreted the Christian pacifism as disloyalty.

156 Laucala is a district of Taveuni, whose people have kinship relations with Vanua Balavu, where the Tongans were strong and where Wainiqolo, one of Ma'afu's leaders, had located himself. He had been expelled from Macuata, where he had been the cause of much political trouble and war about a year before this event. He and his Tongan troops had a bad reputation, and like Ma'afu he had taken advantage of the Wesleyan Mission whose morals and attitude to war were predictable. However, not all the Tongan teachers were pacifist like Joeli. Some became so politically involved that the mission returned them to Tonga. This indiscretion of the Laucala people to bring the Tongan troops to their aid was fatal, and gave them a political alignment against Golea, and was certainly interpreted by him as disloyalty.

157 The annual district meeting, when the church work from all Fiji was discussed and the policy coordinated. The missionaries were predictably antiwar and would always do what they could to terminate these continual disturbances. They supported Fijian chiefs who engaged in peacemaking ventures. In this case the British consul was W. T. Pritchard.

158 Tui Cakau was the paramount chief of the area. Joeli did the right thing culturally in going first to him and in securing one of his men for support. They did not get the endorsement of Tui Cakau, but they were given the right of passage with his approval. He would allow the consul and Mission to speak but not become himself involved—a typical Fijian reaction to a complex situation. He also intimated he wanted a report back with respect to Golea's reactions. Golea would also be able to interpret where Tui Cakau himself stood, from this behaviour complex.

to attack yet another town belonging to the hill folk; and as we also went up on the following morning, we met a great number of prisoners being brought down to the beach, for they had yielded themselves up without a fight. When we found Golea, he met me with a pleasant look and showed so friendly a spirit that my heart grew very glad; and sitting down with him, I made my report.

"We are come," said I, "we two, bringing with us the word of the English consul. This is his messenger whom you see before you, and as for me, I am come to help him in carrying the word—for it was the mind of our elders, and of the consul also, that we should be comrades in the path. Hear, therefore, I beseech you, the word which we bring, even the word of the English chief. Let there be no more fighting. It is enough. Many are dead; wherefore here let the slaughter end."

"Good is your coming," said Golea, "and good are the words you bring. Look, Joeli, here is a whale's tooth, brought to me that the war may go on, but I say it is over. There shall be no more fighting."

So I went back to Waikava with a light heart and thankful, but when I told my tale to our *lotu* folk, great then was their unbelief. "He is deceiving you, Joeli," they cried. "It is his mind to kill us all, because we would not go with him to the war."

In vain did I try to persuade them; they were not to be persuaded; and when the warriors, as they came back, did many despiteful acts towards the *lotu* people—spoiling their gardens, robbing their houses, and wreaking their vengeance even on the graves of the dead by digging up and scattering abroad the bones of them that slept therein—then they said, "Did we not tell you so? He was deceiving you, Joeli. There is no truth in him."[159] Moreover, there were many idle tales going about—as is ever the manner in Fiji at such times—which made them sure that they were in danger. Thus it was reported that four of our [Christian] chiefs were to be killed in revenge for their not going to the war; but I did not believe that this was the mind of Ratu Golea. It was but a foolish story spread abroad by evil men, who were minded to work us a mischief.[160]

At length there came to me Ratu Manasa, who was one of the four, and he told me that they had agreed to put up war fences, for they were sure Golea had evil in his heart against them.

---

159 Joeli accepts Golea's word at its face value, but the Fijian Christians see themselves as victims of intrigue—they detect a plot (*verea*), a regular device of Fijian military strategy, and one for which the Cakaudrove people were famous in pre-Christian times.

160 This may well have been true. The art of intrigue employed the mechanism of gossip as a social institution for serving its purposes—either for causing doubt or uncertainty, or for hiding the strategic purposes from those who were "not in the know." The incident Joeli describes is a good example of how a cohesive social unit can be divided by rumour and counterrumour. That this happened to the Christian community at Waikava might very well have been what the pagans of the area were expecting. The missionaries also knew this, and their reports bewail its obstruction to the growth of the church.

"Do you tell me this," I asked, "because you want to know my mind thereon, or do you only report what you have already resolved upon?"

"No," said he, "but that we may know your mind."

"Well," said I, "if it be so, I will tell you what I think. Forbear, Ratu Manasa; if you love me, forbear. If this thing be done, that chief will say at once that we are defying him. Moreover, these are idle tales which we hear, wherefore let there be no war fences."[161]

"It is good," said he, "there shall be none."

But it was not long before he came to me with another report which he had heard. "Now we *must* fortify our towns, Joeli," he said. "We must put up our fences,[162] that we may live—we, with our women and the children."[163]

Again I strove with him, and again I prevailed, but when he came for the third time, and for the third time I besought him to forbear, he looked sourly and suspiciously upon me, saying, "It is easy for you to say, 'Let there be no fences.' You know well enough that Golea won't kill you. It is our skulls upon which his club will fall" (and here he rapped his head with his clenched fists). "When we are all clubbed, you will be left alive—you and yours; wherefore are you bold to say continually, 'Forbear, forbear; let not the fences be built.'"

My heart was sore when I heard this saying, nor could I urge him any further.[164] "I have told you what is right," I cried, "but you are suspicious of me, wherefore I can say no more. Go now and do as you please, lest, when your warriors are slain, your wives and daughters dragged away, and your children clubbed before your eyes[165]—lest when you have brought this evil upon yourselves by giving heed to these idle tales—you say, 'It is Joeli who has brought these things upon us.'"

So they put up the war fences, and presently a canoe came in bringing two of Wainiqolo's men, whom he had sent to carry his word to our chiefs, and to take back theirs

---

161 The reference to war fences like this is direct. Otherwise they would have spoken symbolically of pig fences. The use of the direct term implies no doubt, no mere precaution—they were expecting and preparing for invasion.

162 The definite use is again strong. This is not strategic retreat. It implies the villages were wholly Christian and united, and suggests the diffusion of Christianity was very like what Fison himself described along the Ra coast at the same time—a Christian village here and a heathen village there. This reflects the conversion pattern.

163 This statement also is symbolic—"live" means survive as persons. Fate for the men killed in the defence of a town meant the cannibal oven. Fate for the women and children who were not killed meant enslavement. Usually the women were given to the heathen warriors, some of them distributed to chiefs, others sent to the men's houses where many died of abuse. This fate was death indeed—and for the pre-Christian Fijian, separation from one's ancestors. An effective defence was to survive—to live. The Fijian word for "live" (bula) had the original meaning of "recovering from sickness" or "escaping from death"—and the causative verb (vakabula) means "to cause to live" or "to keep alive."

164 Ratu Manasa sees no way of saving his skull from the war club but by building a war fence. There is no escape (life) but effective defence. His words to Joeli are hurtful: "My heart was sore." This shows how effectively the Christian group was divided.

165 Sometimes the infants were killed (very infrequently clubbed); sometimes they were tied liked flags to the masts of the war canoes of victorious heathen; sometimes they were taken home for the heathen boys to practise the art of killing; sometimes they were killed to improve a warrior's score, which meant a title for him.

to him. These men came to my house (for they were my countrymen) and began to talk to me about the war, but I would not listen to them. "Why do you come here?" I asked. "Am I a fighting man that you come to me? You have brought evil upon me already, for Golea will think I am one with you in this matter. Go, therefore, both of you, and come to my house no more." So they went sailing back to the land whence they came.

Then came Wainiqolo himself, and he also entered my house, but beyond the customary salutations I spoke no word to him, good or bad, nor he to me, for I grieved at his coming. And on the morrow, in the early morning, I took myself off to a distant town, where I stayed preaching and baptising until there was no more work to do; and when I returned he was gone, whereat I was very glad.[166]

Nevertheless I heard of his doings in this way: He and Ratu Kuila[167] went into a house which they thought to be empty, and there took counsel together, but it so happened that a countryman of mine was lying sick in that very house, and being covered up with a sail mat, they did not see him; wherefore he heard their words and reported them to me—even Ratu Kuila begged for help in fighting against Golea. Whereupon Wainiqolo replied, "Whatsoever you tell me to do, that will I do. War or peace, according to what you tell me."[168]

And when I heard these words, I knew that evil was near; for this Ratu Kuila was a great stirrer-up of evil, who joined himself to us, not because he loved the *lotu*, but because he wanted to kill Golea, who stood in his way.[169]

Nor was it long before the fighting began, which ended in Wainiqolo's death in front of the Wairiki war fence, and the great slaughter of his army; Golea also being wounded in the fight by a musket ball which broke his arm.[170]

---

166   The presence of the Tongan adventurers in Fiji and the exploits of Ma'afu, Semi Fifita, and Wainiqolo were a real embarrassment to Joeli and the Tongan evangelists. We have to recognise two very different types in the group. This is a valuable reference in that it shows this division of opinion among them. Joeli spoke of them as "fighting men" and "nonfighting men." It also shows his courage in dismissing those of his countrymen whose methods he disapproved. Even Wainiqolo himself received no more than the formalities of civility—if he even received this, because to go off preaching and baptising was not a civil way of entertaining a Tongan chief.

167   Ratu Kuila was a high-ranking Cakaudrove chief, whom Fison described as "a dangerous man, and a great stirrer-up of mischief." The very combination was ominous. The early records are filled with accounts of treachery and double-dealing of this kind. To be able to deceive others was a high virtue in pre-Christian Fiji. Many of these tales have been preserved in the traditional songs; e.g., "The Lay of Koroitamana."

168   This is an interesting reference. Unaware of the presence of the sick countryman of Joeli, the secret came out. Ratu Kuila was the instigator of trouble, which was aimed against Ratu Golea. It exposes the mercenary character of the Tongan fighting men, who were available at a price for service under any disgruntled or ambitious Fijian chief, to fight the rival chief of the next territory.

169   Not all conversions were spiritual. Joeli now understood that Ratu Kuila was not a true Christian; but he had joined the cause for the sake of political advantages—a major problem for the evangelists of the first generation that broke away from heathenism.

170   Golea's warriors slaughtered the mercenaries and killed Wainiqolo. We have the date—1862. The Tongans were using Western firearms. Note that Golea was wounded by a musket ball.

Before the fighting began, he sent two messengers for me. "Let Joeli come," said he, "and I will *lotu*." But these men, instead of coming to me, went to Ratu Kuila, who was very angry when he heard their report and sent them away with evil words.[171]

"Go back to Golea," he cried. "Tell him to use his own teacher if he wants to *lotu*. Is not Wesele[172] with him? Why should he rob me of my teacher?"

Golea was wroth at this, and when Wainiqolo was killed, he turned Roman Catholic, forcing his people also to follow him, and doing many things to vex and harass those who still held to the truth.[173] Nor did he spare me in his wrath, for he dragged away a daughter of mine during my absence from home and forced her to live with him.[174]

[Editorial Note: 1862-69

The above is a Wairiki, not a Waikava, narrative. Joeli was at Wairiki from 1858 to 1862. Almost immediately after this event the mission headquarters were removed from Wairiki (Taveuni) across the straits to Waikava (Fawn Harbour) on the mainland of Vanua Levu, but still the kingdom of Cakaudrove. The district meeting (13 May 1862), which I presume was the one to send the message to Golea, also determined to open a major station at Wairiki, and the names of Carey and White were put on the missionary station sheet. In July of the same year Wainiqolo interfered in Cakaudrove military politics as described, and lost his life. This was interpreted as a Protestant defeat, and Golea turned Catholic.

This chapter really leaves us at about July 1862. From late 1862 until 1869 is a gap in the manuscript. We have no record of his experiences during those years except for the one paragraph at the beginning of this chapter. He found himself in teaching work, in charge of a training institution in which he demonstrated remarkable gifts. He was not the only Tongan who was highly effective in both evangelistic thrust and biblical training—Paula Vea, who ultimately evangelised Kadavu, was another.

At this time his appointment was probably a good strategic move. It extracted him from the sociopolitical Fijian/Tongan confrontation situation, in which he had been victimised, and put him in

---

171   This interesting reference shows Ratu Golea's intention to convert after this engagement. Some of his supporters did not want this and relayed his message, not to Joeli as intended, but to Kuila. The chiefs were dependent on the loyalty of messengers. Sometimes the messengers traded on this as their "bargaining power." In this case it stimulated further ill will between Kuila and Golea, with unhappy results for the Wesleyan cause.

172   Wesele Rakusa, a Fijian teacher, was working at the time under Joeli's supervision, but in Golea's town. At the time Joeli composed this account, about ten years later, Wesele was serving as a Fijian missionary to the Rotumans.

173   This is a typical example of how, when two rival chiefs decide to convert to Christianity, they feel they have to choose rival missions. Denominationalism has frequently affiliated itself with existing factionalism within the pre-Christian social and political structures. Many denominationally divided territories in the Pacific Islands today may be traced back historically to some pre-Christian factionalism.

174   Joeli, who had already lost a wife, now lost a daughter, kidnapped by the chief Golea, who associated Joeli with his enemy, Kuila. The kidnapping of Joeli's daughter was an act of contempt—not against her, or against Joeli, but against the chief who supposedly protected them. This was culturally "appropriate," a suitable rejoinder to the offensive message about using his own teacher to *lotu*. Joeli felt it was aimed at him, but it was as much aimed at his "protector"—demonstrating his impotence.

the new and suddenly urgent situation of training evangelists and pastors. The church badly needed armies of such persons—Fijians rather than Tongans—to handle her phenomenal growth since 1854.

As Joeli goes back over his eventful life, his storytelling comes to bear on exciting, tragic, or dramatic events; and the long, faithful, but more routine ministry in training leaders in a school situation receives little attention.

The years 1862-69 were his initial explorations of this dimension of the church's organic growth, and we cannot move on to his Bau ministry without some editorial comment of this kind.

This interim was a period of suffering, yet he never allowed his pain to overpower him. Fison, in 1865, had received a letter from him, written at one of the saddest points in his life.

Fison wrote of that letter: "You know the character Joeli Bulu has gained for himself during all these years. It is all true and I thank God for it. Not for a long time have I read anything which has been so blessed to my own soul" (3 November 1865).

It seems to us that Joeli departed from Waikava in 1866. He was in charge there in 1864. There was no missionary living in the mission house. Tait did a pastoral itineration of six weeks in the area and felt it was a bad location for a mission station, the villages being so widely scattered and difficult to supervise, and the work of a kind which the Fijian pastors could do better than the missionaries.

The mission suffered great loss in these eventful years by serious illness among the missionaries and their families, and a number of deaths. Three families removed to the colonies in mid-1864. These included Waterhouse and Moore, and Calvert was shortly to go. This was the main body of missionary experience.

Joeli, moved by the concern of the district meeting, wrote to Moore in Australia in the following terms:

Bau

13 October 1864

To Mr. Moore,

Oh, my father, I am overwhelmed with sorrow! I am unable to express myself! A dreadful affliction has come upon me and my bowels are black with pain because you are no longer among us.

Then again we have sorrow upon sorrow in that Mr. Waterhouse also has been taken from us, by reason of some disease which I dislike to think about. I have been thinking that if this disease was a man, or something tangible, I would grapple with him; and only if he were stronger than me would I submit to the removal of my father. But it is a disease and not a man: it has no feeling, no sympathy, so what can be done?

I am beginning to fear that the tide in Fiji is ebbing out, to our impoverishment. Are we to be without missionaries? Father, where shall this end? Mr. Waterhouse has gone, and Mr. Calvert will leave in the *Wesley*! I beseech you to have pity on us and come back, come back! Come back! You must judge for yourself; but it is my mind (and I believe this is right) that you should come back and guide us again. I have many things to say, but I cannot write more.

"May the grace of the Lord Jesus be with you" etc. Amen!

  Joeli Bulu.

Calvert visited Fawn Harbour in August 1865, just before his departure from Fiji, and was pleased with Joeli's supervision. The circuit was operating well, and the school was well managed. Four tons of oil had been contributed to the local mission self-support, and for New Testaments.

Joeli visited Bau for the annual meeting that year and participated in the ordination of Taniela Afu and Josefa Nokilevu. It was an interesting year. In spite of troubles, there was much growth—a hundred villages (about ten thousand people) converted to Christianity that year. Thirty new catechists were sent forth from one quarterly meeting. The first consignment of full Fijian Bibles arrived from England, and many Christians who had died in the faith had passed on in glorious triumph.

Yet Joeli himself continued to suffer alone. In 1866 he determined to remarry and went to Lomaloma. He first inspected the Sunday schools and literally wept for joy as he heard the children reading the Scriptures so fluently. Then on Saturday, 11 August 1866, Fison married Joeli to Akesa Muala at Lomaloma and recorded that, "Akesa is, I believe, a wife suitable for him in every respect, and I am thankful that this long-tried and found-faithful servant of God has met with one who will take care of him in his old age" (emphasis his).

Fison had visited Lomaloma from Lakeba, whence he returned by canoe via Cikobia and Tuvuca, passing through some stormy weather in company with Joeli. Thence they both sailed again to Ono (152 miles away), and Fison went on to Vatoa, leaving Joeli in Ono and picking him up a few days later upon return, then back to Lakeba via Moala and Cicia. It was on this trip, not during his earlier stay in Ono, that Joeli shared the deathbed experiences of Taniela Kepa narrated above. (See p. 58). This chronology is confirmed by a reference in one of Fison's letters and another in the Lau circuit records.]

8
MINISTRY AT BAU

After these things[175] I was removed from [Waikava] to Bau, where I have been living ever since,[176] doing what I could to help on the great work; and here the Lord has been very gracious to me, giving me the hearts of the chiefs and of the people, so that I have lived among them in peace and comfort, seeing not a few turn from their evil ways to serve the living God, and burying others who finished their course with joy.[177]

---

175   The death of his wife, the loss of his daughter, and the fracture of his congregation due to political events exacted a heavy toll for Joeli physically. There is a reference to it in a letter of James Calvert:

His troubles have aged him; but, oh! what a heart and mind God has blessed him with.

Apparently he alarmed the missionaries when he went to Ovalau for the 1863 district meeting. Calvert as chairman encouraged Joeli to remarry, and when he wrote that letter in May, he expected Joeli to marry a widow, who was also a class leader of a good devotional type. He thought that each would comfort the other. Calvert said he "approved of her and the offer is accepted," but as we have seen (p. 65), nothing came of it. Eventually Joeli did marry again, but not for three years. Meantime, he was removed from the political scene by the transfer of his responsibilities to Waikava and the training institution, still in the Cakaudrove circuit but at a different location. This would have been for at least three years. Now, in this chapter, he takes up his account again at Bau with a narrative that dates in 1869.

176   This would have been written after three or four years in the appointment. He remained there until his death, serving as Cakobau's chaplain.

177   However, his health was bad. He never did really recover from his Wairiki experiences. In 1868 it appeared he was sick unto death. There is among the Fison papers an old holograph letter book which contains a copy of a letter Fison wrote to Joeli dated 22 November 1868. It is an affectionate letter for no other purpose than comfort and spiritual encouragement, from a dear friend confronting an expectation of death. It is written in nautical terminology (which was typical of both Joeli and Fison), as if a life voyage was nearing the port:

It is reported that you have fallen sick in these days—even that an evil disease has taken hold upon you, so that you have been well-nigh dead. Great indeed is my earnest desire to visit you, that we may look each other in the face once more; but I cannot leave my home at this time. Wherefore do I write to make known my mind to you, Joeli. My mind is that you flee not to heaven in these days; for there is evil astir in the land, and you are wanted. Nevertheless let Him decide who rules us all.

Give strict charge to one of your young men, that he come to me if your sickness attack you again. Let him come running all the way hither, and straightway I will go to you . . .

I write these things that you may know of my keeping you ever in remembrance, and of my warm affection for you. True, indeed, is my love to you, Joeli; and I am sad at heart because you are sick. Often have we two worked together here in Fiji, sailed together, walked together, talked together, rejoiced together, sung together, preached together, prayed together, wept together. But now you are grown old. Sailing far ahead of me, you go; you have neared the land; you see the entrance that leads through the reef into the desired haven. As for me, I come sailing far astern—sailing far out in the midst of the waters. But, Joeli, I know the course: steadfastly I hold on therein. When you have landed, turn then and look seaward. Some day you will see my sail also; or perhaps you will see one swimming over the waves

Many and great also are the deliverances which God has wrought out for me during my stay in this place—deliverances from dangers by sea and by land, for which I bless and praise His holy name. But perhaps the greatest and most wonderful of them all was His saving me, and them that were with me, in the great storm which raged in the month of March [1869], whereof I will now tell you.

In that month our missionary[178] said to me, "How would it be, Joeli, if you were to go to the islands and hold the missionary meetings?" So we asked the *Vunivalu*[179] to lend me a canoe, as ours is rather small for deepwater sailing in March, which is, above all others, the month of storms; and he lent us that large canoe *Kinikinilau.*

After waiting for some days wind-bound at Ovalau, we hoisted sail on a Saturday afternoon, thinking to make some one or other of the islands during the night; but when we had gone only a little way, being then about halfway between Ovalau and Wakaya,[180] my mind misgave me as I saw the threatening look of the sky, for it had grown black with heavy clouds. The wind, moreover, was not steady, but shifted about from point to point, with heavy rain squalls; so I said, "How if we put back, or run in here to Wakaya?" But no one seconded me, and we went sailing onward.

Again, when we had passed Wakaya, I spoke a second time, but none of our ship folk gave heed to my words, and we held on our course until there came rushing down upon us a fierce squall with blinding rain, and then they were all sorry they had not taken my advice. With great difficulty we put the canoe about and tried to run back, but we were too late, for the storm grew in rage, the canoe rolled and plunged so violently as to endanger her fastenings and, to add to our distress, the point of the sailyard was jerked up from its place, where it rests on the bow, and fell deep into the sea. Springing to the work, we tugged and strained until we got it up again, though it was as much as we could do, for many of our crew had hidden themselves in the hold, giving themselves up to death. And still the tempest grew ever fiercer, the raindrops stinging and burning wherever they struck, so that our bodies felt as if they were being burnt with fire; and all hope of life departed from us.

---

on a piece of broken ship. But I shall get safe to land, and then shall we two be together once more. Again shall we walk together, and sing together, and rejoice together; but never again shall we weep together, throughout all eternity.

Then there is a postscript in which he sends his love to "Adi Akesa." Yet Joeli recovered to serve another nine years, during which he wrote his autobiography. We believe it was this "nearness to death" and his recovery which led Fison to pressure him to write down this account of his adventures.

178 Frederick Langham, who was born in Tasmania, Australia, in 1833 and arrived in Fiji in 1858. He served there for over forty years and was eventually honoured by the University of Glasgow with a doctoral degree for his Fijian linguistic work, on the recommendation of Sir William McGregor. Langham died in 1903.

179 *Vunivalu* (War Lord), the civil title of Ratu Cakobau, who was also frequently spoken of as Tui Viti (King of Fiji). However, although the strongest chief, not all Fijian tribes recognised his sovereignty.

180 Wakaya, an island of about three square miles, is only about ten miles from Levuka. The land had been alienated from Bau in 1840, and became a private plantation.

"There is but one thing left," I cried. "Lower the sail, for we can carry it no longer."
And when the sail was lowered on deck and lashed securely, I said, "Come, let us report
ourselves to our God. He can save us alive; and if we are to die, how can we die better than
while praying to Him?" So we knelt down, and Sitiveni the Lasakauan[181] prayed, saying:

> Lord, it is Thou who hast created the heavens and the earth, and all that in
> them is. We also are work of Thy hands. All things are obedient unto Thee, for
> Thou didst fashion them. Thou rulest the winds and the waves, so also the lives
> of men. Thou ordainest, and Thou alone, our life and our death, for Thou art
> our Creator. Wherefore do we now bow down in prayer before Thee. Hear our
> cry, for the sake of Jesus Christ our Saviour. Give unto us, we beseech Thee, Thy
> Holy Spirit to dwell in our hearts, and turn away our thoughts from all earthly
> things, that we may prepare ourselves for eternal life.

When we had said "Amen" to our prayer, a great awe fell upon us, for with the ending
of our prayer the storm also came to an end, not growing weaker and ceasing gradually,
but suddenly, in one moment. And there was a great calm. We looked around for the wind,
but it was gone; and gazing in wonderment at each other's faces, we sat in silence for a long
while, until at length Eroni, the Bauan, cried with a loud voice, "Vekaveka![182] Now I know
the profit of true religion!"

"The Lord has delivered us," I said. "Let us praise Him for His marvellous lovingkindness." And our praises came forth from hearts too full for many words.[183] Then we lowered
the anchor[184] down into the sea, "for," said I, "if the wind should rise again, it will help

---

181   Lasakau is a subdivision of Bau. Almost every influential chief had a community of fishermen, as distinct from
      sailors. One of the most famous fishermen tribes of Fiji was that resident on Bau, in a location which is often known
      by the name of the tribe—Lasakau. The most famous chief of the Lasakauans, Gavidi, lived at the time of which we
      are speaking. He was spoken of as "Cakobau's henchman," and "the provider of bodies." Not only did they secure
      fish, they captured bodies for the cannibal ceremonial. Many indeed are the tales of Gavidi's murderous treach-
      ery. [See Williams and Calvert 1884, 109; Derrick 1950, 16, 58, 97, etc.] He died an ignominious death at Verata, being
      shot in the back.

182   A Fijian expression of surprise.

183   Lorimer Fison asked Sitiveni to write out what he remembered of Joeli's prayer. He did so, and his account runs as
      follows:

      There were two of us who prayed—I first; and when I had done, then Joeli prayed thus:

      Lord, without doubting, that Thou art a prayer-hearing God, ever dost Thou give ear to the cry of them that serve
      Thee. We bow down before Thee in prayer. If it be Thy will that this be our day of rest from our labours, it is well; but
      if Thou wilt make use of us yet for a little while, then let the storm be calm, and the waves thereof be still. We are
      weak, but strength is with Thee. Hear our prayer, for we pray in the name of Jesus. Therefore hear us, and have mercy
      upon us, for His sake. Grant this our request, for the sake of Christ alone.

      Then he broke forth with great earnestness, in these words:

      Come to us, Lord, in the midst of the waters, as Thou camest to Thy disciples in the days of old. The storm was raging
      but Thou saidst, "Be still," and lo, there was a great calm; for Thou art the Almighty One, and all things are obedient
      unto Thee.

184   An anchor might be a large coral rock, or sometimes a strong stake worked into the sand or mud. At this time a few of
      the larger canoes had proper anchors—a sign of acculturation, even before colonial government. However, here it is

to keep her head on to the waves." But there was no more wind. All that night, even till morning, the canoe lay as steady and quiet as if we had been lying in a river, for the waves which had been raging so furiously went down with the ending of the storm; and two great sharks stayed by us all night, one across the bows, and the other across the stern.

At daybreak I roused the scullers out of the hold, that we might go on our way. "Come up here, if fear has not killed you outright," I cried. "Get out the oars, and let us scull to land. If we were all like you, what would become of us?" Slowly, and with much shame and confusion of face, they crawled on deck; and after we had sculled for a while a breeze sprang up, to which we hoisted sail, running before it to Nairai.[185] The wind grew stronger and stronger, driving us swiftly along till, when we entered the passage through the reef, it was blowing a hard gale; and so heavy a sea came rolling into the harbour that our cable parted over and over again after we had let go the anchor. Wherefore, not being able to haul the canoe ashore because it was low tide, we stood by her in the water, holding her with all our might against the waves, that she might not come broadside on and so be dashed to pieces; and as the tide rose, we dragged her further and further up, until we got her high and dry on the shore, out of reach of the sea. By this time a fierce hurricane was blowing, before which many trees and most of the houses fell,[186] but our lives were safe, and throughout all the storm our hearts were singing praises to God for His wonderful goodness.

[Editorial Note:

Joeli Bulu's manuscript ends here. It was written in 1869. Fison immediately prepared the English text and it was printed in 1871 in England.

The account of the Bau ministry is scrappy. Fison rounded it off with his report of an interview or pastoral call he had with Joeli. The words are Joeli's but Fison recorded them, and this we shifted to its appropriate chronological place.

Meantime, Joeli suffered greatly from the effects of the exposures of his years of missionary service and his confrontations with heathenism. The scar of his fight with the shark, like the scar of his troubles at Wairiki, he bore to the end of his life. Although he could lament for his people, he never lost his spiritual radiance or faith. This prophetic Jeremiah-like character is reflected in all the missionary reporting about him, and in all his own utterances through these years of his Bau ministry. Time after time at Fijian gatherings and district meetings of Western and native missionaries, he was

---

used to steady the vessel in the water and permit more effective control to the helmsman. A Fijian anchor has more than one function.

185 An island of about ten square miles, once the location of the famous *Eliza* wreck (1808); one of the first islands to respond to Christianity in a people movement after the conversion of Cakobau in 1854.

186 This is the regular physical structure of a Fijian hurricane—a circular storm moving on its path, first from one direction, then a calm, and finally blowing from the other direction as experienced from a given point in the centre of the disturbance. They had passed through the very centre of the hurricane.

called on to give the inspirational address. This is evidenced by the home church newspaper reports sent from the field.

When he made the voyage to Nairai during the hurricane as just narrated, there were 124,000 persons of all ages attending Christian worship services; over 25,000 of them had progressed far in the faith and had become fully accredited members by Wesleyan standards (which were high). [This was before the measles epidemic which carried off 40,000.] Between 4,000 and 5,000 were in catechumen classes preparing for this status. The church had 893 catechists, 811 local preachers, and 68 native ministers. These figures represented manifest church growth. At the time of the massacre of Baker and his party (1867), the church had 45 native missionaries. The 50 percent increase in a year or so had resulted from the new training programme. A rise of about 400 catechists and local preachers reflected the effectiveness of the district institutions—that is the type of work Joeli had been engaged in at Waikava, and which he merely mentioned in one sentence.

When Joeli left Wairiki to go to Waikava there had been only seven native missionaries, 138 catechists, and 57 local preachers in all Fiji. Australians like Carey, White, and Waterhouse, and Tongans like Bulu and Vea had been responsible for this organic church growth. The 1860s saw 70,000 conversions in Fiji in a growth pattern of steady distribution each year, which explains the need for the training programme policy. Unfortunately, apparently Joeli did not find much adventure for reporting in the experience. We have merely a number of very appreciative references to his work by others.

Just prior to the Nairai episode, Joeli's physical problems produced a type of fit from which it was expected he would die, but he effected a good recovery.

Soon after the district meeting of 1867, Fison had written to Joeli and received the following reply:

Bau

5 July 1867

Dear Mr. Fison,

I, your friend, write this letter to you, that you may know my constant love for you. You came hither to our District Meeting, but therein we were very busy, day and night, so that we could not talk together, we two, and build one another up in the love of our Lord Jesus Christ, as in times gone past.

I have received your letter, wherein you say, that good is the fruit of our sailing to Muala and Matuku [referring to the trip in 1866], and therein does my soul rejoice with exceeding joy. Joeli Keteca also tells me of the good work of God in those lands. Truly the Lord has loved us, in that He has made useful our sailing in that stormy weather.

We are well; but a great trouble has befallen us, even the death of that good lady who was going to Lakeba [Mrs Rooney died 17 June 1867 at Bau, after the birth of a daughter; this event was the subject of a letter by Brooks, Rooney's superintendent, on the need of medical training for missionaries] but who has gone to heaven instead—a grief indeed to us who remain alive.

Salutations from Akesa to you, the lady and the children. I also, your friend, send my great love. Ended now is my letter to you whom I bear continually in my thoughts.

I am,

Joeli Bulu

The stormy weather mentioned in the letter refers to the 1866 voyage with Fison. The Nairai hurricane came in 1869. Joeli was still unwell. It was probably about a year after that Fison encouraged him to write down his autobiographical account which ended at this point we have now reached. He must have written it immediately after the Nairai hurricane. Perhaps he already had it largely written before that event. Fison wrote to England that same year about the publication of his translation.

The following unit is the account of an interview or pastoral call. It is Joeli's testimony as recorded by Fison, perhaps as late as 1870, just four years before the cession of Fiji to Britain.]

Joeli's Testimony ca. 1870

I am now an old man, and my body is weak, but my soul is as strong as ever, rejoicing in the work of the Lord. When I look forward to the Good Land, which is now so near me, my heart burns, and my eyes fill with tears of joy as I think of the glory which I shall soon behold, for the Lord is ever present with me, both night and day; and after putting my trust in Him throughout all these years, I am not going to begin to doubt Him now. No! "I know whom I have believed" (2 Tim 1:12).

Also, when I look around and note what great things our Lord has wrought, and is working—when I see the people moved under my sermons; when sinners come to me crying, "What must I do to be saved?"; when I hear good words in the class meeting, or from the lips of the dying; and when I bury the dead who have died in the Lord—then my soul rejoices with an exceeding great joy.[187]

But when I think of this people's earthly concerns—of the ill blood among the chiefs, of the divisions and hatreds between the various tribes, of how readily a little spark flames up into a blaze of war, and of the impossibility of healing all the breaches and making the common people one in heart—then indeed my heart is sad within me, and I am ready to weep "for the slain of the daughter of my people" (Jer 9:1). For I have seen that the good days of peace have ever been few and short; evil has soon arisen again, undoing the work that was scarce begun; and now, in addition to the causes of evil which we had in the olden times,

---

187 Here is the structure of Joeli's ministry as a pastor—preaching the Word, instructing in class, counselling and comforting. Here he is not engaged in the pioneering thrust into paganism, or the training institution, but is a pastor to his people, ministering with great joy.

very many of the chiefs and of the people are becoming great drunkards—more
and more of them every year. The very boys and girls are now drinking the
white man's *yaqona*, wherefore is my heart very sad within me[188]; and I would
that I could turn mine eyes away, like Hagar of old, that I may not look upon the
destruction of this people, whom I love even as my own sons and daughters.

When he thus spoke, his voice trembled, growing low and faint towards the finish, and
his words ended in a sob. As soon as I could command myself sufficiently to speak, I said to
him, "No, Joeli, but Hagar saw only the dying lad. She did not see the angel who was sent
to deliver her and to save her child alive, that he might be the father of a great and mighty
nation. So also we see the evil which is present with us, but the angel of the Lord is hidden
from our eyes."[189]

The old man looked steadfastly at me for a few moments, then drew a deep breath,
and burst into tears. "Thank you, thank you for that word!" he cried, laying his hand
upon his breast.

"It has entered here. I feel it in my heart, and it comforts me."

[Editorial Note:

*As the first ordained native missionary in Fiji, it was natural that Joeli Bulu would have a par-
ticular standing among his ministerial peers, of whom there were now almost seventy. Although the
task of official district letter writing was normally assigned to the younger men, in times of difficulty
they invariably turned to the old, experienced leader. It was so at the district meeting of 1869, when
the missionary William Moore[190] was returning to Australia after nineteen years of service in Fiji with
one short break. The young men appointed found it impossible to pen a suitable letter of farewell, and
begged Joeli to attend to the task. The following is Fison's translation of the letter which Joeli wrote in
consultation with Taniela Afu and Jemesa Havea, two senior Tongan colleagues. We preserve it in his
autobiography as a true cultural artifact. It is a typical letter of farewell, with Fison's own preamble
on Joeli's testimony as to how it came about that he composed it.]*

---

188   He is not so happy about the politico-social state of the country. This was a period of struggle for national entity,
      and some of his own countrymen were seriously involved. Pressured by a new population group of white plant-
      ers, and with some missionary support, Cakobau had consented to an attempt at establishing a constitutional
      government. The experiment was a dismal failure. A party of missionaries—Thomas Baker and several of Joeli's
      colleagues—had been murdered in the interior of Viti Levu (1867), and the resultant intra-Fijian tensions that
      mark its prolonged aftermath tore the place apart for years. The South Pacific labour trade was at its height as far
      as Fiji was concerned. The forces of acculturation—liquor in particular—were eroding the traditional taboos and
      proscriptions of Fijian society.

      The term *yaqona ni vavalagi* (white man's *yaqona*) was an unfortunate equation, as the only point in common for West-
      ern liquor (which more often than not in those days was gin) and *yaqona* is that they were both beverages.

189   See Genesis 21:13.

190   Moore reached Viwa in the *Wesley*, 23 January 1850, and joined Hazlewood at Nadi in March. [This fell between the
      first and second visits of Joeli Bulu to Nadi.] He moved to Bau in September 1851, and to Rewa in 1854. In 1862 he was
      at Bau but returned to the colonies in 1864. However, in response to requests for his return from missionaries and
      Fijians, he did so. His daughter died at Ovalau in 1867, and his own health deteriorated so that he returned finally to
      the colonies in 1869.

Joeli Bulu, Letter Writer for the Corporate Group

Having made ready pen and paper they sat down and began to talk over what they should write, but when they began to think and speak of all Mr. Moore's lovingkindness to them, they could do nothing but weep, because he was going away from us; and presently they fled from the house. One after another, we tried them all, but they all failed. A few words, and then a great burst of weeping. Thus it was day after day, until the time was far spent. "This will never do," said I. So, calling Taniela Afu and Jamesa Havea,[191] I said to them, "Come now, let us three strengthen our hearts and get this letter written to our elder, lest the meeting be over before anything be done." But indeed, when we sat down to write, we were as foolish as the younger men; only we stuck to our work, writing a little, and weeping much, until it was finished; and when we read it to our brethren, they said, "It is very good," and wrote down their names.[192]

This is a translation of the letter, as it appears in our district meeting records:

To our beloved Elder, the Rev. W. Moore.

This, sir, is the letter of us, the native missionaries, to you; and far indeed from us be words of flattery in this our letter.

Great is our thankfulness to God, in that He chose you to be His ambassador to Fiji; for that he chose you is manifest in very deed and truth to us, from the many proofs thereof which we have seen during your stay in our midst, as a shining example to us.

For your loving spirit—for you have been loving to us native missionaries, to the local preachers also, to the common people, and to all the Church—for this do we thank our God, because of His love to us in giving you such a heart. We know your love to us from the things which we have seen; for you have ever taught us most excellently how we might be saved, and how we might be useful in the work. We cannot set forth in words your great loving-kindness, but the proofs thereof lie in our heart of hearts; and therein appears the truth of Paul's words, which are written—1 Corinthians 13:13: "And now abideth faith, hope, love, these three; but the greatest of these is love." This spirit of yours we shall bear ever in mind, in our thinking of you.

There is also another of your ways which we shall bear in mind—even your steadfast endurance of many sufferings in Fiji. One great trial which befell you was that at Rewa—when, as you lay sleeping in your house, with the children and the lady, the people tried to destroy you, together with your house. And when the house was burnt, with all your goods, you endured it, not wishing for

---

191 Both of these men were Tongans who had settled in Fiji for the sake of the Christian mission.
192 Correct procedure. The letter writers present their composition for discussion and endorsement.

revenge. We saw your friends gather together, that they might take vengeance for this wrong; but you said, "Let them not suffer for this. Let the suffering be mine, and mine only."[193]

Another trial came to you when the lady fell sick, and went away to the white man's land, whether for life or death you knew not; but you endured to stay behind, for the work's sake.[194] And many other sufferings, which cannot be told in this letter, have you endured patiently—sufferings which other men have not been able to endure. Great, very great indeed, is our love to you for this; and we desire that this spirit of yours may abide with us also; for we all know that blessed are they who endure, according to the word of James (5:11): "Behold, we count them happy which endure. Ye have heard of the patience of Job, and have seen the end of the Lord; that the Lord is very pitiful, and of tender mercy."

Another great thing because of which we love you, is that we have seen your zeal for the progress of the work in Fiji. This zeal of yours has been ever manifested in your preaching; for we know that you have prepared yourself so as to fill our souls; and great has been the profit of your sermons to our souls. Your zeal has been shown forth in the books of teaching, also, which you have written to be useful to us Fijians—books which have been useful to us, and more than good.[195] Great indeed is the benefit which we have derived from your earnest and constant teaching, and exhorting and warning us; and it is our earnest desire that we may strive to follow this way of yours, for we believe that it is a most excellent example to us, having moreover, the promise of eternal life, according to the word which is written—Revelation 2:10: "Be thou faithful unto death, and I will give thee a crown of life."

There is yet another thing for which we do indeed love you—even your kindly manner in our midst. Your words have ever tended to foster kindly feeling among both chiefs and people. Never have we known a time when unseemly words fell from your lips. Pure also have been your ways in our midst; just and right have been your doings, and in accordance with the word of the holy Book, which is written—Matthew 5:14: "Ye are the light of the world. A city that is set on a hill cannot be hid"; and because of these your ways our hearts can never forget you.

Yet one thing more is in our minds to tell you—even that we love you in our heart of hearts with an exceeding great love. Know also that our grief is very great in these days, because we are about to be parted from you.

It is in our minds to beseech you to stay yet a little longer with us, but we cannot because of your children. Yes, you will go, and we shall weep; you will be absent

---

193   This event took place in 1855, a year after Moore's transfer from Bau.
194   Actually the district gave him permission to go, but he stayed. His wife was sent to Auckland in 1857.
195   The best known was *Vulagi Lako*, his translation of *Pilgrim's Progress*, printed 1863.

from us, and we shall grieve. We can say nothing more. Only know this, that our souls are full to overflowing with the warmest love for you, and with grief also. We shall not forget you in our prayers. Know this, that great in very deed and truth is the love which we bear you in our inmost heart. We have been thinking whether there were perhaps any gift which we could offer as a token of our love, but we could find none: wherefore did we resolve to write this letter, setting forth our feelings towards you. Our letter is ended. May the grace of our Lord Jesus Christ be with you! Amen. Amen!

Here are our names:

Joeli Bulu	Josefa Ratabua
Joeli Keteca	Wiliame Vutikalulu
Mataiasi Vave	Filimoni Ralawa
Josefa Nokilevu	Penijamani Tora
Kornilio Musuka	Josefa Ravuaka
Eroni Fotofili	Aisea Vunilogologo
Taniela Afu	Aisake Kalou
Iliasa Takelo	Aisea Nasili
Osea Tuni	Joeli Nau
Aisake Rawaidranu	Junia Digova
Jemesa Havea	Kelepi Bai
Necani Dauvere	Tevita Nauhamea
Wesele Ciri	Tomasi Mawi
Marika Tagicakobau	Juliusa Ravai
Melikesiteki Viti	Jonitani Dabea

And herewith let us bid farewell to this good and faithful servant of our Lord Jesus Christ. Yet a little while, and an appendix may perhaps be added to this *Autobiography*, so that it may be known, not only how Joeli Bulu lived, but also how he died. Kindly, just, and honourable towards his fellow men; humble and lowly before God; in quiet times a delightful companion; cool, prompt, and lionhearted in danger; and always ready for every good word and work—such a man should not be without his record and token of remembrance. God grant that this record of his life and labours, imperfect as it is, may stir us all up to a better service of Him whom this war-worn veteran serves; to a firmer trust in the Saviour whom he trusts; to a more earnest striving on behalf of the cause to which he has given the best years of his life, and on which he has spent his strength, even unto old age and grey hairs; so that we may be with him when the great longing of his youth is at last fulfilled and he has become "a dweller among the stars."

[*Editorial Note:*

Thus ends Fison's redaction of the autobiography. It now remains to take up his suggestion and add a brief appendix about the last five years of his life.]

9
LAST YEARS

Fison's redaction of the *Autobiography of Joeli Bulu* left us in 1872. As far as we know, he himself made no attempt to write that appendix he said would need to be written someday, although he outlived Joeli by thirty years. Joeli died on 7 May 1877, so our editorial appendix has to reconstruct briefly the record of the last five years of his life.

Three significant events took place in Fiji during those years, 1871–77: (1) the cession of Fiji to Britain, (2) the measles epidemic, and (3) the Christian mission to New Britain.

(1) The cession of Fiji to Britain has been well discussed by historians in terms of the numerous forces which were also in the background of Joeli Bulu's ministry at Bau. Much of the political drama was played at Bau and a few miles across the water on Ovalau, where Levuka was situated. Joeli was Cakobau's chaplain. Cakobau, under pressure, had accepted a supposedly constitutional government; but the white community exerting the pressure were often themselves involved in the labour trade, and Levuka has been described as "a slave market"—as in one very real sense it was.

The forces at work after the first offer of cession, which was rejected by Britain, gathered impetus through the 1860s and all seemed to converge on the small world of Bau and Levuka. Levuka was on Ovalau, the outline of which lay across the water from Bau. Both Cakobau and Bulu could see it every morning. It reminded them of the growing Western presence—traders, adventurers, planters, and would-be politicians, who continually cried out for titles for their land; and many of whom practised (what they could not have done, at least openly, under a British flag) a form of kidnapping, sometimes called "blackbirding," and marketing the kidnapped labour openly in Levuka in a thoroughly "slave-market" pattern.[196]

Undoubtedly, the main obstruction to any possible success of the constitutional government of 1871–74 was its inability to unify Fiji, and this was most certainly due to the presence of Ma'afu, the Tongan who operated from northern Lau with planter support and linked up with the longstanding Tongan adventuring in Fiji which had dogged Joeli's footsteps for two decades. Ma'afu's presence was a burden to Joeli and to the missionaries. He

---

196 For a detailed and documented description of the trade, including the marketing of labour in Levuka, see Tippett (1956).

claimed to belong to their religious persuasion, but his moral life, and especially his "love for the bottle," put him far away from "the holy life" associated with Wesleyanism. Time after time he was disciplined by the church, then repented, only to "fall from grace" again, as the church records show. Joeli Bulu and Ma'afu were symbolic of the two completely opposite types of Tongan presence in Fiji.

With forces of the establishment of constitutional government ineffective because of rival alignments with Cakobau and Ma'afu, it was apparent that there could be no effective constitutionality without some kind of foreign intervention. It came with the second offer of cession to Britain and its eventual acceptance in 1874. The journey to cession was a highly emotional experience, and both Lorimer Fison, at Rewa, and Joeli Bulu, at Bau, were in the thick of it. It meant a change of British foreign policy and a change of British government before the offer could be accepted.

Several other forces were at work. There was, for example, the longstanding French/British rivalry in the South Pacific, and the fact that when the French flag was raised over a native kingdom where British Protestant missions were at work, invariably the French flag brought with it a Catholic bishop. British missions never did recover from the Tahiti affair[197]; not for that generation, nor for the one which followed it.

One of the tragedies of nineteenth-century Christian missions in the South Pacific (and this includes Fiji) was the tendency of animist communities to exploit Protestant/Catholic competition for the purposes of inherent, indigenous political factionalism. Thus it soon became apparent that the Fijian race would never be unified, and indeed might well exterminate itself,[198] unless colonial government could establish law and order. For this reason, among others, the rapidly increasing Protestant Fijians became alarmed at the shadow of France over their waters. It was not by accident that they thought of cession to Britain, and even to America or Germany rather than to France. And for Joeli Bulu, his sad experience in Wairiki and the loss of years of patient labour to the rival denomination was still a grievous wound.

One of the politico-economic issues that led to cession was pressure from the Manchester cotton interests. The Fijian "cotton boom" came because of the termination of the supply of raw cotton for European markets due to the war between the American states. For the planters the "boom" did not last long, and they turned to the cultivation of sugar; but for the Fijians the cotton market provided an unexpected source of revenue.[199]

The importance here, however, is that over these years—the late sixties and early seventies—cotton was the big issue in Fiji among the planters, who wanted titles for their land

---

197 See Tippett (1973, 158–61) for further detail of the effect of the Tahiti affair on Protestant missionaries.
198 From the introduction of Western arms and ammunition in the first decade of the nineteenth century, this process of steady annihilation continued until cession.
199 The old Fijian wood-and-iron church buildings date from this time. Prior to this they had been built either from forest materials or from coral lime.

to give them equity for the development of their particular form of commerce, and this seemed more likely under a colonial government than a native kingdom. They were not considering native welfare in any way. Most of the planters at this point in history were concerned largely with their own survival.

Arising out of the growth of plantations came the labour question. The Fijians would work only when their own social organisation freed them to do so; i.e., they would not allow the seasonal cotton planting and picking work to disrupt their own hours for organised subsistence farming, communal fishing, religious life, and so on. So the planters had to go elsewhere for labour. Fiji thus became a market for labour—together with Queensland, Samoa, Central America, and the Guano Islands off Peru. Out of this grew the South Pacific kidnapping trade, with Fiji (especially Levuka and Bau) in the centre of it. Neither Cakobau nor the experimental government could control it. Frederick Langham, Joeli Bulu's superintendent and chairman of the Wesleyan Mission, would have no dealings with the government on this matter, although he had a deep personal regard and respect for Cakobau himself. He saw no way of controlling the situation but by external intervention. Britain entrusted the task to her Australian Squadron, and several naval commanders actually intercepted slavers, but they were prevented from carrying out justice because of the inadequacies of international law.[200]

The battle against the slave trade was fought by missionaries on a humanitarian basis through the Australian and British press, and through writing—Fison, in Australia now, Langham in Fiji, Ingliss in the New Hebrides, and Codrington in Mota. It was a concentrated and devastating literary attack over about three years. The murder of Bishop Patteson was used by both Codrington and Fison (both missionary anthropologists) to expose the trade vigorously for anthropological reasons. They were able to name the recruiting ships and the places and numbers of kidnapped persons. It led to law cases in Australia and the state government[201] in session, and various references of a hostile nature were made by several speakers in the House debate on the cession of Fiji to Britain.[202]

So Fiji became British in 1874. These were the "hot topics" of the "road to cession" over the early seventies—the failure of the Fiji government because of the activities of Joeli's fellow countryman, Ma'afu; the continued fear of French (and thus Roman Catholic) intervention, in the face of a British policy of minimum intervention; the alarming inhumanity of the labour trade with its focus in Fiji; the influx of white speculators and the threat of alienation of native lands; and at the local level (which was close to Joeli as a Christian

---

200 E.g., the *Daphne* case. The main obstruction was the unwillingness of a court of law to accept the testimony of an islander against that of a white man.

201 This was before federation.

202 Among them, for example, Alderman McArthur; Eastwick, M.P.; Sir Charles Wingfield; and the Earl of Carnavon himself.

pastor), the temptation to young men and women to separate themselves from the village organisation to serve the white adventurer for a few pence, and for tobacco and liquor.

The effects of acculturation on village life were strong all through the seventies and eighties. For the last seven years of his life Joeli Bulu was pastorally disturbed by the rapid social change among the rising generation. Thus he confessed to Fison as we saw in the last chapter:

> Very many of the chiefs and of the people are becoming great drunkards—more
> and more of them every year. The very boys and girls are now drinking [rum
> and gin], wherefore is my heart very sad within me.[203]

Before Joeli Bulu died, the church had consolidated itself for a vigorous effort against this threat. On the whole the missionaries of the period of cession were more Victorian than those of the pioneering days. Many had been trained in the city missions of the Australian cities and had learned to use "revival techniques" to fight the liquor problem. In Fiji the health danger to women and small children from potent Fiji tobacco[204] (an issue actually aggravated by the new colonial government specifying tobacco cultivation as the means for Fijians paying their taxes)[205] was serious. There are many references to this in the church records, continuing for a decade after Joeli's death.

We now run into *second-generation revivalism* as distinct from *first-generation people movements* (awakenings). A revival "decision for Christ" was made manifest before the group, not by the surrender or destruction of animistic paraphernalia, but by joining the "Anti-smoking and Grogdrinking Society."[206] By being in the early phase of this battle, Joeli Bulu had lived through the period of pioneering evangelism to the period of second-generation evangelism. Fiji had passed into a new era with a new set of social and religious problems, and Joeli Bulu, whose ministry in Fiji lasted for thirty-nine years, was a "bridge" between the two eras—the era of cannibalism and the era of acculturation.

(2) The measles epidemic hit Fiji very soon after cession, and over forty thousand Fijians perished. The effect on the religious life of Fiji and the organisation of the island church was serious. Catechists, preachers, and class leaders had died literally by the hundreds.[207] The whole educational system was temporarily shattered, and hundreds of schools were

---

203 Joeli was now located in an ideal position to observe the effects of acculturation. One by one, the missionary reports show more and more of this, and they frequently called on him to speak on the subject at their gatherings.

204 The Royal Commission on the Decrease of Native Population investigated this in 1896, revealing, among other things, the appalling effect of Fiji tobacco on mothers' milk, and thus on infants, from birth.

205 For a clash on this subject between Langham and the new colonial government, see Tippett (1973, 88–89).

206 This society was actually established a couple of years after Joeli's death, but it was in the process of forming when he died. The mode of handling the problem developed before it was constituted. Lindsay formed the Society at Viwa (two miles across the water from Bau) in 1880, when he found children in "a state of semi-intoxication" from using the strongest Fiji tobacco. At Bau, Langham introduced the total abstinence pledge.

207 This is well documented in the circuit records, and particularly in the personal archives of Lorimer Fison, who was especially interested in the whole question of population decline. Joseph Waterhouse described the measles epidemic in this way:

without teachers. The consolidation of indigenous church structures was put back at least twenty years. The church was deprived of its natural leadership. She was short of cate-chists, preachers, and class leaders, and many of the church meetings had to be conducted by people who were undertrained for the respective statuses. The epidemic left the coun-try physically exhausted, intellectually bewildered, and mentally depressed. The disease left an inherent weakness which was reflected in a further declining birthrate that con-tinued well into the twentieth century.

The 1875 reports provide us with statistics brought in to the annual meetings by the native ministers. Over 8,000 had died in the Rewa circuit; 1,011 of them full members; 90 of them catechists and local preachers. In Kadavu, of 1,811 who perished, 800 were members in full standing. 3237 adherents died in Bau; 1,358 of them full members; 116 of them leaders.

The church statistics from Lakeba showed a congregational decline from 7,129 to 4,404. These were the figures of areas where Joeli had ministered.

The debilitating effect of the measles epidemic, Dr. McGregor[208] argued, was apparent in the general Fijian lack of physical resistance to other epidemics for a generation. Over five thousand died of whooping cough, dengue fever, dysentery, and influenza in the next sixteen years, quite apart from the normal percentage of deaths. The old population de-cline due to deaths by war and cannibalism gave way to decline by infectious disease. The process of decline continued until 1921, by which time there were fewer than eighty-five thousand Fijians alive in the country.

When one considers the thousands of able-bodied persons who died in 1875, it is in-deed remarkable that Joeli, who was himself so close to death, should survive to minister to the sick and dying. His heart was torn apart for the bereaved families and for the young church deprived of its leadership.

(3) *The mission to German New Guinea* [New Britain and New Ireland] is an entry "on the other side of the ledger." By the time of cession Fiji was very largely evangelised. There were no heathen villages left on the coast, and only a few mountain tribes held out against the advance of the gospel. The murder of Thomas Baker, Setareki Seileka, and their party in 1867, far from terminating the mission to the interior of Viti Levu, had been followed by a further burst of fantastic growth. Another 25,995 pagans turned to Christ in 1869 alone, and the in-crease in catechumens, class leaders, and lay preachers shows the growth was as much quali-tative as quantitative. True, there were two important tribes in the Viti Levu interior who

---

Our people are dying by hundreds. In many cases it is more like cholera than measles. If you imagine a country stricken, no work, no amusements, no occupations, no Sunday services, no schools, towns as silent as the grave or deserted, the dead buried without religious funeral rites, graves only half dug because no one is strong enough to dig the grave—you will have a faint idea of Central Fiji at present. (Waterhouse, 16 March 1875)

208 At the time he was chief medical officer of the new colony. Subsequently he became Sir William and was governor of Papua.

were against both Christianity and the gospel, against whom the government had to fight a brief "war" to unify the whole group, but the end was in sight. Fiji had heard the gospel.

This raised a new question for the young church, which for forty years had built into its Christian philosophy of growth the element of evangelistic outreach. Joeli Bulu was not ignorant of the Pacific. He had first come to Fiji from Tonga and learned a new language. He had visited Rotuma with Lyth and had seen a fellow Tongan working there in another language (Rotuman). He thought of the islands further off.

It was natural, with the evangelisation of Fiji almost complete,[209] that this evangelising church should think of new mission fields in more distant islands. It was also natural that any thought of mission outside the Fiji group should be discussed with the Australian church, which supplied Fiji with her missionary personnel. An agreement was reached. The church in Australia would finance the venture and provide the transport. Fiji would provide the personnel. A mission would be established in German New Guinea—a completely untouched field. The only contacts with the outside world had been very unhappy ones, not unlike the sandalwood contacts of pre-Christian Fiji.

The island church in general, and in particular men like Joeli Bulu, were taken up with this idea at the time of cession. Plans were made and set in motion. Then with startling suddenness Fiji was laid waste by the measles epidemic, and German New Guinea seemed "so far away."

Dr. George Brown, the general secretary, who was to supervise the new venture personally, arrived in Fiji in the ship *John Wesley*, the first vessel to enter Fiji after the lifting of quarantine after the epidemic. His ship was provisioned and ready, but many of the selected evangelists had died in the pestilence and others were too weak to go. Still others had scattered and returned home to distant villages. Brown was faced with the complete collapse of his whole venture, and went to the institution at Navuloa with a faint heart.

These hopes and plans were put briefly before the trainees, who were then to go home and talk things over with their wives and pray about it. Brown still hoped to salvage something of the enterprise, but he did not romanticise or hide anything of the dangers of the venture.

The next day, when they assembled, they were asked if any would volunteer to go. There were eighty-three students training in the school. When the request was made, the whole eighty-three to a man rose to their feet. For a time Brown and Waterhouse, Joeli Bulu and others were overwhelmed!

Of course they could not take eighty-three. Neither could the afflicted church spare them. Six married and three single men were chosen and made ready for immediate departure. Joeli Bulu was assigned the task of giving them special instruction on the pioneering missionary confrontation experience.

209　Only two mountain tribes remained unconverted at the time of cession.

A second episode of no less dramatic character occurred when the new Fijian adminis-
trator did his utmost to prevent the departure of the party. He called them all before him
and painted so black a picture that Brown interrupted in protest; and when the adminis-
trator began to labour the notion of their dying away from the land of their ancestors (a
point on which every Fijian at this time was vulnerable—where does one want to die but
at home?) the new leader of the Fijian party, Aminio Baledrokadroka, replied that they
were "not being forced to go," they had volunteered, and there were other volunteers at
the institution who were sad because they had not been selected. Then he added the words
which have gone down in Fijian church history, "We have given ourselves up to God's work.
It is our mind to go. If we die we die; if we live we live!" And that was the end of the matter.[210] The Fijian mission to German New Guinea had begun—1875.

The truth of the warnings the new missionaries had of the perils of pioneering evangelism in areas of pagan animism, which Brown and Bulu had given the new party, were
very soon manifest. The reader will remember we have made several references to Thomas
Baker and his party who were killed and eaten in the Viti Levu interior in 1867.[211] Almost
an identical story (at least in events, if not quite so in motives) took place in New Ireland
when a Christian party under Sailasa Naucukidi, a young Fijian minister, were similarly
murdered. Fiji had now repaid her debt in kind. When the story of this tragedy reached Fiji
in the very year that Joeli Bulu died, Sailasa's own brother, rather than being bitter about
the murder, immediately volunteered to take his place as a missionary to New Ireland. This
was the kind of changed heart brought about in Fiji as a result of the ministry and message
of Joeli Bulu and men like him.

In the last two years of his life Joeli Bulu was concerned with this new outreach in his
prayers and conversation. He was a thorough Wesleyan, seeing the world as his parish to
the end, and dying in confidence—"Best of all God is with us."

*   *   *   *   *

During all his ministry in Fiji, Joeli Bulu has shown us the two sides of Christian mission—on the one hand, the dangers, persecution, and trials; on the other, the glorious experiences of spiritual triumph. The last decade of his life, in the period when the forces of
acculturation were increasingly invading the country, when the church he had fought so
valiantly to plant was subject to quite new and foreign impact, there were two saving factors: (1) the periodic revivals within the land, and (2) the ministry of missionary outreach
to the unchurched islands beyond the Fiji group. Joeli Bulu lived long enough to see both

---

210   The full details of this much retold story may be found in its original source in George Brown's *Autobiography* (1908,
      70–82).

211   The Baker Memorial Hall at Davuilevu, near the location from which Baker and his party departed on that tragic
      journey, is a memorial built by the Fijians themselves as a centre for training teachers and pastors to carry on the
      work in which Baker and his companions died.

of these begin to develop,[212] and to rejoice in them. He also had the fatherly satisfaction of knowing that scores of the younger evangelists who were facing the changing times of the seventies in the full vigour of their strength were his own trainees. He may not have been aware of it, but it was nevertheless true that many of them were little replicas of himself, and they were making a good profession of faith and holding the church together in a worthy fashion.

The Death of Joeli Bulu

Miss Constance Frederica Gordon Cumming wrote a letter from the governor's residence at Nasova[213] on 14 January 1876. She had been to Bau, and with Mrs. Langham had visited Joeli and Akesa, for both of whom she had the highest opinion. Of the early pioneering Tongans, of whom she regarded Joeli as a type, she said:

> Better pioneers could not have been desired. Men of strong energetic character
> and determination, keenly intelligent, physically superior . . . they had always
> taken the lead where-ever they went; and as in their heathen days they had
> been foremost in reckless evil, they now threw their whole influence in the scale
> for good.

Then she went on to differentiate the two types of Tongans, as we have already done in this project. Of the many who became devoted evangelists, she singled out Joeli Bulu:

> Foremost among these was Joeli Bulu, a man whose faith is evidently [mani-
> festly] an intense reality. I have rarely met any man so perfectly simple, or so
> unmistakably in earnest.

A year or so later she was in Bau again, and writing from there (29 April 1877) she described another visit to Joeli. Now she saw that his work was done. She observed the physical wasting away of the last days:

> Alas! His work is well-nigh finished. He is greatly changed this week—wasted to
> a shadow; but his face is perhaps more beautiful than ever, from its sweetness of
> expression and the bright look which at times lights it up—just like some grand
> old apostle nearing his rest. He is very tall and stately, with a halo of white hair
> and a long beard. His skin is very fair, like that of all the Tongans and Samoans.
> Generally he wears only his long white waist-cloth almost to his feet[214] which
> are bare, and the folds of native cloth round his loins. He has been a Christian
> teacher in Fiji . . . from the beginning—amid noise and tumult of war, and in
> the thick of all the devilry of cannibalism. He has been the old king's[215] special

---

212 Joeli was not to be involved in the next confrontation—the Asian migrations. The first shipload of Indians did not come until 1879—two years after his death.
213 She belonged to the governor's family.
214 This is Tongan style. The Fijian cloth is shorter.
215 Cakobau.

teacher—and many a difficult day he has had with him and all his handsome
strong-willed sons and daughters. They are all very much attached to him, and
some are generally with him now, fanning or just watching beside him.

She went on to write of the scars on his arm, and told again of the fight with the shark
years before at Rewa.

Shortly after, she visited him again. The governor's wife had sent him a packet of ju-
jubes and acid drops. His face lit up and he greeted his visitors with words of blessing. He
was calm in spirit, clear in mind, but obviously nearing the end.

On 7 May, Miss Gordon Cumming was still at Bau. Here is the account of the end as she
wrote it down that day immediately after the event:

Bau, 7 May 1877

Last night there was great wailing and lamentation in Bau, for soon after midnight Joeli passed away, and died nobly as he had lived. He was quite conscious
to the very last, and the expression of the grand old face was simply beautiful—
so radiant, as of one without a shadow of doubt concerning the Home he was so
near. No man ever more earned the right to say, "I have fought a good fight—I
have kept the faith," and none ever was more truly humble. If ever the crown of
righteousness is awarded by a righteous Judge to His true and faithful servants,
assuredly Joeli will not fail to stand in that blessed company.

This morning we went to look once more on the face we all loved so truly. He
looked grand in death as in life, lying on a square of rich black-brown *tapa* his
head pillowed on a large roll of native cloth, his beautiful white hair thrown
back as a halo, and his long white beard adding to his patriarchal beauty. Over
his feet were thrown two beautifully fine Samoan mats. His poor widow Akesa,
his pretty grand-daughter, and many other women, and students from the
college, were all weeping bitterly, as those who had lost their wise and loving
counsellor and guide. The king and all his family also mourn sorely, for Joeli has
ever been their true and faithful friend and minister; and many a time has he
vainly pleaded with the old chief in the long years ere he could be brought to
abandon the vile customs of heathenism. All through Joeli's illness I have rarely
entered the house without finding some member of Cakobau's family sitting by
him, watching his sleep, or fanning him.

According to native custom, the costly Samoan mats and native cloth that lay
beneath him and over his feet were buried with him; and had the funeral been
simply *vakaviti*, the body should only have been wrapped in many Fijian mats.
But Cakobau, anxious to do all honour to his old friend, wished that he should
be buried in a coffin. So as there chanced to be a half-caste carpenter on the
island, building a boat, he made a coffin with some planks of red cedar wood. He
did not get the order till 10 a.m., and the funeral was to start at 3 p.m. Just an

hour beforehand it was brought to the mission to be lined and covered, in which work I assisted, and so gained my first experience of undertaker's business.

The place of burial was a beautiful site near an old church on the neighbouring isle of Viwa. The funeral procession was a very touching one. One large canoe carried the dead and the chief mourners. The old king and his three stalwart sons and two daughters, as also Adi Elenoa, Tui Cakau's real wife, followed in others; and nearly all the people of Bau, and from many neighbouring villages, came in canoes and boats, making a very great procession. All the principal mourners, including the royal family, wore a piece of coarse old matting, all frayed out, in token of mourning. It is worn around the waist, over the ordinary dress. We made a beautiful great wreath of white jessamine and blue-grey flowers, with an outer wreath of scarlet leaves, and this we laid on the coffin. The grave was upwards of a mile from the shore; and about twenty young teachers—fine young fellows—took it by turns to carry the coffin up a steep hill, and through green forest-glades, to the place of rest. Part of our beautiful funeral service was repeated in the rich Fijian tongue (which to my ear always resembles Italian); and then Joeli was laid beside his old friend and teacher, the Rev. John Hunt, one of the early Wesleyan missionaries, with whom he had shared many an anxious day, and who died here in 1848, at the early age of thirty-six.

REFERENCES

Birtwhistle, Allen. 1954. *In his armour: The life of John Hunt of Fiji.* London: Cargate.

Brown, George. 1908. *Pioneer, missionary and explorer: An autobiography.* London: Hodder & Stoughton.

Bulu, Joeli. 1871. *Joeli Bulu: The autobiography of a native minister in the South Seas.* Trans. Lorimer Fison. London: Wesleyan Mission House.

———. n.d. *Ai Tukutuku ni Noqu Bula.* Manuscript.

Capell, A., ed. 1941. *A new Fijian dictionary.* Sydney: Australasian Medical Publishing Co.

Cargill, David. 1841. *Memoirs of Mrs. Margaret Cargill.* London: John Mason.

Correspondence. 1864–70. *Wesleyan Missionary Notices.*
    Letters of: James Calvert
    Jesse Carey
    Lorimer Fison
    Thomas Jaggar
    Federick Langham
    Joseph Nettleton

Deller, T. N. 1934. Tonga and Fiji. *Missionary Review* (September).

Derrick, R. A. 1950. *A history of Fiji.* Suva, Fiji: Government Printing Office.

———. 1951. *The Fiji Islands.* Suva, Fiji: Government Printing Office.

Farmer, Sarah S. 1855. *Tonga and the Friendly Islands.* London: Hamilton, Adams & Co.

Fiji Times and Herald, 17 April, 1953.

Fison, Lorimer. 1864–70. Correspondence in *Wesleyan Missionary Notes.*

———. 1867–69. Holograph Letter Book.

———. 1873–78. Letters to General Secretary. Microfilm.

———. n.d. Correspondence with Lewis Henry Morgan.

———. n.d. Published Articles [Cuttings Book].

———. n.d. Reading and Research Notes. Microfilm.

Gordon Cumming, Constance Frederica. 1883. *At home in Fiji*. New York: Armstrong & Sons.

Havea, Jemesa. n.d. *Ai Tukutuku ni Noqu Bula*. Manuscript.

Hazlewood, David. 1850. *A Feejeen and English dictionary*. Viwa, Fiji: Wesleyan Mission Press.

Henderson, G. C. 1931a. *Fiji and the Fijians 1835-1856*. Sydney: Angus & Robertson.

———. 1931b. *The journal of Thomas Williams: Missionary in Fiji, 1840-53*. 2 vols. Sydney: Angus & Robertson.

Hunt, John. 1846. *Memoir of the Rev. William Cross*. London: John Mason.

Lawry, Walter. 1850. *Friendly and Feejee Islands: Missionary visit 1847*. London: Charles Gilpin.

———. 1851. *Second Missionary Visit to the Friendly and Feejee Islands 1850*. London: John Mason.

Methodist Church in Fiji. Archives.
    Annual Reports: Bau
    Bua
    Cakaudrove
    Lau
    Nadi
    Rewa
    Somosomo
    Viwa

Methodist Church of Australasia. Archives. Methodist Overseas Missions. Reports, Correspondence, Journals: Baker, Fison, Horsley, Hunt, Jaggar, Lyth, Waterhouse.

Missionary journals.
    Thomas Baker
    John Hunt
    Thomas Jaggar
    Thomas Williams

Mitchell Library, Sydney.
    Assorted items: Lorimer Fison
    Richard Lyth
    Thomas Williams

Nettleton, Joseph. 1906. *John Hunt: Missionary pioneer and saint*. London: Charles H. Kelly.

Parham, H. B. R. 1953. A brief account of a well-known chief: Ra Masima, Tui Bua. *Proceedings and Transactions of the Fiji Society of Science and Industry*. 97–106.

Parham, J. W. 1972. *Plants of the Fiji Islands*. Suva, Fiji: Government Printer.

Rowe, George Stringer. 1860. *The life of John Hunt, missionary to the cannibals*. London: Hamilton, Adams & Co.

Seemann, Berthold. 1862. *Viti: An account of a government mission to the Vitian or Fijian Islands (1860-1861)*. Cambridge: Macmillan.

Tippett, Alan R. 1953. Historic mission graves moved over the Rewa River to Lomanikoro. *Fiji Times and Herald*, April 17.

——. 1956. The nineteenth-century labour trade in the South West Pacific. MA thesis, American University.

——. 1968. *Fijian material culture: A study of cultural context, function, and change.* Honolulu: Bishop Museum Press.

——. 1970. "Church Growth in Fiji." (Various published and unpublished items). Bound volume, 17.

——. 1971. *People movements of Southern Polynesia.* Chicago: Moody Press.

——. 1973. *Aspects of Pacific ethnohistory.* Pasadena: William Carey Library.

Ward, J. M. 1948. *British policy in the South Pacific.* Sydney: Australasian Publishing Co.

Waterhouse, Joseph. 1866. *The king and people of Fiji.* London: Wesleyan Conference Office. Reprint, 1997, Honolulu: University of Hawaii Press.

Wilkes, Charles. 1850. *United States exploring expedition during the years 1838–1842.* Philadelphia: Sherman.

Williams, Thomas, and James Calvert. 1860/1870/1884. *Fiji and the Fijians*, and *Missionary labours among the cannibals.* London: Charles H. Kelly.

Wood, A. Harold. 1975. Tonga and Samoa. Vol. 1 of Overseas missions of the Australasian Methodist Church. Melbourne: Aldersgate.

INDEX

The Road to Bau

INDEX

The Autobiography of Joeli Bulu

130077